The Literary Almanac

THE BEST OF THE PRINTED WORD

1900 TO THE PRESENT

MJF BOOKS
NEW YORK

Published by MJF Books
Fine Communications
Two Lincoln Square
60 West 66th Street
New York, NY 10023

The Literary Almanac
ISBN 1-56731-328-0

Cover illustrations (left to right): Samuel Beckett, Norman Mailer, Virginia Woolf, and James Baldwin

Book Design: Patrick Seymour
Cover Design: Doris Straus
Design Coordinator: Christine S. Shaw

This edition published by arrangement with Andrews McMeel Publishing.

Manufactured in the United States of America on acid-free paper

10 9 8 7 6 5 4 3 2 1

"What is the answer? [*I was silent.*] In that case, what is the question?"
Gertrude Stein's last words. From Alice B. Toklas, What Is Remembered *(1963)*

Table of Contents

1900

HARDCOVER BESTSELLERS
fiction
To Have and to Hold, Mary Johnston
Red Pottage, Mary Cholmondeley

was considered too grim for publication at the time, so it wasn't until *The Red Badge of Courage* (1895), the realistic story of an inexperienced soldier trapped in battle, that he became known. The novel demonstrated Crane's remarkable imagination, for he derived his military knowledge solely from Tolstoy and books on the Civil War. It also convinced the newspaper establishment that Crane would be a worthy war correspondent. And thus for the rest of his life he reported from the front, an occupation that provided him ample fodder for his later writing, such as the story "The Open Boat," based on the sinking of his ship in Atlantic waters, and *Wounds in the Rain* (1900), journalistic sketches of the Spanish-American war. A year before his death, Crane returned to New York, his health broken; he died of tuberculosis in Germany, mythologized as a drug addict and a man depraved by war.

STEPHEN CRANE (1871-1900) was born in New Jersey and raised in Upstate New York. He attended Lafayette and Syracuse universities, each for a year, but at twenty opted for the life of a struggling writer in New York City, where he occasionally filed stories for the *Herald* and the *Tribune*. Crane's first novel, *Maggie: A Girl of the Streets* (1893),

[*8*]

BIRTHS
Jorge Luis Borges
Antoine de Saint-Exupery
Margaret Mitchell
Thomas Wolfe

DEATHS
Stephen Crane
Friedrich Wilhelm Nietzsche
John Ruskin

Oscar Wilde

OSCAR WILDE (1854-1900) was born in Dublin, the son of a surgeon and literary hostess, and educated at Trinity and Oxford, where he was known as a glib, sexually ambiguous dandy. He was an unapologetic egotist; when asked upon arriving for his U.S. lecture tour whether he had anything to declare, he replied, "Only my genius." In the 1880s, Wilde published plays and poems, married, and wrote the children's tale *The Happy Prince* (1888). His only novel, *A Picture of Dorian Gray*, modeled on his presumed lover, the poet John Gray, was issued in 1890 to great scandal. Over the next five years, Wilde built a dramatic reputation, notably for *The Importance of Being Earnest* (1895) and *Salome* (1894), the latter of which was translated by the Marquis of Queensbury's son, who publicly insulted the playwright and set off a chain of events that led to Wilde's 1895 imprisonment for sexual offenses. Released two years later, he went to France, wrote a prison memoir, and spent his last years wandering the continent.

1901

HARDCOVER BESTSELLERS

fiction

The Crisis, Winston Churchill

Alice of Old Vincennes,
Maurice Thompson

**THE ALFRED B. NOBEL
PRIZE FOR LITERATURE**

Sully Prudhomme, France

BIRTHS

Zora Neale Hurston
André Malraux
Margaret Mead

*Booker T. Washington publishes
Up from Slavery.*

WINSTON CHURCHILL (1841–1947)—not to be confused with Sir Winston S. Churchill, the statesman—was born in St. Louis and graduated from Annapolis. In the 1890s, he moved to New Hampshire and began writing historical romances, the most popular of which, **The Crisis (1901)** and *The Crossing* (1904), celebrated the forces that shaped early America. His later novels, such as *Coniston* (1906), focused on contemporary politics, an interest that led him to engage in politics directly; Churchill in his lifetime served as a member of the New Hampshire legislature and even became a candidate for governor.

No race can prosper till it learns that there is as much dignity in tilling a field as in writing a poem.

Booker T. Washington,
Up from Slavery (1901)

• • •

The past is but the beginning of a beginning, and all that is and has been is but the twilight of the dawn.

H. G. Wells,
Anticipations (1901)

1 9 0 2

> *A work of art is a corner of creation seen through a temperament.*
>
> Émile Zola, *My Hates* (1866)

ÉMILE ZOLA (1840–1902) was born in Paris, but spent his childhood in Aix-en-Provence, where he befriended the painter Cézanne. After the death of  his father, he and his family moved to Paris, where he went to university but failed the *baccalauréat.* Desperate and broke, Zola took a job as a publishing publicist, wrote his first works of fiction, and then became an outspoken journalist. He was sentenced to prison for his powerful article against the Dreyfus affair, 'J'Accuse,' but the verdict was quashed. A second trial was called, but Zola fled to England and remained there until an amnesty permitted his return to France. In the 1880s, Zola formed with a group of prominent nineteenth-century intellectuals the Naturalist School, promoting realism in art and literature. Its influence resulted in his multivolume Rougon-Macquart series, "a natural history of a family during the Second Empire," as the subtitle described it, which was serialized and made Zola a popular novelist. He died accidentally from inhalation of charcoal fumes in his Paris apartment.

BIRTHS

Arna Bontemps
Langston Hughes
Carlo Levi
Beryl Markham
Ogden Nash
John Steinbeck

DEATHS

Bret Harte
Émile Zola

> The first living master of psychological fiction . . . one of its author's high successes.
>
> Review of *The Wings of the Dove* by Henry James, *NY Times Book Review,* December 4, 1902

1903

HARDCOVER BESTSELLERS

fiction

Lady Rose's Daughter,
  Mrs. Humphrey Ward

Gordon Keith, Thomas Nelson Page

THE ALFRED B. NOBEL PRIZE FOR LITERATURE

Björnstjerne Björnson, Norway

*Nobel Prize winner
Björnstjerne Björnson*

BIRTHS

*Kay Boyle
Erskine Caldwell
Nora Zeale Hurston
Clare Boothe Luce
George Orwell
Evelyn Waugh
Nathanael West
Marguerite Yourcenar*

Many passages of the book will be very interesting to the student of the negro character who regards the race ethnologically and not politically, not as a dark cloud threatening the future of the United States, but as a peculiar people, and one, after all, but little understood by the best of its friends or the worst of its enemies outside of what the author of "The Souls of Black Folk" is fond of calling the "Awful Veil."

Review of
The Souls of Black Folk
by W. E. B. Du Bois,
NY Times Book Review,
December 25, 1903

1 9 0 4

HARDCOVER BESTSELLERS
fiction
The Crossing, Winston Churchill
The Deliverance, Ellen Glasgow

THE ALFRED B. NOBEL PRIZE FOR LITERATURE
Frédéric Mistral, France
José Echegaray, Spain

considered paradigms of the genre for their unique combination of comedy, tragedy, and pathos—are "Ward No. Six" (1892), "My Life" (1896), and "Lady with the Lapdog" (1899). He also wrote subtle, brilliant plays of upper-class life, including *Uncle Vanya* (1900), *Three Sisters* (1901), and *The Cherry Orchard* (1904). In the early 1900s, Chekhov gained immense success abroad, where, particularly in England, his work was admired by the writers E. M. Forster, Virginia Woolf, and G. B. Shaw, the latter declaring that reading Chekhov's plays made him want to destroy his own. Chekhov is undoubtedly Russia's greatest twentieth-century short story writer and dramatist.

BIRTHS
James T. Farrell
Graham Greene
Moss Hart
Christopher Isherwood
Cecil Day Lewis
Pablo Neruda
S. J. Perelman
Dr. Seuss (Theodore Seuss Geisel)
William I. Shirer
Isaac Bashevis Singer

DEATHS
Anton Chekhov
Kate Chopin

ANTON CHEKHOV (1860-1904) was born in Taganrog, Russia, the son of an unsuccessful shopkeeper and grandson of a serf. He began writing short stories for journals while studying medicine in Moscow. Among his greatest stories—

> *I think we ought to read only the kind of books that wound and stab us.*
>
> Franz Kafka,
> letter to Oskar Pollak,
> January 27, 1904

> *A book must be the axe for the frozen sea inside us.*
>
> ibid.

demnation (her book was labeled "unwholesome" by the all-male publishing establishment), and it was not until 1991 that her later short story collection saw publication. She is credited today for her sensitive and prescient literary treatment of women and blacks.

> *For the first time in her life she stood naked in the open air, at the mercy of the sun, the breeze that beat upon her, and the waves that invited her.*
>
> Kate Chopin,
> *The Awakening* (1901)

> *There are some people who leave impressions not so lasting as the imprint of an oar upon the water.*
>
> ibid.

KATE CHOPIN (1850-1904). Born into a bourgeois New Orleans family of strong widows who emphasized learning, curiosity, and financial independence, Kate O'Flaherty had many of the prerequisites for literary success. In 1870, after surviving the perils of the Civil War (her family supported the Confederacy), she married Oscar Chopin, a Louisiana planter, who in 1882 died of malaria, leaving her twelve thousand dollars in debt. But being resourceful, Chopin managed to come out ahead, and even survived a scandalous affair with a married local farmer. Her first story, "A Point at Issue!," published when she was thirty-nine, became an immediate success and was followed by several equally popular novels. With the publication of *The Awakening* (1899), the tale of a Louisiana wife and mother with two lovers, however, Chopin met vigorous con-

1905

JULES VERNE (1828–1905) was born in Nantes, France, the son of a lawyer whose career path he was expected to follow. He obtained his license in Paris in 1849, but being more interested in theater, spent his time writing plays, the first of which was performed in 1850. From then, Verne's literary direction changed. Through association with a number of scientists, explorers, and experimental artists such as Nadar, he realized a new vein in fiction—adventures in exotic places depicting the possibilities offered by new scientific inventions. His first success, the novel *Cinq Semaines en ballon* (1863), examined scientific preoccupations of the day, namely balloon travel, but in his later novels, such as *Journey to the Centre of the Earth* (1864), *Twenty Thousand Leagues Under the Sea* (1870), and *Around the World in Eighty Days* (1873), Verne expanded his scientific repertoire to include the inner appearance of the earth, submarines, and space travel. Long viewed as a minor author for young people, Verne today is celebrated as a science fiction innovator.

BIRTHS

Lillian Hellman
Arthur Koestler
John O'Hara
Ayn Rand
Jean Paul Sartre
C. P. Snow
Lionel Trilling
Robert Penn Warren

DEATHS

John Bartlett
Jules Verne

1 9 0 6

HARDCOVER BESTSELLERS
fiction

Coniston, Winston Churchill
Lady Baltimore, Owen Wister

THE ALFRED B. NOBEL PRIZE FOR LITERATURE

Giosuè Carducci, Italy

Laws are sand, customs are rock. Laws can be evaded and punishment escaped but an openly transgressed custom brings sure punishment.

Mark Twain,
"The Gorky Incident" (1906)

---

journalist, theater director, and, after the publication of *The Pretenders* (1857), as head of the Norwegian Theater in Oslo. In 1862, the theater went bankrupt and Ibsen went into voluntary exile in Rome, Dresden, and Munich (1864–1892), during which he wrote most of his superb dramas. Today Ibsen is acknowledged as the founder of modern drama for his plays of realism and social issues. The impact of these dramas—including *A Doll's House* (1879), *Hedda Gabler* (1890), and *The Master Builder* (1892)—revolutionized European theater and earned him the praise of such writers as Henry James, Bernard Shaw, and Sigmund Freud.

BIRTHS

Hannah Arendt
Samuel Beckett
Anne Morrow Lindbergh
Clifford Odets
T. H. White
Henry Roth

DEATHS

Henrik Ibsen
Margaret E. Rey

[16]

HENRIK IBSEN (1828–1906) was born in Skien, Norway, the son of a wealthy merchant who went bankrupt. He first took a position as a chemist's assistant, intending to study medicine, but found that his passion was for theater. Beginning in the 1850s, he worked as a

1907

THE ALFRED B. NOBEL PRIZE FOR LITERATURE

Rudyard Kipling, England

Nobel Prize winner Rudyard Kipling

RUDYARD KIPLING (1865–1936) was born in Bombay, where his father was principal of an art school, and at six was sent to England to live with foster parents. A mediocre student, Kipling forwent university and returned to India as a journalist. There he spent seven years and produced verse and stories championing the virtues of British imperialism. In 1892, he married his agent's sister, Carrie Balestier, a domineering woman who gave him two sons. The next decade was his most productive: he wrote the verse collection *Barrack Room Ballads* (1892), the children's stories collected in *The Jungle Book* (1894-1895), and *Kim* (1901), a novel set in India about a boy spy. Though many of Kipling's views are considered unacceptable today—he has been accused of imperialism, jingoism, and sexism—his value as a poet and prose writer continues to endure. He was awarded the **1907 Nobel Prize**.

BIRTHS

W. H. Auden
Rachel Carson
Daphne du Maurier
Leon Edel
James Michener
Jesse Stuart

1908

HARDCOVER BESTSELLERS

fiction

Mr. Crewe's Career,
  Winston Churchill

The Barrier, Rex Beach

THE ALFRED B. NOBEL PRIZE FOR LITERATURE

Rudolf Eucken, Germany

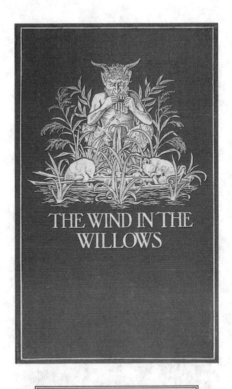

THE WIND IN THE
WILLOWS

The President's tremendous enjoyment infects his pen, and the reader catches the contagion from the printed page.

Review of *Outdoor Pastimes of an American Hunter* by Theodore Roosevelt,
NY Times Book Review,
December 26, 1908

[*18*]

BIRTHS

Simone de Beauvoir
Ian Fleming
John Kenneth Galbraith
Louis L'Amour
Theodore Roethke
Sinclair Ross
William Saroyan
Richard Wright

Mr. Upton Sinclair's new book is not important, is not literature, is not "a good story." To say of it that it has a sneer on every page and on many an incendiary utterance might be giving the author too much credit ... disgusts educated people because of the falsity of the picture, and ought to make the multitude laugh.

Review of *The Metropolis* by Upton Sinclair,
NY Times Book Review,
March 14, 1908

W. E. B. DU BOIS (1868-1963) was born in Great Barrington, Massachusetts, of French Huguenot, Dutch, and African ancestry. Raised by his mother, who died when he was sixteen, Du Bois struggled to receive an education. He won a scholarship to the all-black Fisk University, and then to Harvard, becoming in 1895 the first man of color to receive a Ph.D. from the university. Du Bois soon developed a reputation as America's most dynamic black leader. He taught economics and history at Atlanta University (1897-1910), organized young black intellectuals in the Niagara Movement (1905), helped to

W. E. B. Du Bois

[21]

found the National Association for the Advancement of Colored People (1909), edited the chief black publication of the day, *Crisis* (1910-1934), as well as wrote the most significant historical and sociological studies of African-America: *The Suppression of the African Slave Trade to the U.S.A.* (1896), his doctoral thesis; *The Souls of Black Folk* (1903); and **John Brown (1909),** among other works. He also wrote novels. Du Bois also served as a powerful advocate for African self-government, earning the title the "Father of Pan-Africanism." In 1900, he made the famous prophecy that "the problem of the Twentieth Century is the problem of the color line." In 1961, he joined the Communist Party, and a year before his death moved to Ghana to become a citizen of that nation.

• • •

H. G. Wells

H. G. WELLS (1866-1946) was born in Bromley, Kent, England, the son of an unsuccessful shopkeeper who abandoned the family when Wells was fourteen. He had a checkered education, but managed a position as a grammar school teacher and in 1884 won a scholarship to London's Normal School of Science, where he fell under the influence of T. H. Huxley. Wells married his cousin in 1891, but left her three years later to marry Amy Catherine Robbins, whom he regularly cheated on (Wells was a dedicated womanizer and strongly advocated sexual freedom). He rose to prominence in 1895 with the publication of *The Time Machine*, a class analysis set in the year 802701, and remained a best-selling author with *The Island of Dr.*

Moreau (1896), *The Invisible Man* (1897), and *The War of the Worlds* (1898), all science fiction novels elucidating his political idealism and socialist tendencies. Wells also wrote realistic novels of middle-class life, such as the successful *Tono Bungay* **(1909)**, and *Ann Veronica* **(1909)**, a tale of female sexual liberation. He was frequently involved in scandals—for the content of his fiction and his harsh political and literary criticism—but remained a prominent citizen, after World War I attending meetings at the League of Nations and traveling to the U.S.S.R. and the U.S. to interview Stalin and Roosevelt.

1910

LEO TOLSTOY (1828–1910) was born in Yasnaya Polyana, Russia, into an aristocratic family. Orphaned at nine, he was brought up by an elderly aunt and studied at Kazan University but did not graduate. After several aimless years in town and countryside, Tolstoy served as an officer in the Caucasus, wrote his first novels,  and after the Crimean War retired as commander. He returned to St. Petersburg a literary star, traveled abroad, and in 1862 married Sophie Behrs, who bore him thirteen children. Thereafter he settled on his Volga estate, combining the duties of a progressive landlord with that of a literary toiler, the latter culminating in his great novels—some of the most important fiction ever written—*War and Peace* (1869) and *Anna Karenina* (1877). Toward the end of his life, Tolstoy, as part of a religious quest, denounced all sophistication and luxury and handed over his fortune to his wife, with the resolution to live as a peasant under her roof. He died in a wintry railroad station after a quarrel with his wife.

> *Art is a human activity having for its purpose the transmission to others of the highest and best feelings to which men have risen.*
>
> Leo Tolstoy,
> *What Is Art?* (1898)

BIRTHS
Paul Bowles
Jean Genet

DEATHS
Björnstjerne Björnson
O. Henry (William Sydney Porter)
Leo Tolstoy
Mark Twain

spend several years lecturing and writing to keep his family in their Connecticut mansion. By the end of his life, he had achieved this goal but had become a bitter skeptic, despairing of human nature and the values of twentieth-century America.

> *I have had a "call" to Literature, of a low order— i.e. humorous. It is nothing to be proud of, but it is my strongest suit . . . seriously scribbling to excite the laughter of God's creatures.*
>
> Mark Twain, letter to Orion and Mary Clemens, October 19, 1865

MARK TWAIN (1835-1910) was born Samuel Clemens in Florida, Mississippi. He worked first as a printer and then as a river-boat pilot, where he adopted the name Mark Twain, which in boatman's terms means the mark of two fathoms. The Civil War put an end to the river traffic, and so he tried his hand at silver prospecting, journalism, and fiction, publishing his first story in 1865. Twain's literary career was central to the development of American letters; his greatest masterpieces, *Tom Sawyer* (1876) and *Huckleberry Finn* (1884), legitimized vernacular story-telling methods, while humorously and graphically portraying America's frontier mentality. After the success of these two novels, Twain invested in a publishing firm that failed, forcing him to

O. Henry 1862-1910

1911

HARDCOVER BESTSELLERS
fiction
The Broad Highway, Jeffrey Farnol
The Prodigal Judge, Vaughan Kester

THE ALFRED B. NOBEL PRIZE FOR LITERATURE
Maurice Maeterlinck, Belgium

BIRTHS
Elizabeth Bishop
William Golding
Tennessee Williams

It is always a mistake not to close one's eyes, whether to forgive or to look better into oneself.

Maurice Maeterlinck,
Pelleas et Melisande (1892)

• • •

A home run narrative
as vivid as the flight
of the ball in a world
championship game.

Review of *The Young Pitcher*
by Zane Grey,
Boston Globe, 1911

A charming character is
portrayed—that of a
man who because of his
love and pity for a woe-
fully afflicted boy, makes
a plaything of himself,
responsive to the little
fellows whimsical
demands, and does a
great many extraordinary
and ridiculous things.

Review of
Beasley's Christmas Party
by Booth Tarkington,
NY Times Book Review,
December 3, 1911

• • •

A remarkable study
of Russian character . . .
while the story is psy-
chological in treatment,
it is full enough of
dramatic climaxes and
gripping emotional
situations to make it an
absorbing tale. Its attempt
to translate the Russian
into terms a little more
intelligible to the
Western understanding
ought to make it very
interesting to those
readers who wish to
follow the course
of Russian events with
comprehension.

Review of
Under Western Eyes
by Joseph Conrad,
NY Times Book Review,
December 10, 1911

1912

HARDCOVER BESTSELLERS

fiction

The Harvester, Gene Stratton Porter

The Street Called Straight, Basil King

nonfiction

The Promised Land, Mary Antin

The Montessori Method,
Maria Montessori

**THE ALFRED B. NOBEL
PRIZE FOR LITERATURE**

Gerhart Hauptmann, Germany

August Strindberg, by Edvard Munch

AUGUST STRINDBERG (1849–1912) was born in Stockholm, Sweden, the son of a grocer and shipping agent. After failing to complete his studies at Uppsala University, and failing in his ambition to become an actor, he tried his hand at playwriting and realized he had talent. Strindberg's personal life was as turbulent as his work; he had three unsuccessful marriages and periods of severe persecution mania. His first major play was *Mäster Olof* (1872), an historical drama written in realistic and colloquial speech, which was quickly denounced by cultural authorities. His breakthrough came with the historical novel *The Red Room* (1879), based on his Bohemian experiences. It too created an uproar, but like much of his work was prescient; it is now viewed as a founding work of modern Swedish literature. Strindberg is largely remembered for his plays—such as *Miss Julie* (1888) and *A Dream Play* (1902)—which reflected his philosophical transitions (he was variously a follower of naturalism, Neitzsche, mysticism, and scientific realism) and, above all, foreshadowed the tenets of modern European theater.

> *I loathe people who keep dogs. They are cowards who haven't got the guts to bite people themselves.*
>
> August Strindberg,
> *A Madman's Diary* (1985)

[*24*]

There is an utter absence of sanity in the book which is delicious. The characters do idiotic things, their reason, doubtless, being that they must give the author something to describe.

Review of
The Prince and Betty
by P. G. Woodhouse,
NY Times Book Review,
March 17, 1912

•　　•　　•

No one can build his security upon the nobleness of another person.

Willa Cather
Alexander's Bridge

Russia is little better than a vast mad-house in which the keepers share the affliction of the kept. And yet the reader in spite of this presumption will not be able to deny that everybody— every man, woman, and child introduced into these 840 pages is human—convincingly and horribly human.

Review of
The Brothers Karamazov
by Fyodor Dostoyevsky,
NY Times Book Review,
June 30, 1912

BIRTHS

John Cheever
Lawrence Durrell
Jean Garrigue
Eugéne Ionesco
Mary McCarthy
Studs Terkel
Patrick White
Garth Williams

DEATH
August Strindberg

1913

HARDCOVER BESTSELLERS

fiction

The Inside of the Cup,
Winston Churchill

V.V.'s Eyes, Henry Sydnor Harrison

nonfiction

Crowds, Gerald Stanley Lee

Germany and the Germans,
Price Collier

**THE ALFRED B. NOBEL
PRIZE FOR LITERATURE**

Rabindranath Tagore, India

RABINDRANATH TAGORE (1861–1941) was born in Calcutta, India, the son of a distinguished scholar and religious reformer. Raised amidst the influences of three revolutionary movements—in religion, literature, and politics—Tagore came to embody the new India. Jawaharlal Nehru, India's first prime minister, described his work as being as influential as Gandhi's, and said, "More than any other Indian, he has helped to bring into harmony the ideals of the East and West." Tagore is primarily known as a poet, but he was prolific and versatile as a dramatist, novelist, short story writer, and writer of nonfiction prose. He published nearly sixty volumes of verse, the most famous of which, *Gitanjali* (1912), Yeats called "the work of supreme culture" and Pound compared to "the Paradiso of Dante." Tagore received the **1913 Nobel Prize**, the first Asian to do so, and was knighted in 1915—although he resigned in 1919 to protest British policy in the the Punjab. His major works include *Binodini* (1902), the first truly modern novel by an Indian writer, and the nonfictional meditation *The Religion of Man* (1931).

[26]

The beautiful bond between the restless son and the mother whom "his soul could not leave" even when she slept and "dreamed her young dream" . . . makes this book one of rare experience.

Review of *Sons and Lovers* by D. H. Lawrence, *NY Times Book Review,* September 12, 1913

BIRTHS

Pierre Boulle
Albert Camus
Robertson Davies

1914

AMBROSE BIERCE (1842–1914) was born in Horse Creek Cave, Ohio, and after fighting in the Civil War moved to San Francisco where he gained a reputation as a vitriolic journalist. In 1872, he sailed for London and found work writing caustic sketches of British politics and society. Back in San Francisco in 1877, Bierce joined Hearst's *Examiner* and as such became the most provocative pen on the West Coast, earning the nickname "Bitter Bierce." His short stories about the Civil War, such as "Chickamauga" and "An Occurrence at Owl Creek Bridge," established him as a creative writer, and his subsequent works, including the story collection *Can Such Things Be?* (1893) and *The Devil's Dictionary* (1911)—a collection of newspaper articles attacking politicians, materialistic values, and bourgeois life—made him even more popular. In 1913, tired of American society, Bierce traveled to revolutionary Mexico in search of "the good, kind darkness," and was never heard from again.

BIRTHS

John Berryman
William Burroughs
Marguerite Duras
Ralph Ellison
Howard Fast
John Hersey
Bernard Malamud
Octavio Paz
Dylan Thomas

DEATH

Ambrose Bierce

1915

HARDCOVER BESTSELLERS

fiction

The Turmoil, Booth Tarkington

A Far Country, Winston Churchill

THE ALFRED B. NOBEL PRIZE FOR LITERATURE

Romain Rolland, France

BIRTHS

Roland Barthes
Saul Bellow
Arthur Miller
Jean Stafford
Orson Welles
Herman Wouk

DEATH

Booker T. Washington

[*28*]

BOOKER T. WASHINGTON (1856-1915) was born in Franklin County, Virginia, the son of an unknown white man and a slave cook. He too was born into slavery, and as such spent his childhood packing salt, digging in a coal mine, and working as a general's houseboy. At sixteen, Washington altered the course of his life by entering Hampton Institute, where he adopted his symbolic surname and began to develop his influential racial and educational theories. Ten years later, at age twenty-five, he was chosen to become founding principal of a teacher-training school for blacks in Tuskegee, Georgia, which under his jurisdiction became the most prominent African-American vocational school in the country. Washington did not emphasize academics or political rights as the path to progress and self-enlightenment for blacks, but rather argued that hard work, thrift, and self-help were the keys to improved social status. His views were well received by the Roosevelt and Taft administrations, where he wielded more political power than any other black man of his generation, and by philanthropists such as Andrew Carnegie, who helped fund his Tuskegee Institute. Washington's fame was spread by his writing, especially his autobiography *Up from Slavery* (1901), which became a bestseller.

People ask you for criticism, but they only want praise.

W. Somerset Maugham,
Of Human Bondage (1915)

1916

HENRY JAMES (1843–1916) was born in New York City, but spent his youth traveling between England and America with his father, James Sr., a brilliant theologian; his brother, William, soon to emerge as the founder of modern psychology; and his sister, Alice, an important diarist. Together they became the most remarkably creative family America has ever known. By the time he was twenty-one, James had spent one-third of his life in foreign coun-

> *So it has come at last—the Distinguished Thing.*
>
> Henry James, of his final illness, December 2, 1915

tries, and thus it is not surprising that one of his recurring themes is the contrast between New World innocence and Old World sophistication. He wrote his great novels, such as *The Portrait of a Lady* (1881), *The Turn of the Screw* (1898), and *The Wings of the Dove* (1902), from a new perspective, employing the feelings and dialogue of his characters rather than an objective narrative. This new technique revolutionized fiction and made James the acknowledged master of the psychological novel.

BIRTHS

Roald Dahl
James Herriot
Walker Percy

DEATHS

Henry James
Jack London

JACK LONDON (1876-1916) was born in San Francisco, a "bastard," as he recalled, but actually the son of a medium and "professor" of astrology who lived in poverty. At age ten, he

trouble reconciling his fame with his fortune (which he squandered on a round-the-world schooner, *The Shark*). He drank heavily, was brutal and adventurous, and simultaneously adhered to socialism and Anglo-Saxon supremacy. He died at age forty of uremia, hastened by a morphine overdose.

> *I am the people—the mob—the crowd—the mass. Do you know that all the great work of the world is done through me?*
>
> Carl Sandburg,
> "I Am the People, the Mob"
> (1916)

Jack London

took employment as a newspaper vendor, subsequently working as a sailor, seal-hunter, political activist, and gold prospector, while finding time for furious self-education. London's first book of stories about gold miners led him to be dubbed "The Kipling of Klondike," but it wasn't until his novels, *The Call of the Wild* (1903) and *The Sea Wolf* (1904), that he became a bestselling author, earning, by the age of thirty, a million dollars. London had

Franz Kafka publishes "Metamorphosis" (1916).

1917

HARDCOVER BESTSELLERS

fiction

Mr. Britling Sees It Through,
H. G. Wells

The Light in the Clearing,
Irving Bacheller

general nonfiction

Rhymes of a Red Cross Man,
Robert W. Service

The Plattsburg Manual, O. O. Ellis
and E. B. Garey

war books

The First Hundred Thousand, Ian Hay

My Home in the Field of Honor,
Frances W. Huard

THE ALFRED B. NOBEL PRIZE FOR LITERATURE

Karl Gjellerup, Denmark

Henrik Pontoppidan, Denmark

THE PULITZER PRIZE

biography or autobiography

Julia Ward Howe, Laura E. Richards
and Maude Howe Elliott, assisted
by Florence Howe Hall

*Who shall say I am not the
happy genius of my household?*

William Carlos Williams,
"Danse Russe" (1917)

• • •

A new novel by Edith
Wharton is in itself quite
enough to arouse the
curiosity and pleasurable
anticipation of those who
care for what is the best in
contemporary fiction …
In one or two places, the
reader is a little surprised at
the slight way in which
certain important episodes
are touched on. But to say
that it is artistic and well
worth reading is merely to
report something which all
readers of modern fiction
will accept as a matter of
course.

Review of *Summer*
by Edith Wharton,
NY Times Book Review,
July 8, 1917

1918

HARDCOVER BESTSELLERS

fiction

The U. P. Trail, Zane Grey

The Tree of Heaven, May Sinclair

general nonfiction

Rhymes of a Red Cross Man,
Robert W. Service

Treasury of War Poetry, G. H. Clark

war books

My Four Years in Germany,
James W. Gerard

The Glory of the Trenches,
Coningsby Dawson

THE ALFRED B. NOBEL PRIZE FOR LITERATURE

No award

GUILLAUME APOLLINAIRE (WILHELM KOSTROWITZKI) (1880-1918). The son of a father of unknown nationality and a Polish adventuress supposedly of aristocratic birth, Apollinaire spent his childhood in constant travel from one international resort to another. At twenty, he arrived in Paris, changed his name, and became the perfect incarnation of the Left Bank Bohemian. There he socialized and is credited for having "discovered" the painters Picasso, Rousseau, and Braque. Apollinaire is known more for his persona than for his prose or poetry (his best-known work, *The Poet Assassinated* (1923), was described as "sheer premeditated insanity"). He was said to resemble a Roman emperor of the decadent period, and was variously described as "the Heliogabalus of the Intellect" and "the Marco Polo of the new spirit in art."

BIRTHS

Muriel Spark
Mickey Spillane
Aleksandr Solzhenitsyn

DEATHS

Guillaume Apollinaire
Joyce Kilmer
Edmond Rostand

THE PULITZER PRIZES

fiction

His Family, Ernest Poole

biography or autobiography

Benjamin Franklin, Self Revealed,
William Cabell Bruce

drama

Why Marry?, Jesse Lynch Williams

1919

tion at fourteen. After serving in the Spanish-American War, he became manager of an Ohio paint factory, but one day abandoned his post, leaving the impression that he had gone insane. Anderson is best known for his short story collection, ***Winesburg, Ohio* (1919)**, which with its careful studies of thwarted personalities earned him the appellation "the Chekhov of Middle America." In 1924, he moved to Marion, Virginia, where he became editor simultaneously of the two town papers—one Republican and one Democratic. Though he loved writing, toward the end of his life he announced it a dead art in America, soon to be replaced by the cinema, and said he was ready to devote himself to the new craft.

SHERWOOD ANDERSON (1876–1941) was born in Camden, Ohio, the son of a roaming, improvident, but highly imaginative father who moved his family aimlessly around Ohio. To help out, young Anderson worked odd jobs, and as a result ended his formal educa-

BIRTHS

Shirley Jackson
Doris Lessing
Iris Murdoch
J. D. Salinger

DEATH

L. Frank Baum

1920

HARDCOVER BESTSELLERS

fiction

The Man of the Forest, Zane Grey

Kindred of the Dust, Peter B. Kyne

nonfiction

Now It Can Be Told, Philip Gibbs

The Economic Consequences of the Peace, John Maynard Keynes

THE ALFRED B. NOBEL PRIZE FOR LITERATURE

Knut Hamsun, Norway

THE PULITZER PRIZES

fiction

No award

biography or autobiography

The Life of John Marshall, Albert J. Beveridge

drama

Beyond the Horizon, Eugene O'Neill

Nobel Prize winner Knut Hamsun

BIRTHS

Isaac Asimov
Ray Bradbury
P. D. James
Mario Puzo
Richard Scarry

DEATH

William Dean Howells

[34]

As for literature
It gives no man a sinecure.
And no one knows, at sight,
a masterpiece.
"And give up verse, my boy,
There's nothing in it."

Ezra Pound,
Hugh Selwyn Mauberley (1920)

Marcel Proust completes his masterpiece,
Remembrance of Things Past.

1921

HARDCOVER BESTSELLERS

fiction

Main Street, Sinclair Lewis

The Brimming Cup,
Dorothy Canfield

nonfiction

The Outline of History, H. G. Wells

White Shadows in the South Seas,
Frederick O'Brien

THE ALFRED B. NOBEL PRIZE FOR LITERATURE

Anatole France, France

Bestselling author Sinclair Lewis

BIRTHS

Betty Friedan
Alex Haley
Andrei Sakharov
Richard Wilbur

Pulitzer Prize winner Edith Wharton

THE PULITZER PRIZES

fiction

The Age of Innocence, Edith Wharton

biography or autobiography

The Americanization of Edward Bok,
Edward Bok

drama

Miss Lulu Bett, Zona Gale

1922

HARDCOVER BESTSELLERS

fiction

If Winter Comes,
  A. S. M. Hutchinson

The Sheik, Edith M. Hull

nonfiction

The Outline of History, H. G. Wells

The Story of Mankind,
  Hendrik Willem Van Loon

THE ALFRED B. NOBEL PRIZE FOR LITERATURE

Jacinto Benavente, Spain

THE PULITZER PRIZES

fiction

Alice Adams, Booth Tarkington

biography or autobiography

A Daughter of the Middle Border,
  Hamlin Garland

poetry

Collected Poems,
  Edwin Arlington Robinson

drama

Anna Christie, Eugene O'Neill

THE NEWBERY MEDAL

The Story of Mankind,
  Henrik Willem van Loon

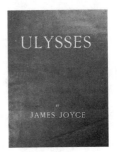

A few intuitive, sensitive visionaries may understand and comprehend "Ulysses," James Joyce's new and mammoth volume, without going through a course of training or instruction, but the average intelligent reader will glean little or nothing from it.

Joseph Collins, review of
Ulysses by James Joyce,
NY Times Book Review,
May 28, 1922

BIRTHS

Kingsley Amis
William Gaddis
Jack Kerouac
Howard Moss
Grace Paley
Kurt Vonnegut

DEATH

Marcel Proust

MARCEL PROUST (1871-1922) was born in Paris, a town he rarely left, to a professor of medicine. An asthmatic and semi-invalid all his life, he was cosseted by his mother, whose death in 1905 robbed him of all desire to continue his "social butterfly" life. He studied law and political science, but his health problems precluded any regular profession: besides, his devotion was to writing. In his early years, Proust contributed to literary reviews and indulged in the world of the Parisian salons. But this, as noted, did not last. At thirty-four, he withdrew from

> *What artists call posterity is the posterity of the work of art.*
>
> Marcel Proust,
> *Within a Budding Grove*
> (1919)

society, immured himself in a sound-proof flat, and between 1912 and 1920 wrote his masterpiece, *Remembrance of Things Past*, a seven-volume work devoted to the depiction and distillation of one man's emotional life. Though few had taken Proust seriously earlier—in fact most had considered him a neurotic literary aristocrat—by the time of his death it was clear that his psychological novel was to be a milestone in twentieth-century literature.

T. S. Eliot publishes his ground-breaking poem, "The Waste Land."

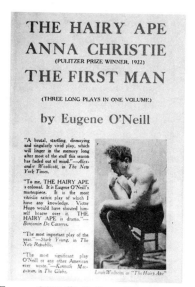

Eugene O'Neill's Pulitzer Prize–winning play Anna Christie

1923

HARDCOVER BESTSELLERS

fiction

Black Oxen, Gertrude Atherton

His Children's Children, Arthur Train

nonfiction

Etiquette, Emily Post

The Life of Christ, Giovanni Papini

THE ALFRED B. NOBEL PRIZE FOR LITERATURE

W. B. Yeats, Ireland

Unlike most of the younger writers who have left the old, beaten tracks, Miss Woolf is not pessimistic. There is no disillusionment in her work, but instead of that, a fine realization of the intrinsic beauty of life and a dominant sympathy with her characters. This book again impresses upon the reader of English fiction the great quality of the women now writing in that country, headed, of course, by May Sinclair. Miss Woolf is certainly one of the foremost figures in this group.

Review of *Jacob's Room*
by Virginia Woolf,
NY Times Book Review,
March 4, 1923

Mr. Forster is brilliant, humorous, subtle, original, but never unconvincing. His books are packed with life, observation and good sense, and always they ring true. His books, it has been said, are not about life; they are life . . . though his audiences in both England and America are still limited, it is very obvious that soon they will be widespread.

Henry James Forman, review
of *A Room with a View*
by E. M. Forster,
NY Times Book Review,
February 4, 1923.

BIRTHS

Italo Calvino
James Dickey
Nadine Gordimer
Joseph Heller
Denise Levertov
Norman Mailer

as senator of the Irish Free State from 1922 to 1928). Yeats was also a maverick of the essay, biography, the short story, and drama. In his later years, he devoted himself largely to modernist, stylistically rigorous poetry, which among his manifold literary achievements won him the **1923 Nobel Prize**. He died in France, the most respected and prolific poet of his day.

> *Let there be spaces in your togetherness.*
>
> Kahlil Gibran, *The Prophet* (1923)

W. B. YEATS (1865-1939) was born in Dublin, Ireland, the son of John Butler Yeats, a portrait painter, whose theories about art profoundly shaped his son's career. In 1884, he became a student of painting, but soon realized his talent lay in words. His early narrative poem, *The Wanderings of Oisin* (1889), and the collection *The Wind among the Reeds* (1899) drew on his dissatisfaction with scientific rationalism and interest in occultism and Irish nationalism. In 1885, he founded the Hermetic Society with a group of like-minded Irish intellectuals, and thus began his lifelong devotion to Irish politics and literary culture. Four years later, he met and fell in love with Maud Gonne, an actress and national agitator, whom he pursued unsuccessfully for thirteen years and who inspired much of his literary and political work (he served

THE PULITZER PRIZES

fiction
One of Ours, Willa Cather

biography or autobiography
The Life and Letters of Walter H. Page, Burton J. Hendrick

poetry
Ballad of the Harp-Weaver, Edna St. Vincent Millay

drama
Icebound, Owen Davis

THE NEWBERY MEDAL

The Voyages of Doctor Dolittle, Hugh Lofting

1924

HARDCOVER BESTSELLERS

fiction

So Big, Edna Ferber

The Plastic Age, Percy Marks

nonfiction

Diet and Health, Lulu Hunt Peters

The Life of Christ, Giovanni Papini

THE ALFRED B. NOBEL PRIZE FOR LITERATURE

Wladyslaw Reymount, Poland

instructed that they be destroyed after his death, a request that was thankfully disregarded by his friend and executor Max Brod, leading to the posthumous publication of *The Trial* (1925, 1937), *The Castle* (1926, 1937), and *Amerika* (1927, 1938), now considered paradigms of the modern European novel.

> *All interest in disease and death is only another expression of interest in life.*
>
> Thomas Mann,
> *The Magic Mountain*
> (1924)

FRANZ KAFKA (1883–1924) was born in Prague, the son of a prosperous Jewish businessman who insisted his son study law. Reluctantly, Kafka heeded his father's wishes, and in 1908 took a position at a workers' accident insurance company, where he began to keep a meticulous diary analyzing his inner life. Anxiety-ridden and deeply introspective, Kafka was never pleased with his personal or creative life, never married, and never had much confidence in his influential work. In 1917, he was diagnosed with tuberculosis and relegated to life in sanatoria. Though his short stories and essays, such as "Metamorphosis" (1916), were published in his lifetime, Kafka refused to do the same for his novels. In fact, he

BIRTHS

Kobo Abe
James Baldwin
Truman Capote
José Donoso
Leon Uris
Malcolm X

DEATHS

Joseph Conrad
Anatole France
Franz Kafka

JOSEPH CONRAD (1857–1924) was born Josef Teodor Konrad Korzeniowski of Polish parents in Russian-dominated Ukraine. His father's political sympa-

Joseph Conrad

Narcissus (1897), *Heart of Darkness* (1899), *Lord Jim* (1900), and *Under Western Eyes* (1911), were generally ill-received by critics and the public alike (they were read as simple sea stories), but by the end of his life he was recognized as one of the English language's finest modern novelists.

thies caused the family to be exiled to Volagda in northern Russia, where Conrad's mother died when he was seven. Four years later, his father died, and he was taken under the wing of his uncle, Thaddeus Bobrowski, who lived in Switzerland and tutored him in the classics. In 1874, Conrad, desiring to see the world, embarked on a vessel headed for Marseilles. From there, he traveled to the French territories, gambled away a small fortune, and survived a self-inflicted shotgun wound. In 1886, he became a British subject and a master mariner, and in 1894, after twenty years at sea, settled in England and devoted himself to writing in English—his third tongue, first heard at age twenty-one. Conrad's famous works of fiction, *The Nigger of the*

THE PULITZER PRIZES
fiction
The Able McLaughlins, Margaret Wilson

biography or autobiography
From Immigrant to Inventor, Michael Pupin

poetry
New Hampshire: A Poem with Notes and Grace Note, Robert Frost

drama
Hell-Bent for Heaven, Hatcher Hughes

THE NEWBERY MEDAL
The Dark Frigate, Charles Hawes

ANATOLE FRANCE (1844-1924) was born Jacques-Anatole-François Thibault, the son of a Parisian bookseller, and spent the early part of his career as a reviewer and publisher's editor before gaining

Anatole France

recognition as a writer. In 1877, he was appointed keeper at the Senate Library, but lost his position after a literary quarrel and then his wife after a too-public affair with his patron Madame de Caillavet. France is chiefly known for his witty, urbane novels, short stories, and nonfictional meditations, the most famous of which are *Le Petit Pierre* (1919), an autobiographical novel of his childhood, his short story collection *Balthasar* (1889), and *Les Dieux ont soif* (1912), a masterly study of revolutionary fanaticism and corruption. The Dreyfus affair stirred France into politics as an opponent of church and state as well as a vociferous advocate of internationalism. He was awarded the 1921 Nobel Prize in Literature.

There are some novelists who creep into public esteem rather imperceptibly, and Mr. E. M. Forster is one of these ... "A Passage to India" is both a challenge and an indictment ... "A Passage to India" should greatly widen that rather small audience that has relished his novels in the past. And that rather small audience should congratulate itself on its acumen.

Herbert S. Grossman,
review of
A Passage to India
by E. M. Forster,
NY Times Book Review,
August 17, 1924

Pulitzer Prize winner Robert Frost. In his lifetime, he earned four Pulitzer Prizes.

1925

HARDCOVER BESTSELLERS

fiction

Soundings, A. Hamilton Gibbs

The Constant Nymph,
Margaret Kennedy

nonfiction

Diet and Health, Lulu Hunt Peters

The Boston Cooking School Cook Book, Fannie Farmer [new ed.]

THE ALFRED B. NOBEL PRIZE FOR LITERATURE

George Bernard Shaw, Ireland

THE PULITZER PRIZES

fiction

So Big, Edna Ferber

biography or autobiography

Barrett Wendell and His Letters,
M. A. DeWolfe Howe

poetry

The Man Who Died Twice,
Edwin Arlington Robinson

drama

They Knew What They Wanted,
Sidney Howard

THE NEWBERY MEDAL

Tales from Silver Lands,
Charles Finger

The philosopher of the flapper has escaped the mordant, but he has turned grave. A curious book, a mystical, glamourous story of today. It takes a deeper cut at life than hitherto has been essayed by Mr. Fitzgerald. He writes well—he always has—for he writes naturally, and his sense of form is becoming perfected.

Edwin Clark, review of
The Great Gatsby
by F. Scott Fitzgerald,
NY Times Book Review,
April 4, 1925

There is no room for the impurities of literature in an essay.

Virginia Woolf,
The Common Reader (1925)

[43]

BIRTHS

William F. Buckley
Art Buchwald
James Clavell
Elmore Leonard
Yukio Mishima
Flannery O'Connor
William Styron
Gore Vidal

DEATH

Amy Lowell

A French critic . . . described Marcel Proust as a man shut up in his ego as in a railway carriage, indefatigably looking out of his window at the landscape passing by . . . It should also be added that M. Proust directs his own route and, however much he may seem to be deflected into the byways of associative memory, his side trips are never absolutely involuntary. On the contrary, he knew where he was going, and throughout his long, reminiscent journey his hand controlled the throttle . . . in spite of the piquant nature of much of his material, Proust will never be a widely popular writer.

Rose Lee, review of
The Guermantes Way
by Marcel Proust,
NY Times Book Review,
July 5, 1925

No one has ever made of the novel so potent an instrument for social satire or administered, through its medium, so many rough jolts to national complacency . . . One closes the novel with a feeling that, if eternal verities be the ultimate objective, no great progress has been made . . . This novel is full of passages of a quite noble felicity and the old skill in presenting character through dialogue never fails.

Henry Longan Stuart,
review of *Arrowsmith*
by Sinclair Lewis,
NY Times Book Review,
March 8, 1925

The New Yorker *will
not be edited for the old
lady from Dubuque.*

Harold Ross, upon founding
The New Yorker, 1925

1926

HARDCOVER BESTSELLERS

fiction

The Private Life of Helen of Troy, John Erskine

Gentlemen Prefer Blondes, Anita Loos

nonfiction

The Man Nobody Knows, Bruce Barton

Why We Behave Like Human Beings, George A. Dorsey

THE ALFRED B. NOBEL PRIZE FOR LITERATURE

Grazia Deledda, Italy

Bestselling author Anita Loos

BIRTHS

Robert Bly
Allen Ginsberg
John Knowles
James Merrill
W. D. Snodgrass

DEATH

Rainer Maria Rilke

If any less well established writer than Mr. Dreiser had brought the manuscript of these two volumes into a publisher's office it is easy to guess what would have happened to him. He would have been told that his work was very promising indeed, and asked to take it away and cut it in half . . . "An American Tragedy" is not to be recommended as fireside reading for the tired businessman: yet, as a portrayal of one of the darker phases of the American character, it demands attention.

Robert L. Duffus, review of
An American Tragedy
by Theodore Dreiser,
NY Times Book Review,
January 1, 1926

THE PULITZER PRIZES

fiction
Arrowsmith, Sinclair Lewis

biography or autobiography
Life of Sir William Osler,
  Harvey Cushing

poetry
What's O'Clock, Amy Lowell

drama
Craig's Wife, George Kelly

THE NEWBERY MEDAL

Shen of the Sea, Arthur Chrisman

> *Death is the side of
> life which is turned away
> from us.*
>
> Rainer Maria Rilke,
> letter to W. von Hulewicz

SELECTED POEMS of CARL SANDBURG Edited by Rebecca West

ISAAC BABEL (1894–?1941) was born in a Jewish ghetto in Odessa, Ukraine, the son of a shopkeeper, who brought him up in the Orthodox faith. In 1915, he moved to Petrograd where he worked as a journalist and wrote short stories, which Maxim Gorky published in his literary review. Beginning in 1917, Babel served as a soldier in the tsar's army, and after the Revolution in various Bolshevik campaigns as a Cossack supply officer. These experiences led to his masterpiece, **Red Calvary (1926–1929)**, which describes the harshness and savagery of war. Babel also wrote a cycle of stories about a Jewish Odessan gangster, collected in *Odessa Tales* (1924). In the 1920s, he came under increasing pressure from the Soviet authorities, and in 1939 was arrested and disappeared into the Soviet penal system: the date of his death is unknown. Babel was posthumously rehabilitated and today his work is widely read and translated.

1927

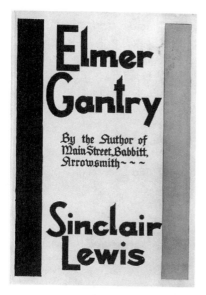

Bestselling novel

Like some of the modern composers he is a heretic so far as the dogmas of composition are concerned, and he mingles freely a dozen traditions ranging from the manner of the ancient Chinese and the Provençal troubadours to the most modern vers libre in order to attain his effects . . . his work is always the personal reflex of his furious opinions on life, love and art . . . one may call him the finest American warrior for a liberalized expression in contemporary poetry.

Review of *Personae, The Collected Poems of Ezra Pound* by Ezra Pound, *NY Times Book Review,* January 23, 1927

> The great poet, in writing himself, writes his time.
>
> T. S. Eliot,
> "Shakespeare and the
> Stoicism of Seneca" (1927)

THE PULITZER PRIZES

fiction
Early Autumn, Louis Bromfield

biography or autobiography
Whitman: An Interpretation in Narrative, Emory Holloway

poetry
Fiddler's Farewell, Leonora Speyer

drama
In Abraham's Bosom, Paul Green

THE NEWBERY MEDAL

Smoky, the Cowhorse, Will James

BIRTHS

Erma Bombeck
Günter Grass
Robert Ludlum
W. S. Merwin
Neil Simon

THE MAGIC MOUNTAIN
BY THOMAS··MANN

The reader looks in vain through "The Magic Mountain" for the docketed views and pat opinions of Thomas Mann . . . "The Magic Mountain" falls just short of being that work upon which the thoughtful wanderer among contemporary perplexities may build a serene, untroubled, understanding acceptance of life. But it goes far on the way.

John W. Crawford, review of
The Magic Mountain
by Thomas Mann,
NY Times Book Review,
May 28, 1927

1928

THOMAS HARDY (1840-1928) was born in Dorset, England, to common rural folk. His mother taught him to read at three and by the time he finished grammar school, he knew the classics, French, and German. In 1856, he was apprenticed to a Dorchester and then a London architect, but despite winning awards, he was determined to be a writer. Hardy published his first novel at thirty-one, and with the sale of his fourth book, *Far from the Madding Crowd* (1874), proposed marriage to Emma Gifford, a woman whose considerable social standing led him to cut off relations with his own family. Yet Hardy's simple origins proved indispensable. His empathetic depiction of country people in *The Return of the Native* (1878) and *Tess of the d'Urbervilles* (1891) won him readers; however, these books also earned him condemnation—from the public and his wife—who believed them to be somewhat amoral. Today his books feel modern and he remains a giant of English literature.

BIRTHS

Edward Albee
Maya Angelou
John Ashbery
Noam Chomsky
Philip K. Dick
William Kennedy
Judith Krantz
Gabriel García Márquez
Maurice Sendak
Anne Sexton
Elie Wiesel

DEATH
Thomas Hardy

[*50*]

MARGARET MEAD (1901–1978) was born in Philadelphia, Pennsylvania, and earned a Master's degree in anthropology from Columbia University. An authority on more than a dozen aspects of human science and a perennial student of human cultural evolution, Mead made an impact on the field of anthropology that is unmistakable. She is credited with revolutionizing her field—making it broad-based and interdisciplinary as well as accessible to a wide public. Much of her career was devoted to the study of native people of the Pacific. In 1925, she traveled to the Samoan Islands to study adolescent girls, which led to perhaps her most influential work, **Coming of Age in Samoa (1928)**. She also studied various tribes inhabiting New Guinea, all the time questioning the problems of cultural stability, sex difference, gender socialization, education, generational change, cooperation and competition, and family life. One obituarist described her ambition the "greater understanding of human harmony."

1929

THE ALFRED B. NOBEL PRIZE FOR LITERATURE

Thomas Mann, Germany

Nobel Prize winner Thomas Mann

THOMAS MANN (1876-1955), the **1929 Nobel Prize** winner, was born in Lübech, Germany, into a patrician family of merchants and senators. His mother was a talented musician of part Portuguese, part Creole descent, and these clashing influences of Nordic and Latin, industry and artistry, and rationalism and mysticism served as a strong motif in Mann's life. At nineteen, he left school and settled with his mother in Munich, where he wrote his first masterpiece, *Buddenbrooks* (1901), a saga of a family like his own, which made him a leading German novelist at the age of twenty-four. Over the next few years, he produced remarkable essays and novels, including *A Death in Venice* (1913) and *The Magic Mountain* (1924), mostly dealing with the problem of the artist's salvation and the dying traditions of nineteenth-century Europe. World War I revealed Mann's militant German patriotism, but in 1933 he retracted this position and fled the Nazi regime, living in exile in Switzerland. His German citizenship was revoked in 1936. He moved to California in 1938, became a U.S. citizen in 1944, but spent his final years in Switzerland.

[53]

BIRTHS

Anne Frank
Martin Luther King
Milan Kundera
Ursula LeGuin
Ira Levin
John Osborne
William Safire

ALL QUIET ON THE WESTERN FRONT
ERICH MARIA REMARQUE

Bestselling novel

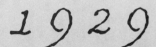

1929

THE PULITZER PRIZES

fiction
Scarlet Sister Mary,
Julia M. Peterkin

biography or autobiography
*The Training of an American:
The Earlier Life and Letters
of Walter H. Page*,
Burton J. Hendrick

poetry
John Brown's Body,
Stephen Vincent Benét

drama
Street Scene,
Elmer Rice

THE NEWBERY MEDAL

The Trumpeter of Krakow,
Eric P. Kelly

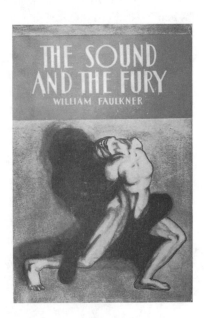

THE SOUND AND THE FURY
WILLIAM FAULKNER

A FAREWELL TO ARMS
ERNEST HEMINGWAY

1930

SIR ARTHUR CONAN DOYLE (1859–1930) was born in Edinburgh, England, to devout Roman Catholics and studied medicine at the city's university, where one of his professors served as the model for his irascible literary character, Sherlock Holmes. Doyle said that his writing developed because his patients were so few and thus his business so bad. In 1888, his first book featuring Holmes was published, followed by two dozen riotously popular stories. But by this time, he had come to hate the character and decided—against his publisher's advice—to kill him off. Eight years later, though, he consented to public protest and revived Holmes in *The Hound of the Baskervilles* (1902). Doyle then turned to politics: twice he ran unsuccessfully for Parliament; in 1900, he sailed to South Africa eager to witness the Boer War; and in 1909, he defended a man wrongly condemned to capital punishment. By the end of his life, he announced he was a convert to spiritualism.

[53]

D. H. LAWRENCE (1885-1930) was born in Eastwood, Nottinghamshire, the son of a miner. He attended public school on scholarship, became a reluctant teacher, and when his childhood sweetheart sent his poems to Ford Madox Ford (who accepted them immediately), he began to give serious

thought to becoming a writer. After the publication of his first novel, *The White Peacock* (1911), Lawrence gave up teaching, and with the wife of his former professor from Nottingham University, eloped to Bavaria and traveled throughout Europe. The war years were difficult for Lawrence, who was exempt from military service due to tubercular tendencies (which killed him at age forty-four), and whose books, including *The Rainbow* (1915), were considered scurrilous and banned by the authorities. After the war, he again traveled widely, writing poetry, essays, and novels, including *Women in Love* (1920) and *Lady Chatterly's Lover* (1928), which drew just as much criticism for their explorations of sex and marriage.

Our American professors like their literature clear and cold and pure and very dead.

Sinclair Lewis, "The American Fear of Literature," Nobel lecture, December 12, 1930

• • •

This novel is distinguished and unusual. It is a lucid exposition of the mind and the life of an English village woman who—after some sixteen years of fortitude—has been driven by her circumstances to murder . . . The book, so the publishers inform us, is satire. It seems, rather, a dizzy nightmare.

Review of *The Defendant Soul* by Charles Forrest, *NY Times Book Review*, March 23, 1930

1931

HARDCOVER BESTSELLERS

fiction

The Good Earth, Pearl S. Buck

Shadows on the Rock, Willa Cather

nonfiction

Education of a Princess,
  Grand Duchess Marie

The Story of San Michele,
  Axel Dunthe

THE ALFRED B. NOBEL PRIZE FOR LITERATURE

Erik A. Karlfeldt, Sweden

THE PULITZER PRIZES

fiction

Years of Grace,
  Margaret Ayer Barnes

biography or autobiography

Charles W. Eliot, Henry James

poetry

Collected Poems, Robert Frost

drama

Alison's House, Susan Glaspell

THE NEWBERY MEDAL

The Cat Who Went to Heaven,
  Elizabeth Coatsworth

Bestselling author Willa Cather

BIRTHS

Donald Barthelme
Mary Higgins Clark
E. L. Doctorow
John le Carré
Toni Morrison
Alice Munro
Mordecai Richler
Tom Wolfe

DEATHS

Kahlil Gibran
Vachel Lindsay

[55]

BY THE AUTHOR OF
THE SOUND AND THE FURY
SANCTUARY
WILLIAM FAULKNER

1932

ALDOUS HUXLEY (1894–1963) was born of the blood of two of England's most eminent intellectual families, the Huxleys and the Arnolds. At fourteen his mother died and at sixteen he developed serious eye trouble, which made

him nearly blind, but Huxley nonetheless graduated from Oxford with honors in English. His first novel, *Crome Yellow* (1921), established him as a precocious and brilliant cynic, and his **1932** novel, **Brave New World**, depicting a dystopian view of the future, made him world famous. In 1937, Huxley emigrated to America with the guru-figure Gerald Heard and became interested in mysticism. He settled in California, collaborated on Hollywood films, experimented with consciousness-expanding drugs, and wrote essays and works of fiction that went mostly unnoticed. It wasn't until after his death that Huxley's literary importance was resurrected.

> It is Mr. Huxley's habit to be deadly in earnest. One feels that he is pointing a high moral lesson in satirizing Utopia. Yet it is a little difficult to take alarm . . . the bogy of mass production seems a little overwrought . . . if Mr. Huxley is unduly bothered about the impending static world, let him go back to his biology and meditate on the possibility that even in laboratory-created children mutations might be inevitable.
>
> John Chamberlain,
> review of
> *Brave New World*
> by Aldous Huxley,
> *NY Times Book Review*,
> February 7, 1932

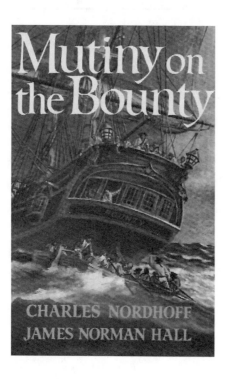

**CHARLES NORDHOFF
JAMES NORMAN HALL**

BIRTHS
*John Gregory Dunne
Umberto Eco
V. S. Naipaul
Sylvia Plath
John Updike*

DEATHS
*Hart Crane
Kenneth Grahame*

"1919" is primarily a
"news" novel. It is, of
course, a satire on expan-
sionist, "on the make,"
raffish and vulgar America
... Mr. Dos Passos is ...
the most adventurous, the
most widely experienced,
the man with the broad-
est sympathies (we do not
say the deepest), among
our novelists since Sinclair
Lewis bade goodbye to
Martin Arrowsmith.
Hemingway, who is Dos
Passos's closest competitor
in exploring the modern
jungle, has been almost
solely orientated in per-
sonal problems raised by
the war.

John Chamberlain, review of
1919 by John Dos Passos,
NY Times Book Review,
March 13, 1932

1933

HARDCOVER BESTSELLERS

fiction
Anthony Adverse, Hervey Allen

As the Earth Turns,
  Gladys Hasty Carroll

nonfiction
Life Begins at Forty,
  Walter B. Pitkin

Marie Antoinette, Stefan Zweig

THE ALFRED B. NOBEL PRIZE FOR LITERATURE

Ivan G. Bunin, U.S.S.R.

THE PULITZER PRIZES

fiction
The Store, T. S. Stribling

biography or autobiography
Grover Cleveland, Allan Nevins

poetry
Conquistador, Archibald MacLeish

drama
Both Your Houses,
  Maxwell Anderson

THE NEWBERY MEDAL

Young Fu of the Upper Yangtze,
  Elizabeth Lewis

... ostensibly a piece of humorous fiction. But do not class it with the clever wisecracking little volumes that emerge ... to carry on the tradition of bald American exaggeration. It is ostensibly satiric. But its irony has roots to it. The wit is hard, brilliant and very funny.

Review of *Miss Lonelyhearts*,
by Nathanael West,
NY Times Book Review,
April 23, 1933

BIRTHS
Jerzy Kosinski
Cormac McCarthy
Reynolds Price
Philip Roth
Susan Sontag

DEATHS
John Galsworthy
Ring Lardner

1934

HARDCOVER BESTSELLERS

fiction

Anthony Adverse, Hervey Allen

Lamb in His Bosom, Caroline Miller

nonfiction

While Rome Burns,
Alexander Woollcott

Life Begins at Forty, Walter B. Pitkin

THE ALFRED B. NOBEL PRIZE FOR LITERATURE

Luigi Pirandello, Italy

THE PULITZER PRIZES

fiction

Lamb in His Bosom, Caroline Miller

biography or autobiography

John Hay, Tyler Dennett

poetry

Collected Verse, Robert Hillyer

drama

Men in White, Sidney Kingsley

THE NEWBERY MEDAL

Invincible Louisa, Cornelia Meigs

BIRTHS

Amiri Baraka (LeRoi Jones)
Joan Didion
David Halberstam
Wole Soyinka
Gloria Steinem
Mark Strand

DEATH

Mary Austin

[*59*]

Call It Sleep *by Henry Roth, originally published in 1934, as reissued in 1991*

HENRY MILLER (1891–1980) was born in New York and brought up by German-American parents in Brooklyn. Rebellious from the start, he dropped out of City College, went from job to job, ran a speakeasy in Greenwich Village, and at thirty, with money attained from his wife June's wealthy lovers, moved to Paris to write fiction. There he met Anaïs Nin, who underwrote (with money from her lover and psychiatrist Otto Rank) the publication of **Tropic of Cancer (1934)** and with whom Miller and June had a triangular love affair, described in Nin's journal *Henry and June* (1986). With the outbreak of the war, Miller returned to the United States, settled in Big Sur, wrote *The Rosy Crucifixion* trilogy, and finally saw American editions of his *Tropic*(s) *of Cancer and Capricorn* (considered sexually obscene when written). Until the late 1970s (when he fell afoul of feminist critics), he was one of the most read American authors.

[60]

James T. Farrell publishes The Young Manhood of Studs Lonigan, *the second volume in the Studs Lonigan trilogy.*

1935

*Bestselling author
Anne Morrow Lindbergh*

BIRTHS

*Woody Allen
Ken Kesey
E. Annie Proulx
Carol Shields
Calvin Trillin*

DEATH

Edwin Arlington Robinson

1936

HARDCOVER BESTSELLERS

fiction

Gone with the Wind,
Margaret Mitchell

The Last Puritan, George Santayana

nonfiction

Man the Unknown, Alexis Carrel

Wake Up and Live!,
Dorothea Brande

**THE ALFRED B. NOBEL
PRIZE FOR LITERATURE**

Eugene O'Neill, U.S.

THE PULITZER PRIZES

fiction

Honey in the Horn, Harold L. Davis

biography or autobiography

*The Thought and Character of
William James,*
Ralph Barton Perry

poetry

Strange Holiness,
Robert P. Tristram Coffin

drama

Idiot's Delight, Robert E. Sherwood

THE NEWBERY MEDAL

Caddie Woodlawn, Carol Brink

[62]

EUGENE O'NEILL (1888-1953) was born in New York, the son of a successful romance actor. He attended Princeton for one year, then worked as a secretary in New York, a seaman in South America, and a gold prospector in Honduras. At twenty-four—perhaps confounded by his experiences—O'Neill attempted suicide and was sent to a sanitarium where he decided to become a playwright. His first one-act plays were considered remarkable for their combination of symbolic representation and realism, and his 1916 *Bound East for Cardiff* is generally viewed as the beginning of modern American theater. In 1920, O'Neill was awarded the Pulitzer Prize for his first full-length play, *Beyond the Horizon*, and over the next fourteen years became the most famous dramatist in the United States. By 1934, however, he had again become immobilized by depression, destroying all that he produced, even though the honor of the **1936 Nobel Prize** fell to him. It was not until *The Iceman Cometh* (1946) that O'Neill broke his theatrical silence, and it was not until after his death that many of his finest plays, including *Long Day's Journey into Night* (1956)—often regarded as the most important twentieth-century American play—were published.

> *In the United States there is more space where nobody is than where anybody is. This is what makes America what it is.*
>
> Gertrude Stein,
> *The Geographical History of America*
> (1936)

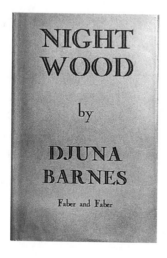

Bestselling author Margaret Mitchell

This is beyond a doubt one of the most remarkable first novels produced by an American writer. It is also one of the best . . . a book of uncommon quality, a superb piece of story-telling . . . only a rash critic would make any prophecies as to Miss Mitchell's future. She has set herself a hard mark to match with a second book, and I hope only that she will not set too soon about it.

J. Donald Adams, review of
Gone with the Wind
by Margaret Mitchell,
NY Times Book Review,
July 5, 1936

Rudyard Kipling 1865-1936

BIRTHS

Don DeLillo
Václav Havel
Larry McMurtry
Luigi Pirandello

DEATHS

Federico García Lorca
Rudyard Kipling
Lincoln Steffens

Art is unthinkable with-
out risk and spiritual self
sacrifice.

Boris Pasternak,
"On Modesty and Bravery,"
speech at Writers'
Conference, 1936

1937

HARDCOVER BESTSELLERS

fiction

Gone with the Wind,
Margaret Mitchell

Northwest Passage, Kenneth Roberts

nonfiction

*How to Win Friends and Influence
People*, Dale Carnegie

An American Doctor's Odyssey,
Victor Heiser

**THE ALFRED B. NOBEL
PRIZE FOR LITERATURE**

Roger Martin du Gard, France

> *Women forget all those
> things they don't want to
> remember, and remember
> everything they don't want
> to forget. The dream is the
> truth. Then they act and do
> things accordingly.*
>
> Zora Neale Hurston,
> *Their Eyes Were Watching God*
> (1937)

Bestselling author *Dale Carnegie*

EDITH WHARTON (1862–1937) was born Edith Newbold Jones in New York to an aristocratic American family, and grew up in New York, Newport, and Paris. In 1885, she married a Boston banker, Edward Robbins Wharton, who was mentally unstable and with whom she had an unhappy marriage (they divorced in 1913). She began writing as a means of relief, publishing stories, and in 1905 became a cause célèbre for her second novel, *The House of Mirth*, a tragedy about a beautiful and sensitive society girl, which sold one hundred thousand copies within ten days of publication. *The Age of Innocence* (1920), was awarded a Pulitzer Prize. Wharton is known for her keen, witty observations of high society and her gripping portraits of women and men constrained by social norms and sexual hypocrisy. In her later years, she lived mostly in Europe, and by the end of her life had authored almost fifty novels, poetry collections, and travelogues.

[66]

> It belongs not with the many novels that horrify, but with the many fewer novels which terrify.
>
> Louis Kronenberger, review of *The Trial* by Franz Kafka, *NY Times Book Review*, October 24, 1937

BIRTHS

Thomas Pynchon
Robert Stone
Tom Stoppard
Joseph Wambaugh

DEATHS

James M. Barrie
Ralph Conner
Edith Wharton

THE PULITZER PRIZES

fiction
Gone with the Wind, Margaret Mitchell

biography or autobiography
Hamilton Fish: The Inner History of the Grant Administration, Allan Nevins

poetry
A Further Range, Robert Frost

drama
You Can't Take It With You, George S. Kaufman and Moss Hart

THE NEWBERY MEDAL

Roller Skates, Ruth Sawyer

1938

HARDCOVER BESTSELLERS

fiction

The Yearling,
Marjorie Kinnan Rawlings

The Citadel, A. J. Cronin

nonfiction

The Importance of Living, Lin Yutang

With Malice Toward Some,
Margaret Italsay

**THE ALFRED B. NOBEL
PRIZE FOR LITERATURE**

Pearl S. Buck, U. S.

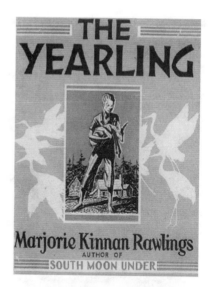

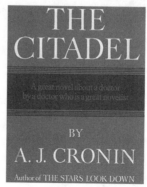

*Pearl S. Buck receives the Nobel Prize
from King Gustav in Stockholm, Sweden.*

There was a young belle of
old Natchez
Whose garments were
always in patchez.
When comment arose
On the state of her clothes,
She drawled, When Ah
itchez, Ah scratchez!

Ogden Nash, "Requiem,"
I'm a Stranger Here Myself
(1938)

Pulitzer winner John P. Marquand

I don't know which is more discouraging, literature or chickens.

E. B. White,
letter to James Thurber,
November 18, 1938

THE PULITZER PRIZES

fiction

The Late George Apley,
John P. Marquand

biography or autobiography

Divided between *Pedlar's Progress*,
Odell Shephard, and *Andrew
Jackson*, Marquis James

poetry

Cold Morning Sky,
Marya Zaturenska

THE NEWBERY MEDAL

The White Stag, Kate Seredy

THE CALDECOTT MEDAL

Animals of the Bible,
Helen Dean Fish, Illustrated by
Dorothy P. Lathrop

[*68*]

DAPHNE DU MAURIER (1907-1989) was born in London, England, the daughter of the renowned actor Gerald du Maurier. Despite a happy and financially secure childhood, she felt "inadequate" and turned to writing as a means of escape. Du Maurier wrote her first novel, *The Loving Spirit* (1931), a romantic family chronicle, at age twenty-four during ten weeks of isolation in her parents' country home. It became a bestseller and even succeeded in attracting her a husband, Major Frederick "Boy" Browning, with whom she led an equally romantic existence. Her fifth novel, **Rebecca (1938)**, became a literary sensation, praised by critics in England and America as a marvel of Gothic fiction. Du Maurier continued to write novels with seductive storylines in the melodramatic vein, but she was often accused of creating two-dimensional characters and sticking to similar themes. As defense, she once explained, "I am interested in types who represent forces of good and evil . . . [and] am passionately interested in human cruelty, human lust and human avarice—and, of course, their counterparts in scale and virtue."

THOMAS WOLFE (1900-1938) was born in Asheville, North Carolina, the son of a gloomy mason and an estranged wife who ran a boarding house. After graduating from the University of North Carolina with a predilection for theater, Wolfe studied playwriting at Harvard, but soon realized he had little talent and decided to become a college instructor. He spent his twenties teaching at NYU and writing his first novel, *Look Homeward, Angel* (1929), a largely autobiographical work, like all his novels, that took cues from Dreiser, Lewis, and Joyce and earned him enough money to devote himself full-time to writing. He also authored *Of Time and the River* (1935), a sequel to his first novel, and *The Web and the Rock* (1939), an exploration of the web of experience and the desire for freedom from ancestry, which he concluded with the maxim "you can't go home again." Wolfe died of a cerebral infection before reaching forty.

OSIP MANDELSTAM (1891-1938) was born in Warsaw, the son of a Jewish merchant, and spent his childhood in St. Petersburg and Pavolvsk. He studied at the universities of Heidelberg and St. Petersburg, at the latter joining Gumilev's poetry guild and taking up the Futurist cause. In 1908, he published his first poems, and in 1913 his first book, *Kamen*, appeared, followed by two other collections; Mandelstam produced little but his poems are considered some of the best to come out of twentieth-century Russia. Like many writers of his generation, his circumstances were transformed by the Bolshevik Revolution. Beginning in the 1930s, his work was surressed, and in 1934, he was arrested—supposedly for writing a caustic epigram on Stalin—and exiled, returning briefly to Moscow only to be arrested again in 1938. He died of a heart attack on the way to the gulag.

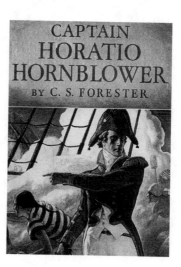

[69]

1939

HARDCOVER BESTSELLERS

fiction

The Grapes of Wrath,
John Steinbeck

All This, and Heaven Too,
Rachel Field

nonfiction

Days of Our Years,
Pierre van Paassen

Reaching for the Stars, Nora Waln

THE ALFRED B. NOBEL PRIZE FOR LITERATURE

Frans Eemil Sillanpää, Finland

No. 1 fiction bestseller

It is a very long novel, the longest that Steinbeck has written, and yet it reads as if it had been composed in a flash, ripped off the type-writer and delivered to the public as an ultima-tum . . . Steinbeck has written a novel from the depths of his heart with a sincerity seldom equaled. It may be an exaggera-tion, but it is the exag-geration of an honest and splendid writer.

Peter Monro Jack, review of
The Grapes of Wrath
by John Steinbeck,
NY Times Book Review,
April 16, 1939

BIRTHS

Margaret Atwood
Raymond Carver
Seamus Heaney
William Least Heat Moon
Hunter S. Thompson
Robert James Waller

DEATHS

Havelock Ellis
Sigmund Freud
Zane Grey
Ford Madox Ford
William Butler Yeats

WILLIAM SAROYAN (1905–1981) was born in Fresno, California, the son of an Armenian minister-writer turned immigrant farm laborer. After the death of his father, his mother placed him in an orphanage so that she could work, and at age seven Saroyan began working himself as a newspaper boy to help ameliorate his family's "amazing and comical poverty." Saroyan never finished high school, but upon reading his father's prose started writing his own narratives. In 1933, *Star* magazine accepted one of his short stories, and soon enough he was a regular contributor, publishing his first collection in 1934. His break came with the play *My Heart's in the Highlands* (1938), followed by **The Time of Your Life (1939)**, which was awarded a Pulitzer Drama Prize, though Saroyan rejected it on the basis that commerce should not judge the arts. He spent his life traveling, living unconventionally and often chaotically, and writing dozens of novels, plays, and stories, which depicted a range of American characters who, like himself, were optimistically entangled in the American dream.

Pulitzer Prize winner
Marjorie Kinnan Rawlings

Lillian Hellman

LILLIAN HELLMAN (1905–1980) was born into a Jewish family in New Orleans. She attended university in New York, but rather than graduate decided to work as a reader for a Manhattan publisher, a reviewer for the *Herald Tribune*, and beginning in 1930, a reader for MGM. In L.A., she met the crime novelist Dashiell Hammett, "who was getting over a five day drunk," and though she was married immediately returned with him to New York. Hellman quickly became a well-known dramatist under Hammett's tutelage, with plays such as **The Little Foxes** (**1939**), a compelling study of Southern decadence, and *Watch on the Rhine* (1941), the first American anti-Nazi play. During these years, she also emerged a left-wing activist and, many said, a

[*72*]

Communist Party member. When brought before the Un-American Activities committee, Hellman's reply was: "I can't cut my conscience to fit this year's fashions." Known to exaggerate the truth, Hellman won many enemies for her later autobiographical works, but today is remembered as one of the most persuasive voices in modern American theater.

> *Now I know*
> *That twenty centuries of*
>   *stony sleep*
> *Were vexed to nightmare by*
>   *a rocking cradle,*
> *And what rough beast, its*
>   *hour come round at last,*
> *Slouches towards Bethlehem*
>   *to be born?*
>   W. B. Yeats,
>   "The Second Coming,"
>   *Michael Robartes and*
>   *the Dancer* (1921)

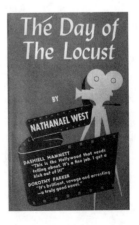

1940

HARDCOVER BESTSELLERS

fiction

How Green Was My Valley,
Richard Llewellyn

Kitty Foyle, Christopher Morley

nonfiction

I Married Adventure, Osa Johnson

How to Read a Book,
Mortimer Adler

THE ALFRED B. NOBEL PRIZE FOR LITERATURE

No award

THE PULITZER PRIZES

fiction

The Grapes of Wrath,
John Steinbeck

biography or autobiography

Woodrow Wilson, Life and Letters,
Ray Stannard Baker

poetry

Collected Poems, Mark Van Doren

drama

The Time of Your Life,
William Saroyan

This is the best book Ernest Hemingway has written, the fullest, the deepest, the truest. It will, I think, be one of the major novels in American literature . . . There is nothing obtrusive about the manner in which this book is written; the style is a part of the whole; there is no artifice to halt the eye. It has simplicity and power, delicacy and strength . . . "For Whom the Bell Tolls" is the book of a man who knows what life is about, and who can convey his knowledge.

J. Donald Adams,
review of
For Whom the Bell Tolls
by Ernest Hemingway,
NY Times Book Review,
October 20, 1940

BIRTHS

Peter Benchley
Joseph Brodsky
Angela Carter
J. M. Coetzee

DEATHS

F. Scott Fitzgerald
Nathanael West

and high-living, first in the United States and later in Europe. Together they became the mythical representatives of the American Jazz Age, living in a style Fitzgerald depicted most perfectly in his novel *The Great Gatsby* (1925). But the glitter faded quickly for the Fitzgeralds: the next decades were overshadowed by money troubles, alcoholism, and frequent illnessses. Zelda was permanently institutionalized in 1934, and six years later F. Scott died of a heart attack.

F. SCOTT FITZGERALD (1896-1940), like most of his characters, was a Midwesterner, born in St. Paul, Minnesota, who moved East in search of high society and education. After dropping out from Princeton, he made a beeline to New York City, where at twenty-four he published *This Side of Paradise*, an autobiographical novel that established him as the leading chronicler of his generation. In 1919, he married Zelda Sayre, a beautiful, talented, but unstable woman, with whom he embarked upon a decade of drinking, socializing,

> *They were careless people, Tom and Daisy—they smashed up things and creatures and then retreated back into their money or their vast carelessness, or whatever it was that kept them together, and let other people clean up the mess they had made.*
>
> F. Scott Fitzgerald,
> *The Great Gatsby* (1925)
>
> • • •
>
> *Draw your chair up close to the edge of the precipice and I'll tell you a story.*
>
> F. Scott Fitzgerald,
> *Notebooks* (1978)

NATHANAEL WEST (1903-1940) was born Nathan Wallenstein Weinstein in New York City, the eldest child of Russian-Jewish immigrants. He left high school without graduating, but by forging his school record was accepted to Tufts, which soon discovered his handiwork. Fortunately, there was another Nathan Weinstein at Tufts and somehow their records were "confused," allowing him sufficient credits for acceptance to Brown. West then went to Paris, where he wrote his first novel, the avant-garde *The Dream Life of Balso Snell* (1931). He returned to New York in 1926, mismanaged a hotel, and helped William Carlos Williams edit the magazine *Contact*. In 1933, his *Miss Lonelyhearts*, a macabre tale about an agony columnist, was published to great acclaim but garnered low sales (West's publisher was bankrupt). The script was bought by Twentieth Century Fox, though, and brought him to Hollywood, where he worked on scripts for several years. West died young in a car accident in 1940.

> There is always one moment in childhood when the door opens and lets the future in.
>
> Graham Greene,
> *The Power and the Glory*
> (1940)

THE NEW NOVEL BY

ZANE GREY

Zane Grey, our greatest writer of Western adventure, has never had a serious rival. Literally millions of readers have known and loved his famous stories of the out-of-doors. *Western Union—Riders of the Purple Sage—The Light of Western Stars—The Thundering Herd*—titles like these echo down the years, the most typically *American* literature which our country has produced. In 30,000 ON THE HOOF, the new 1940 novel by the acknowledged leader in his field, the reader will find all the romance, excitement, adventure, the color and beauty of the out-of-doors which have contributed to Zane Grey's enormous popularity.

During recent years each succeeding Zane Grey novel has outsold its predecessor; and the critical reception of Zane Grey as an American novelist has increased with the volume of his sales. 30,000 ON THE HOOF, his latest novel, shows this beloved writer in the full tide of his remarkable career.

30,000 ON THE HOOF
NOT PUBLISHED SERIALLY

2. 1599

[75]

> I believe that we are lost here in America, but I believe we shall be found.
>
> Thomas Wolfe,
> *You Can't Go Home Again*
> (1940)

A ready way to show the importance of this novel is to call it the Negro "American Tragedy" and to compare it roughly with Dreiser's master-piece . . . The startling difference in Mr. Wright's "Native Son" is that the injustice is a racial, not merely a social one . . . The story is a strong and powerful one and it alone will force the Negro issue into our attention. Certainly, "Native Son" declares Richard Wright's impor-tance, not merely as the best Negro writer, but as an American author as distinctive as any of those now writing.

Peter Monro Jack, review of
Native Son
by Richard Wright,
NY Times Book Review,
March 3, 1940

*Goddammit, look! We live
here and they live there.
We black and they white.
They got things and we
ain't. They do things
and we can't. It's just like
living in jail.*

Richard Wright,
Native Son (1940)

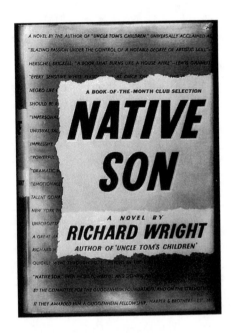

Wolfe believed that enduring fiction must be written out of its author's personal experience of life . . . This is the story of a man who found himself, in relation to life, in relation to his time.

J. Donald Adams, review of
You Can't Go Home Again
by Thomas Wolfe,
NY Times Book Review,
September 22, 1940

1941

HARDCOVER BESTSELLERS

fiction

The Keys of the Kingdom,
A. J. Cronin

Random Harvest, James Hilton

nonfiction

Berlin Diary, William L. Shirer

The White Cliffs, Alice Duer Miller

THE ALFRED B. NOBEL PRIZE FOR LITERATURE

No award

Rabindranath Tagore 1861-1941

[77]

BIRTHS

Philip Caputo
Nora Ephron
Anne Rice
Ricardo Sánchez
Paul Theroux
Anne Tyler

DEATHS

Sherwood Anderson
Isaac Babel
James Joyce
Rabindranath Tagore
Virginia Woolf

THE PULITZER PRIZES

fiction

No award

biography or autobiography

Jonathan Edwards,
Ola Elizabeth Winslow

poetry

Sunderland Capture, Leonard Bacon

drama

There Shall Be No Night,
Robert E. Sherwood

THE NEWBERY MEDAL

Call It Courage, Armstrong Sperry

THE CALDECOTT MEDAL

They Were Strong and Good,
Robert Lawson

James Joyce, photograph by Josef Breitenbach

JAMES JOYCE (1882–1941) was born in Dublin and educated at Jesuit schools and University College, Dublin. Distressed by what he saw as Catholicism's bigotry, he left home in 1902 for Paris, where he lived in poverty and composed poetry. For the next few years, he moved his family around Europe, writing and trying to make ends meet. In 1914, Joyce published *Dubliners*, a collection of short stories about ordinary Irish people, which caught the attention of Ezra Pound, who urged him to continue writing and gave him financial support. The next year, he published his only play, *Exiles*, and went into permanent exile himself, where he wrote, among other books, *A Portrait of the Artist as a Young Man* (1916) and his masterpiece, *Ulysses* (1922), a book revolutionary for its time, considered one of the greatest literary achievements of the century.

(1925), *To the Lighthouse* (1927), and *A Room of One's Own* (1929), and though a literary celebrity—and a female one at that—she lived with great sadness. At fifty-nine, she loaded her pockets with stones and drowned herself in the River Ouse.

VIRGINIA WOOLF (1882-1941) was born in London, into the late Victorian intellectual aristocracy. Her teens were fraught with family difficulties (her mother died and her half-brother sexually abused her), and by early adulthood, Woolf suffered the first of several mental breakdowns. After the death of her father, Woolf moved with her siblings to a London brownstone, which became the epicenter of the famous—and for her inspiring—Bloomsbury Group. In 1912, she married Leonard Woolf, with whom she founded Hogarth Press. Three years later she published her first book. Woolf's third novel, *Jacob's Room* (1922), marked the beginning of her experimentation with narrative and language and made her a champion of Modernist literature. She then wrote her masterpieces, *Mrs. Dalloway*

1942

HARDCOVER BESTSELLERS

fiction

The Song of Bernadette, Franz Werfel

The Moon Is Down, John Steinbeck

nonfiction

See Here, Private Hargrove,
Marion Hargrove

Mission to Moscow, Joseph E. Davies

**THE ALFRED B. NOBEL
PRIZE FOR LITERATURE**

No award

THE PULITZER PRIZES

fiction

In This Our Life, Ellen Glasgow

biography or autobiography

Crusader in Crinoline, Forrest Wilson

poetry

The Dust Which Is God,
William Rose Benet

drama

No award

THE NEWBERY MEDAL

The Matchlock Gun, Walter Edmonds

THE CALDECOTT MEDAL

Make Way for Ducklings,
Robert McCloskey

BERYL MARKHAM (1902–1986) was born in Melton Mowbray, in the Leicester-shire area of England, and raised in Kenya. An independent woman, unconventional to the core, Markham refused the life of female idleness known to her class and made her living as a horse trainer and freelance commercial pilot. In 1936, she became famous as the first person to fly solo across the Atlantic from east to west. Departing from Abingdon Royal Air Force field in England, Markham flew her single-engine plane for twenty-one hours and twenty-five minutes before lack of fuel forced her to make a crash landing in a Nova Scotia bog.

Although her plane was heavily damaged, she escaped with minor injuries and when brought to New York City—her original destination—was honored with a ticker-tape parade. Markham then returned to Kenya where she subsequently trained eight winners of the Kentucky Derby. Her spectacular memoir, *West with the Night* (1942), though ignored when it was first published, was reissued in 1983 to great fanfare. "She had written so well," remarked Ernest Hemingway, "that I am completely ashamed of myself as a writer."

BIRTHS

Michael Crichton
Stephen Hawking
John Irving
Erica Jong
Garrison Keillor

DEATH

Lucy Maude Montgomery

ROBERT MCCLOSKEY (1914-) was born in Hamilton, Ohio, where his parents encouraged him to pursue his interests. And so as a child, he taught himself to play four instruments and studied the basic structures of mechanical and electric objects. Young McCloskey next discovered art, and by his senior year in high school had won a scholarship to a renowned Boston art school. In 1936, he moved to New York City to study at the National Academy of Design, but school prizes did not pay bills, so he worked as a commercial artist and then in 1938 returned to Ohio to focus on illustration. The next year McCloskey won the Prix de Rome and published his first children's book, *Lentil*. In 1942, he won his first **Caldecott Medal** for **Make Way for Duckings.** Since then, McCloskey has been hailed as one of America's preeminent children's book illustrators and authors, who with stories such as *Homer Price* (1943), *Blueberries for Sal* (1948), and *Time of Wonder* (1957), has shaped the style of American juvenile literature.

1943

HARDCOVER BESTSELLERS

fiction

The Robe, Lloyd C. Douglas

The Valley of Decision,
Marcia Davenport

nonfiction

Under Cover, John Roy Carlson

One World, Wendell L. Willkie

THE ALFRED B. NOBEL PRIZE FOR LITERATURE

No award

THE PULITZER PRIZES

fiction

Dragon's Teeth, Upton Sinclair

biography or autobiography

Admiral of the Ocean Sea,
Samuel Eliot Morison

poetry

A Witness Tree, Robert Frost

drama

The Skin of Our Teeth,
Thornton Wilder

Bestselling author Wendell Wilkie

Pulitzer Prize winner Thornton Wilder

Ayn Rand

Ayn Rand is a writer of great power . . . Her characters are romanticized, larger than life as representations of good and evil. But nothing she has to say is said in a second-rate fashion. You have to think of "The Magic Mountain," you have to think of "The Master Builder" when you think of "The Fountainhead."

Lorine Pruette,
review of *The Fountainhead*
by Ayn Rand,
NY Times Book Review,
May 16, 1943

It is only with the heart that one can see rightly; what is essential is invisible to the eye.

Antoine de Saint-Exupéry,
The Little Prince (1943)

BIRTHS
Nikki Giovanni
Sam Shepard

DEATHS
Stephen Vincent Benét
Beatrix Potter
Sir Charles G. D. Roberts

1944

HARDCOVER BESTSELLERS
fiction
Strange Fruit, Lillian Smith

The Robe, Lloyd C. Douglas

nonfiction
I Never Left Home, Bob Hope

Brave Men, Ernie Pyle

THE ALFRED B. NOBEL PRIZE FOR LITERATURE
Johannes V. Jensen, Denmark

THE PULITZER PRIZES
fiction
Journey in the Dark, Martin Flavin

biography or autobiography
The American Leonardo: The Life of Samuel F. B. Morse, Carleton Mabee

poetry
Western Star, Stephen Vincent Benét

drama
No award

THE NEWBERY MEDAL
Johnny Tremain, Esther Forbes

THE CALDECOTT MEDAL
Many Moons, James Thurber, Illustrated by Louis Slobodkin

BIRTHS
Carl Bernstein

Alice Walker

DEATHS
Jean Giraudoux

Stephen Leacock

Antoine de Saint-Exupéry

STEPHEN VINCENT BENÉT (1898–1943) was born in Bethlehem, Pennsylvania, into an Army family. His first poetry collection, *Five Men from Pompey*, appeared when he was still in his teens, and his second, *Young Adventure*, was published a year before he graduated from Yale. Benét is best known for

"John Brown's Body," a long patriotic poem about the Civil War, which earned him the 1929 Pulitzer Prize. In addition to poetry, he wrote five novels and five collections of short stories, the most famous of which is "The Devil and Daniel Webster," a Faustian story set in rural America, which Walter Dieterle made into the popular film *All That Money Can Buy* (1941). After his death, his unfinished narrative poem, *Western Star*, was awarded the **1944 Pulitzer Prize**. He was married to the writer Rosemary Carr.

Bestselling author Bob Hope performing with Bing Crosby

"Dangling Man" is set down in diary form, which is always an excuse for formlessness ... Bellow brings home the ultimate horror of war without ever getting close to the front lines.

John Chamberlain, review of
Dangling Man
by Saul Bellow,
NY Times Book Review,
March 25, 1944

• • •

The invasion of Sicily is barely six months old— yet here, hot off the griddle of war, is a first novel dealing with a town in Sicily taken by the Americans ... Mr. Hersey has told a story that needed to be told as soon as possible.

Jerre Mangione,
review of
A Bell for Adano
by John Hersey,
NY Times Book Review,
February 6, 1944

• • •

In spite of everything I still believe that people are really good at heart.

Anne Frank, *Anne Frank: The Diary of a Young Girl*,
March 7, 1944

1945

HARDCOVER BESTSELLERS

fiction

Forever Amber, Kathleen Winsor

The Robe, Lloyd C. Davis

nonfiction

Brave Men, Ernie Pyle

Dear Sir, Juliet Lowell

THE ALFRED B. NOBEL PRIZE FOR LITERATURE

Gabriela Mistral, Chile

THE PULITZER PRIZES

fiction

A Bell for Adano, John Hersey

biography or autobiography

Brahmin Rebel, Russell Blaine Nye and George Bancroft

poetry

V-Letter and Other Poems, Karl Shapiro

drama

Harvey, Mary Chase

journalism at *Time* magazine and then to writing nonfictional accounts of World War II. In 1945, he was awarded the **Pulitzer Prize** for his first novel, *A Bell for Adano*, realistically depicting the atmosphere of Allied rule in a Sicilian village. Hersey was wonderfully prolific in his lifetime, writing scores of essays and short stories as well

John Hersey

as over a dozen novels, such as *The Wall* (1950), a well-researched depiction of the Warsaw ghetto uprising, and *The Child Buyer* (1960), a satirical parable about modern education. His life and work were largely inspired by the bloodshed and chaos of the midcentury.

JOHN HERSEY (1914–1993) was born in Tianjin, China, to American missionary parents, and was educated in China, the United States, and England. One of his first jobs was as secretary to Sinclair Lewis, but he soon moved on to

THE NEWBERY MEDAL

Rabbit Hill, Robert Lawson

THE CALDECOTT MEDAL

Prayer for a Child, Rachel Field,
Illustrated by
Elizabeth Orton Jones

GEORGE ORWELL (1903-1950) was born Eric Arthur Blair in Bengal, the son of a British civil servant in the opium department, and educated on scholarship at England's Eton College, where he developed a lifelong antipathy to the British class system. At twenty-one, he joined the Indian Imperial Police in Burma, but soon left, sickened by the hypocrisies of imperialism. Determined to escape the oppression he saw everywhere, he decided to "go native," and disguised himself as a bum to live among the underclass, resulting in his first book *Down and Out in Paris and London* (1933). During the next two decades, Orwell supported himself as a war correspondent (he fought on the side of the Loyalists in the Spanish Civil War) and freelance journalist, vehemently espousing the necessity for democratic socialism. In 1945, his anti-Soviet barnyard allegory ***Animal Farm*** was published, followed in 1949 by *Nineteen Eighty-Four*, a futurist vision of a scientifically perfected totalitarian state, now considered his masterpiece.

All animals are equal, but some animals are more equal than others.

George Orwell,
Animal Farm (1945)

BIRTHS
Pat Conroy
Annie Dillard
August Wilson
Tobias Wolff

DEATHS
Robert Benchley
Theodore Dreiser
Anne Frank
Paul Valéry

1946

HARDCOVER BESTSELLERS

fiction

The King's General,
Daphne du Maurier

The Side of Innocence,
Taylor Caldwell

nonfiction

The Egg and I, Betty MacDonald

Peace of Mind, Joshua L. Liebman

THE ALFRED B. NOBEL PRIZE FOR LITERATURE

Hermann Hesse, Switzerland

Bestselling author Daphne du Maurier

> "Hiroshima" penetrated the tissue of complacency we had built up. It penetrated it all the more inexorably because it told its story not in terms of graphs and charts but in terms of ordinary human beings . . . "Hiroshima" seems destined to become about the most widely read article and book of our generation.
>
> Charles Poore, review of
> *Hiroshima* by John Hersey,
> *NY Times Book Review*,
> November 10, 1946

THE PULITZER PRIZES

fiction

No award

biography or autobiography

Son of the Wilderness,
Linny Marsh Wolfe

poetry

No award

drama

State of the Union, Russel Crouse
and Howard Lindsay

THE NEWBERY MEDAL

Strawberry Girl, Lois Lenski

THE CALDECOTT MEDAL

The Rooster Crows,
Maude and Miska Petersham

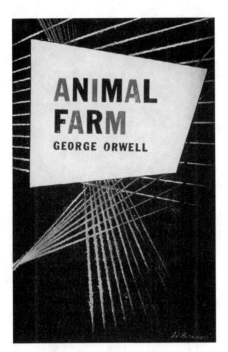

ANIMAL FARM

GEORGE ORWELL

Animal Farm, *published in England in 1945, was released in the United States in 1946.*

The story should be read in particular by liberals who cannot understand how Soviet performance has fallen so far behind Communist professions. "Animal Farm" is a wise, compassionate and illuminating fable for our times.

Arthur M. Schlesinger, Jr.,
review of *Animal Farm*
by George Orwell,
NY Times Book Review,
September 25, 1946

DEATHS
Damon Runyon
Gertrude Stein
Booth Tarkington
H. G. Wells

GERTRUDE STEIN (1874-1946) was born in Allegheny, Pennsylvania, of educated German-Jewish immigrants, and schooled at Radcliffe College, where she studied psychology under William James. In 1903, she decided to move to Paris with her brother Leo, an art collector, to participate in the world of experimental arts and letters. Stein soon became determined to revolutionize literature the way her friends Cézanne, Matisse, and Picasso were revolutionizing art, and in the 1910s wrote a number of anti-nineteenth-century novels, including *The Making of Americans* (1925). When the First World War came, Stein and her lover Alice B. Toklas remained in Paris. She did not return to the United States until 1934, when she gave a series of influential lectures and paid a visit to New York to witness the popularity of her modernist opera, *Four Saints in Three Acts*, featuring an all-black cast. Though Jewish, Stein stayed in the countryside of France during World War II, but upon returning to Paris was diagnosed with cancer and the next year died from it.

announced himself a devotee of writing. He left behind a large and fairly versatile body of work that includes novels, plays, short stories, and juvenile fiction, centering largely on Midwestern middle-class life and morals. His best novels include the Pulitzer Prize-winning *The Magnificent Ambersons* (1918), the chronicle of three generations of a leading Indiana family, and *Alice Adams* (1921), the story of a middling girl's love affair with a man above her social rank, which gained him a second Pulitzer Prize.

BOOTH TARKINGTON (1869-1946) was born in Indianapolis, Indiana, the son of a lawyer. He attended Princeton University, but could not graduate because of his inadequate Greek. Tarkington dabbled in several professions in his early years, including politics—he was elected a Republican member of the Indiana Senate in 1902—but by his late thirties

> Isherwood is a real novelist, a real minor novelist.
>
> Alfred Kazin, review of
> *The Berlin Stories*
> by Christopher Isherwood,
> *NY Times Book Review*,
> February 12, 1946

1947

HARDCOVER BESTSELLERS

fiction

The Miracle of the Bells,
Russell Janney

The Moneyman, Thomas B. Costain

nonfiction

Peace of Mind, Joshua L. Liebman

Information Please Almanac 1947,
John Kieran, ed.

THE PULITZER PRIZES

fiction

All the King's Men,
Robert Penn Warren

biography or autobiography

*The Autobiography of William Allen
White,* William Allen White

poetry

Lord Weary's Castle, Robert Lowell

drama

No award

ROBERT PENN WARREN (1905–1989) was born in Kentucky, the son of a banker with unfulfilled literary aspirations. Unable to become a naval officer because of the loss of his left eye, he opted for a university education at Vanderbilt, where he began to forge a brilliant academic career. Warren held many academic posts, the longest at Yale, eventually as Professor Emeritus of English. The range of his literary ability as well as his varied concerns have made him a twentieth-century writer hard to match. In 1947, he was awarded the **Pulitzer Prize** for *All the King's Men*, a novel about a well-intentioned politician corrupted by megalomania, and nine years later was awarded a second Pulitzer for his poetry collection *Promises* (1957), making him the only author to win the prize in different genres. He also wrote important nonfiction works on subjects as diverse as John Brown, the Southern economy, and modern fiction and poetry. Three years before his death, he became America's first Poet Laureate.

BIRTHS

Ann Beattie
Tom Clancy
Stephen King
David Mamet
Salman Rushdie
Danielle Steele

DEATHS

Willa Cather
Hugh Lofting

THE ALFRED B. NOBEL PRIZE FOR LITERATURE
André Gide, France

THE NEWBERY MEDAL
Miss Hickory, Carolyn Bailey

THE CALDECOTT MEDAL
The Little Island,
Golden MacDonald,
Illustrated by Leonard Weisgard

ANDRÉ GIDE (1869-1951), the prolific French novelist, essayist, and man-of-letters, was born in Paris and brought up to conform to the strict Protestant traditions of the French bourgeoisie, against which he eventually rebelled. In his early adulthood, he devoted himself to literature, music, and travel, and in 1892 married his cousin, although he was bisexual and strongly attracted to men. Gide made his international literary reputation with *The Immoralist* (1902, 1930), his short novel about a young man who follows every impulse. During the next three decades, he made a profound influence on avant-garde literature and by 1917 emerged as the prophet of the French youth. His most widely read works in English are his novel *The Counterfeiters* (1925, 1927) and his revealing autobiography *If I Die* (1926, 1935). Gide was awarded the **1947 Nobel Prize**.

WILLA CATHER (1873-1947) was born in Virginia, and at the age of nine moved with her family to Nebraska settler county, where she was reared among European immigrants. She attended the University of Nebraska and in 1896 moved to Pittsburgh to work as a journalist and teacher. After her book of poems and short story collection were published, she was asked to become an editor at the influential *McClure's Magazine* in New York, where she lived for the rest of her life. Cather's early novels dealt with sophisticated Easterners, but she is best known for her middle work, including *O Pioneers!* (1913) and *My Antonia* (1918), which depict strong women enduring life in the sparsely populated American west. She also wrote popular historical novels, such as *Death Comes for the Archbishop* (1927), which show her growing affinity for Christianity and distaste for modern life. Cather was awarded the **1922 Pulitzer Prize** for *One of Ours*.

1948

HARDCOVER BESTSELLERS

fiction

The Big Fisherman,
Lloyd C. Douglas

The Naked and the Dead,
Norman Mailer

nonfiction

Crusade in Europe,
Dwight D. Eisenhower

*How to Stop Worrying and Start
Living,* Dale Carnegie

**THE ALFRED B. NOBEL
PRIZE FOR LITERATURE**

T. S. Eliot, England

T. S. ELIOT (1888–1965) Although born in St. Louis, Missouri, and educated at Harvard, Eliot spent the majority of his life in England, his philosophical home. He received diplomas from the Sorbonne and Oxford, and in 1922 founded and edited *The Criterion*, a quarterly British review, in which he published his ground-breaking poem *The Waste Land*, which established him as the decisive voice of a disillusioned generation. In the next two decades, Eliot's influence spread quickly: he published poems (*Four Quartets*, 1943), produced his own plays (*Murder in the Cathedral*, 1935), and became a leading literary critic as well as director of Faber and Faber, where he published Ezra Pound and W. H. Auden. Eliot today is credited with shaping the development of Anglo-American literature; his preoccupation with the ills of rationalism and shallow gentility of early nineteenth-century society as well as his emphasis on symbolism, form, and poetic control still hold enormous sway. He won the 1948 **Nobel Prize**.

DEATH

Mahatma Gandhi

JAMES MICHENER (1907?–1997) was raised near Doylestown, Pennsylvania, by a foster parent, and never discovered anything about his actual family background. Naturally inquisitive, he hitchhiked through forty-six states at age fourteen, and after entering Swathmore College with a sports scholarship graduated summa cum laude. Michener did not publish his first novel until he was forty-one, working variously as a professor of education, textbook editor, and World War II Navy lieutenant in the South Pacific. His first work of fiction, *Tales of the South Pacific,* earned him the 1948 **Pulitzer Prize** and was successfully adapted into the musical *South Pacific.* It wasn't until his fourth novel, *Hawaii* (1959), however, that he found the formula that would make him America's leading bestselling author. Since the 1960s, he has success-

fully repeated this formula—of writing fictionalized history to depict monolithic places—with books such as *The Source* (on Israel, 1965) and *The Covenant* (on South Africa, 1980).

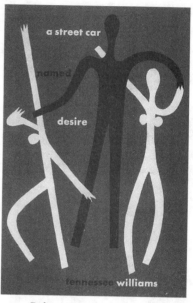

Pulitzer Prize–winning play

*Bestselling author
Dwight D. Eisenhower*

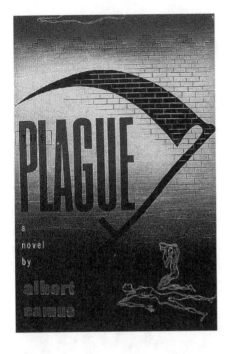

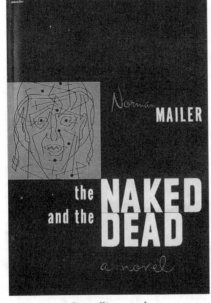

Bestselling novel

"The Plague" is parable and sermon, and should be considered as such ... "The Plague" stands or falls by its message. The message is not the highest form of creative art, but it may be of such importance for our time that to dismiss it in the name of artistic criticism would be to blaspheme against the human spirit.

Stephen Spender, review of
The Plague
by Albert Camus,
NY Times Book Review,
September 1, 1948

•   •   •

This is a beautiful novel, a rich, firm and moving piece of prose ... There is not much current writing that goes deeper than this.

Richard Sullivan, review of
Cry the Beloved Country
by Alan Paton,
NY Times Book Review,
February 1, 1948

1949

HARDCOVER BESTSELLERS

fiction

The Egyptian, Mika Waltari

The Big Fisherman,
Lloyd C. Douglas

nonfiction

White Collar Zoo, Clare Barnes, Jr.

How to Win at Canasta,
Oswald Jacoby

THE ALFRED B. NOBEL PRIZE FOR LITERATURE

William Faulkner, U.S.

Nobel Prize winner William Faulkner

PAUL BOWLES (1910-) Born in New York City and educated at the University of Virginia, Bowles studied music composition with Aaron Copland and became a composer himself, writing scores for movies and operas. Though a rising musical talent, he decided to dedicate himself to writing (Gertrude Stein discouraged him, but later changed her mind), and in the 1940s left New York for Morocco, where he remained for over fifty years. There he became a key figure of the ever-renewing "lost generation," gaining cult status as the quintessential ex-patriate writer. His best novels, **The Sheltering Sky** (1949) and *Let It Come Down* (1952), depict Occidentals in the Arab world in defiance of the West's rote morality but incapable of completely escaping it. In the 1990s, Bowles returned to composing music, and in 1995 made a rare trip back to New York—his first in twenty-six years—to attend a festival of his compositions.

[*97*]

This has always been a man's world, and none of the reasons hitherto brought forward in explanation of this fact has seemed adequate.

Simone de Beauvoir,
The Second Sex (1949)

THE PULITZER PRIZES

fiction

Guard of Honor,
James Gould Cozzens

biography or autobiography

Roosevelt and Hopkins,
Robert E. Sherwood

poetry

Terror and Decorum, Peter Viereck

drama

Death of a Salesman, Arthur Miller

THE NEWBERY MEDAL

King of the Wind, Marguerite Henry

THE CALDECOTT MEDAL

The Big Snow,
Berta and Elmer Hader

GWENDOLYN BROOKS (1917–) was born in Topeka, Kansas, but lived almost her entire life on Chicago's South Side. She began publishing poetry as a teenager, and in 1945 achieved national recognition when *Mademoiselle* named her among the "Ten Young Women of the Year" in response to the publication of her first poetry volume, *A Street in Bronzeville*. *Annie Allen* (**1949**) , a verse narrative about a young black woman, earned her the **1950** Pulitzer Prize, the first ever awarded to an African-American. Next she published *Maud Martha* (1953), a novel, and another poetry collection (1960). In the following decades, Brooks published over twenty-five books of poetry and fiction. She is the recipient of over fifty honorary degrees and was the first black woman to be named Library of Congress Poetry Consultant. Her influence on contemporary black American writers is unquestionable.

[*98*]

Pulitzer Prize winner Arthur Miller

BIRTHS

Martin Amis
Scott Turow

DEATH

Margaret Mitchell

1950

HARDCOVER BESTSELLERS

fiction

The Cardinal,
  Henry Morton Robinson

Joy Street, Frances Parkinson Keyes

nonfiction

Betty Crocker's Picture Cook Book,
  Betty Crocker

The Baby

THE ALFRED B. NOBEL PRIZE FOR LITERATURE

Bertrand Russell, England

THE PULITZER PRIZES

fiction

The Way West, A. B. Guthrie, Jr.

biography or autobiography

John Quincy Adams and the Foundations of American Foreign Policy,
  Samuel Flag Bernis

poetry

Annie Allen, Gwendolyn Brooks

drama

South Pacific, Richard Rodgers,
  Oscar Hammerstein II, and
  Joshua Logan

THE NEWBERY MEDAL

The Door in the Wall,
  Marguerite de Angeli

Nobel Prize winner Bertrand Russell

THE CALDECOTT MEDAL

Song of the Swallows, Leo Politi

THE NATIONAL BOOK AWARDS

fiction

The Man with the Golden Arm,
  Nelson Algren

nonfiction

Ralph Waldo Emerson,
  Ralph L. Rusk

poetry

Paterson: Book III and Selected Poems,
  William Carlos Williams

DEATHS

William Rose Benet
Edgar Rice Burroughs
Edgar Lee Masters
Edna St. Vincent Millay
George Orwell
George Bernard Shaw

---

quately received, but it wasn't until his plays of the 1900s and 1910s, such as *Androcles and the Lion* (1912) and *Pygmalion* (1913), that he was heralded as the new voice of drama. Shaw was obsessed by the necessity of self-enlightenment through creativity, and consequently presented himself as a fierce opponent of outdated social mores. At the 1909 Joint Committee on Stage Censorship (before which he was brought for his frank portrayals of politics, family life, and prostitution), he declared himself an "immoralist and heretic." Shaw died in his mid-nineties, England's most wealthy and envied public intellectual.

GEORGE BERNARD SHAW (1856-1950) was born in Dublin, Ireland, the son of an unsuccessful, alcoholic corn merchant whose wife abandoned him. In 1876, after unhappily apprenticing to an estate agent, he moved to London and began writing novels, the first five of which he was unable to publish. Shaw next turned to socialist criticism and playwriting. *Widowers' House* (1892) and his other early plays were ade-

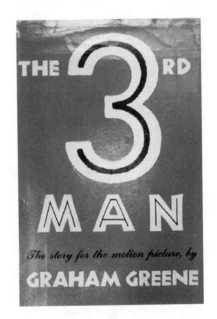

THE **3**RD **MAN**

The story for the motion picture, by
GRAHAM GREENE

1951

HARDCOVER BESTSELLERS

fiction

From Here to Eternity, James Jones

The Caine Mutiny, Herman Wouk

nonfiction

Look Younger, Live Longer,
 Gayelord Hauser

Betty Crocker's Picture Cook Book,
 Betty Crocker

THE ALFRED B. NOBEL PRIZE FOR LITERATURE

Pär Lagerkvist, Sweden

THE PULITZER PRIZES

fiction

The Town, Conrad Richter

biography or autobiography

John C. Calhoun: American Portrait,
 Margaret Louise Colt

poetry

Complete Poems, Carl Sandburg

drama

No award

DEATHS

André Gide

Sinclair Lewis

Harold Wallace Ross

SINCLAIR LEWIS (1885–1951), the son of a country doctor, was born in Sauk Center, Minnesota, a small Midwestern town that became the inspiration for his now-classic American novels. After attending a local high school, Lewis went to Yale, and then on to jobs in journalism and publishing—a few from which he was fired—and worked for a period as Jack London's ghostwriter. In 1920, he achieved enormous success with *Main Street*, a novel satirizing the vapid materialism and intolerance of American small-town life. Two years later he published *Babbitt*, perhaps his best-known novel, which also dealt with American philistinism. His later fictional works were less effective, and in his later years Sinclair was accused of living the very ideologies he so vigorously had opposed. He refused the 1926 Pulitzer Prize for *Arrowsmith*

(1925), but accepted the 1930 Nobel, the first awarded to an American writer.

also a popular and critical success and led to the implementation of the first antipesticide bills. Carson is remembered as one of our most important female environmentalists.

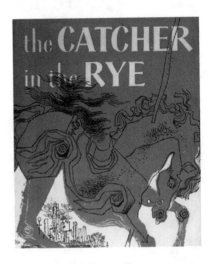

RACHEL CARSON (1907–1964) grew up on a farm near Springdale, Pennsylvania, where she developed an early interest in nature conservation. After the death of her father and sister, Carson took her mother and two nieces to Maryland and supported them as a nature-oriented pamphlet and radio script writer. Meanwhile, she composed two books, the most famous of which, **The Sea Around Us (1951)**—detailing the sea's creation and creatures—won the National Book Award and spent eighty-six weeks on the bestseller list. It also, at last, allowed her to become a full-time writer. Her fourth book, *Silent Spring* (1961), a riveting denunciation of pesticides, was

This Salinger, he's a short story guy. And he knows how to write about kids. This book though, it's too long. Gets kind of monotonous. And he should've cut out a lot about these jerks and all at that crumby school. They depress me. They really do. Salinger, he's best with real children.

James Stern, review of *The Catcher in the Rye* by J. D. Salinger, *NY Times Book Review*, August 11, 1951

1952

HARDCOVER BESTSELLERS

fiction

The Silver Chalice,
Thomas B. Costain

The Caine Mutiny, Herman Wouk

nonfiction

*The Holy Bible: Revised
Standard Version*

A Man Called Peter,
Catherine Marshall

THE ALFRED B. NOBEL PRIZE FOR LITERATURE

François Mauriac, France

THE PULITZER PRIZES

fiction

The Caine Mutiny, Herman Wouk

biography or autobiography

Charles Evans Hughes,
Merlo J. Pusey

poetry

Collected Poems, Marianne Moore

drama

The Shrike, Joseph Kramm

THE NEWBERY MEDAL

Ginger Pye, Eleanor Estes

Pulitzer Prize and National Book Award
winner Marianne Moore

THE CALDECOTT MEDAL

Finders Keepers, Will Lipkind,
Illustrated by Nicolas Mordvinoff

THE NATIONAL BOOK AWARDS

fiction

From Here to Eternity, James Jones

nonfiction

The Sea Around Us, Rachel Carson

poetry

Collected Poems, Marianne Moore

[*103*]

BIRTH

Amy Tan

DEATHS

Knut Hamsun
George Santayana

but his sympathetic critics also compared him to Tolstoy, one describing him as "the only living nineteenth-century novelist." He also has written fictional accounts of post-1947 Israel and nonfiction works on Jewish-American life.

HERMAN WOUK (1915-) was brought up in the Bronx, the son of a first-generation Russian Jewish industrialist, and educated at Columbia University. After graduation, he worked as a radio scriptwriter, then serving in the Navy during World War II, the experience of which he drew on for his classic war novel, *The Caine Mutiny* (1951). The novel was awarded the **1952 Pulitzer Prize** and even-

tually became a successful film starring Humphrey Bogart. Wouk's two other noteworthy bestsellers were *Marjorie Morningstar* (1955), the story of a gorgeous Jewish girl, praised as a "modern Jewish Vanity Fair," and *Youngblood Hawke* (1962), based on the life of the writer Thomas Wolfe. Wouk was often accused of being a highbrow soap opera writer, for he loved large, epic-style novels exploring moral dilemmas,

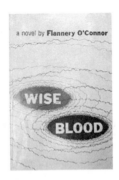

a novel by **Flannery O'Connor**

WISE BLOOD

There is in Flannery O'Connor a fierceness of literary gesture, an angriness of observation, a facility for catching, as an animal eye in a wilderness, cunningly and at one sharp glance, the shape and detail and animal intention of enemy and foe. The world of "Wise Blood" is one of clashing in a wilderness.

William Goyen,
review of *Wise Blood*
by Flannery O'Connor,
NY Times Book Review,
May 18, 1952

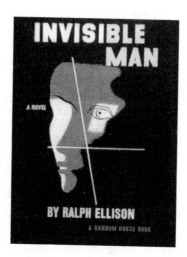

The reader who is familiar with the traumatic phase of the black man's rage in America will find something more in Mr. Ellison's report. He will find the long anguished step toward its mastery. The author sells no phony forgiveness. He asks none himself. It is a resolutely honest, tormented, profoundly American book ... "Invisible Man" belongs on the shelf with the classical efforts man has made to chart the river Lethe from its mouth to its source.

Wright Morris, review of
Invisible Man
by Ralph Ellison,
NY Times Book Review,
April 13, 1952

Because the diary was not written in retrospect, it contains the trembling life of every moment—Anne Frank's voice becomes the voice of six million vanished Jewish souls.

Meyer Levin, review of
The Diary of a Young Girl
by Anne Frank,
NY Times Book Review,
June 6, 1952

● ● ●

What the book is about is friendship on earth, affection and protection, adventure and miracle, life and death, trust and treachery, pleasure and pain, and the passing of time. As a piece of work it is just about perfect, and just about magical in the way it is done.

Eudora Welty, review of
Charlotte's Web
by E. B. White,
NY Times Book Review,
October 19, 1952

1953

DYLAN THOMAS (1914-1953) was born in Swansea, Wales, son of a school master. After leaving university in 1931, he became a reporter for the South Wales *Evening Post*, but after fifteen months decided to move to London. In 1934, his first book of poems, *19 Poems*, was published to great success. Three years later, he married Caitlin Macnamara, a former dancer, and they had three children. Thomas then embarked on a second career as a bohemian drinker and literary party man, having uncountable love affairs. (A fellow poet once complained that when Thomas sat on a sofa he left a stain.)

His bouts of drinking and partying, however, were interspersed with stays at his aunt's Carmarthenshire dairy farm, where he wrote many of his famous poems, including "Fern Hill" and "The Hunchback in the Park." During the war, Thomas, unfit for service, gained more popular attention as a freelance BBC reporter, and in 1950, during a drunken lecture tour of the United States, collapsed from alcohol poisoning. He died of pneumonia caused by acute alcoholism in 1953.

THE NATIONAL BOOK AWARDS

fiction

Ralph Ellison, *Invisible Man*

nonfiction

Bernard A. De Voto,
The Course of an Empire

poetry

Archibald MacLeish,
Collected Poems, 1917-1952

---

*I am an invisible man . . .
I am a man of substance, of
flesh and bone, fiber and
liquids—and I might even
be said to possess a mind. I
am invisible, understand,
simply because people refuse
to see me.*

Ralph Ellison,
Invisible Man (1952),
1953 National Book Award

It is a truly magnificent
book, even if sometimes
irritating to a mere male.
It should be a required
companion volume to all
who read the forth-
coming report of Kinsey
and his associates. For
Mlle. de Beauvoir says
much about sexuality
that is important which
we are not likely to get
from the Indiana group.
Statistical tables of the
incidence of various
types of sexual acts need
to be balanced by the
historical depth, philo-
sophical sophistication
and exquisite psycholog-
ical sensibilities of a
Simone de Beauvoir.

Clyde Kluckhohn, review of
The Second Sex
by Simone de Beauvoir,
NY Times Book Review,
February 22, 1953

Ralph Ellison

THE NEWBERY MEDAL

Secret of the Andes, Ann Nolan Clark

THE CALDECOTT MEDAL

The Biggest Bear, Lynd Ward

Pulitzer Prize winner

praise. *Death of a Salesman*, the story of a disillusioned traveling salesman whose sons turn against him, has been called the greatest American play of the century. Miller's fame escalated in the 1950s and 1960s: his clever indictment of the McCarthy trials, **The Crucible (1953)**, became a popular and critical hit; and in 1956 he married Hollywood's most glamorous actress, Marilyn Monroe. He has written over thirty plays to date.

ARTHUR MILLER (1915–) was born in Harlem, New York, the son of an Austro-Hungarian Jewish immigrant who ran a clothing manufacturing business. A mediocre student, Miller nevertheless believed he had potential as a writer and spent his early twenties saving money for college. In 1934, he enrolled at the University of Michigan, and three years later was awarded a Theatre Guild's Bureau Prize for his first play, *Honors at Dawn*. Full of hope, Miller returned to New York in 1938 and landed jobs with CBS and NBC as a radio playwright. His first professionally produced play closed after four performances, but his third one, *Death of a Salesman* (1948), won him extraordinary

DEATHS
Eugene O'Neill
Marjorie Kinnan Rawlings
Ricardo Sánchez
Dylan Thomas

1954

HARDCOVER BESTSELLERS

fiction

Not as a Stranger,
Morton Thompson

Mary Anne, Daphne du Maurier

nonfiction

*The Holy Bible: Revised
Standard Edition*

The Power of Positive Thinking,
Norman Vincent Peale

**THE ALFRED B. NOBEL
PRIZE FOR LITERATURE**

Ernest Hemingway, U.S.

COLETTE (1873–1954) was born Sidonie Gabrielle Colette in the Burgundian village of Sauveur-en-Puisaye. At twenty, she married Henry Gauthier-Villars, a journalist and popular novelist, who enlisted poor writers to produce under his name. This group soon included Colette, who wrote the phenomenally successful *Claudine* novels. Tired of literary slavery and her husband's constant infidelities, Colette left the marriage in 1906, began to write her own novels, and embarked on a period of scandalous independence, which included a stint as a music-hall artiste and mime and an affair with the marquise de Morny. In 1912, Colette left the bohemian life, married again, and published novels such as *Chéri* (1920). In the 1930s and 1940s, she turned to autobiographical and semifictional work, and during World War II courageously protected her Jewish husband (her third) in Paris. Colette, in her lifetime, was regarded as a writer limited to psychological and nature writing and overly concerned with women, but since the 1970s has been recast as a great twentieth-century female writer.

BIRTH
Louise Erdrich

DEATH
Colette

Mr. Tolkien has succeeded superbly . . . No fiction I have read in the last five years has given me more joy than "The Fellowship of the Ring."

W. H. Auden, review of
The Fellowship of the Ring
by J. R. R. Tolkien,
NY Times Book Review,
October 31, 1954

THE PULITZER PRIZES

fiction

No award

biography or autobiography

The Spirit of St. Louis,
Charles A. Lindbergh

poetry

The Waking, Theodore Roethke

drama

Teahouse of the August Moon,
John Patrick

THE NEWBERY MEDAL

. . . And Now Miguel,
Joseph Krumgold

THE CALDECOTT MEDAL

Madeline's Rescue,
Ludwig Bemelmans

*Pulitzer Prize winner Charles Lindbergh
with his wife, writer Anne Morrow Lindbergh*

William Golding
Lord of the
Flies

*Ralph wept for the end of
innocence, the darkness of
man's heart, and the fall
through the air of the true,
wise friend called Piggy.*

William Golding,
The Lord of the Flies (1954)

THE NATIONAL BOOK AWARDS

fiction

The Adventures of Augie March,
Saul Bellow

nonfiction

A Stillness at Appomattox,
Bruce Catton

poetry

Collected Poems, Conrad Aiken

1955

HARDCOVER BESTSELLERS

fiction

Marjorie Morningstar, Herman Wouk

Auntie Mame, Patrick Dennis

nonfiction

Gift from the Sea,
Anne Morrow Lindbergh

The Power of Positive Thinking,
Norman Vincent Peale

THE ALFRED B. NOBEL PRIZE FOR LITERATURE

Halldor K. Laxness, Iceland

JAMES AGEE (1909-1955) was born in Knoxville, Tennessee, and educated at Harvard. After graduation, he worked for several publications before being commissioned by *Fortune* magazine to report on several "typical" Alabama sharecropper families with the photographer Walker Evans. *Fortune* found the piece unsuitable for publication, but it was eventually published, along with Evan's photographs in 1941 as a book, *Let Us Now Praise Famous Men*. An overnight literary celebrity, Agee next found himself being wooed by Hollywood, where he wrote the film scripts for *The African Queen* (1952) and *The Night of the Hunter* (1955) as well as popular *Nation* film reviews. His first work of fiction, the novella, *The Morning Watch*, was published in 1951, and was followed by the semi-autobiographical *A Death in the Family*, which was unfinished at the time of Agee's death and was awarded a posthumous Pulitzer Prize.

BIRTH

John Grisham

DEATHS

James Agee
Thomas Mann
Wallace Stevens

THE PULITZER PRIZES

fiction

A Fable, William Faulkner

biography or autobiography

The Taft Story, William S. White

poetry

Collected Poems, Wallace Stevens

drama

Cat on a Hot Tin Roof,
Tennessee Williams

THE NEWBERY MEDAL

The Wheel on the School,
Meindert Dejong

THE CALDECOTT MEDAL

Cinderella, Illustrated and retold from Perrault by Marcia Brown

[111]

Pulitzer Prize winner Tennessee Williams

My life, my real life, was
in danger, and not from
anything other people might
do but from the hatred
I carried in my own heart.

James Baldwin,
Notes of a Native Son (1955)

ALLEN GINSBERG (1926–1997) was born in Newark, New Jersey, the son of a poet-teacher and Russian-born mother, whose political commitments (she was an ardent Communist) degenerated into paranoia, and eventually institutionalism, lobotimization, and death in an asylum. Her gruesome life became the subject of Ginsberg's long memorial poem, "Kaddish." Ginsberg received a scholarship to study law at Columbia, but changed his major to English and became Lionel Trilling's star pupil. He then attached himself to the members of the soon-to-be-christened Beat movement: Jack Kerouac and William S. Burroughs, with whom he took drugs, broke laws, and experimented literarily. This life was challenging and Ginsberg found himself twice in short-term psychiatric care. In **1955**, he made his literary debut with the incantatory **"Howl,"** which was declared obscene for its explicit expression of homosexuality. Ginsberg is widely regarded as a father figure to the 1960s counterculture. He coined the term "flower power," and spent the majority of his life demonstrating against the collective evils of the establishment.

THE NATIONAL BOOK AWARDS

fiction
A Fable, William Faulkner

nonfiction
The Measure of Man,
Joseph Wood Krutch

poetry
*The Collected Poems of
Wallace Stevens,* Wallace Stevens

1956

HARDCOVER BESTSELLERS

fiction

Don't Go Near the Water,
William Brinkley

The Last Hurrah, Edwin O'Connor

nonfiction

Arthritis and Common Sense, Revised
Edition, Dan Dale Alexander

*Webster's New World Dictionary of the
American Language,* Concise
Edition, David B. Guralnik, ed.

**THE ALFRED B. NOBEL
PRIZE FOR LITERATURE**

Juan Ramón Jiménez, Spain

DEATHS
*Bertolt Brecht
H. L. Mencken
A. A. Milne*

BERTOLT BRECHT (1898–1956) was born in East Berlin, studied medicine in Munich, and by the age of thirty was recognized as a versatile writer of plays and lyric poetry as well as a radical opponent of nationalism and war. In 1933, he went into exile in Switzerland, Denmark, Finland, and Russia,

*Bertolt Brecht, photograph
by Josef Breitenbach*

finally landing in California in 1941, where he worked on film scripts with Charles Chaplin and Charles Laughton. After the war, he returned to East Berlin and founded the Berliner Ensemble in deliberate contrast to the Weimar theater of Goethe and Schiller. Brecht believed that theater was the most effective means of communication; he experimented enormously with political theater, language, and dramatic form, and dismissed the idea that drama should seek to create the illusion of reality. His best known works are *Man Is Man* (1927), *The Threepenny Opera* (1928), and *Mother Courage* (1941).

[*113*]

A. A. MILNE (1882–1956) was born in London, the son of a prep school headmaster of Scottish origin. He attended Cambridge's Trinity College, where he edited the still extant literary journal *Granta*. Milne began his career as a London journalist and editor. During World War I, he wrote propaganda for England's intelligence service and spent his free time writing fantasy plays, which after the war were staged to great acclaim. Although he wrote in almost every literary form, Milne today is remembered solely as the creator of cheerful children's books, such as *When We Were Very Young* (1924), *Now We Are Six* (1927), and, most famously, *Winnie the Pooh* (1926), featuring Christopher Robin, a character named for his estranged son. (Oddly, Milne had an uncanny ability to understand the world of children but trouble communicating with his own progeny.) He spent most of his life in the Chelsea area of London and in his country home in Sussex near the Ashdown Forest, where his Pooh books are set.

The story of "Long Day's Journey Into Night" is no more devastating than others he told. But it seems more devastating because it is personal and as literal as a drama can be. This was the environment, respectably middle class on the surface, obsessed and tortured inside, out of which our most gigantic writer of tragedy emerged.

Brooks Atkinson,
review of
Long Day's Journey Into Night by Eugene O'Neill,
NY Times Book Review,
February 19, 1956

A single sentence will suffice for modern man: he fornicated and read the papers.

Albert Camus,
The Fall (La Chute) (1956)

THE PULITZER PRIZES

fiction
Andersonville, MacKinlay Kantor

biography or autobiography
Benjamin Henry Latrobe,
Talbot F. Hamlin

poetry
Poems, North and South,
Elizabeth Bishop

drama
The Diary of Anne Frank,
Frances Goodrich and
Albert Hackett

Pulitzer Prize winner Elizabeth Bishop

America I'm putting my
queer shoulder to the wheel.

Allen Ginsberg,
"America" (1956)

You and I
Are suddenly what the trees
try
To tell us we are:
That their merely being
there
Means something; that soon
We may touch, love,
explain.

John Ashbery,
"Some Trees" (1956)

HERMANN

HESSE

The Journey to the East

[115]

In pornographic novels,
action has to be limited to
the copulation of clichés.
Style, structure, imagery
should never distract the
reader from his tepid lust.

Vladimir Nabokov,
"On a Book Entitled *Lolita*"
(1956)

1957

HARDCOVER BESTSELLERS

fiction

By Love Possessed,
James Gould Cozzens

Peyton Place, Grace Metalious

nonfiction

Kids Say the Darndest Things!,
Art Linkletter

The FBI Story, Don Whitehead

THE ALFRED B. NOBEL PRIZE FOR LITERATURE

Albert Camus, France

THE PULITZER PRIZES

fiction

No award

biography or autobiography

Profiles in Courage, John F. Kennedy

poetry

Things of This World, Richard Wilbur

drama

Long Day's Journey into Night,
Eugene O'Neill

DEATHS

Nikos Kazantzakis
Malcolm Lowry
Christopher Morley

*Pulitzer Prize winner John F. Kennedy,
with his brother Robert.*

"On the Road" belongs to the new Bohemianism in American fiction in which an experimental style is combined with eccentric characters and a morally neutral point of view ... As a portrait of a disjointed segment of society acting out of its own neurotic necessity, "On the Road" is a stunning achievement. But it is a road, as far as the characters are concerned, that leads nowhere—and which the novelist himself cannot afford to travel more than once.

David Dempsey,
review of *On the Road*
by Jack Kerouac,
NY Times Book Review,
September 8, 1957

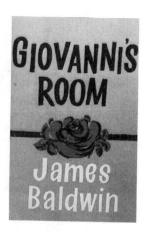

he was condemned for writing in the Demotic Greek, the language of ordinary people. Kazantzakis today is regarded as the most important figure in twentieth-century Greek literature.

NIKOS KAZANTZAKIS (1883?–1957) was born in Heraklion, Crete, the son of a peasant farmer, and grew up among Cretan shepherds, farmers, and fishermen. As a teenager he was sent to the Greek island of Naxos to study in a monastery. From there he went on to earn a law degree from the University of Athens, and then studied in France under the philosopher Henri Bergson. Kazantzakis's life and literary work were bound up in philosophical quests; "My principal anguish," he once said, "and the source of all my joys and sorrows . . . has been the incessant, merciless battle between the spirit and the flesh." Kazantzakis boldly brought these themes to bear in his two best-known novels, *Zorba the Greek* (1946, 1953) and *The Last Temptation of Christ* (1955, 1960), which made his literary reputation in the West but whose unconventional themes brought him harsh criticism at home. Particularly,

THE NEWBERY MEDAL

Miracles on Maple Hill,
  Virginia Sorensen

THE CALDECOTT MEDAL

A Tree Is Nice, Janice Udry,
  Illustrated by Marc Simont

THE NATIONAL BOOK AWARDS

fiction

The Field of Vision, Wright Morris

nonfiction

Russia Leaves the War,
  George F. Kennan

poetry

Things of This World, Richard Wilbur

[117]

1958

BORIS PASTERNAK (1890–1960) was born in prerevolutionary Moscow, the son of artistic parents who belonged to the day's most culturally prestigious social circle. Pasternak's first wish was to be a great music composer, but after several years of eager study gave it up, realizing for him a musical career "was against the will of fate and heaven." He chose poetry as an alternative, and in 1923 published his first volume of poems, *My Sister, Life*, which made him an instant literary sensation. At first supportive of the 1917 Russian Revolution, Pasternak by the 1930s hid in its shadows ("Don't touch this cloud dweller," Stalin was rumored to have ordered), while witnessing the "disap-pearance" of the great writers of his generation. This among other experiences inspired his fictional masterpiece, *Dr. Zhivago*, which when submitted for publication in 1956 earned him the wrath of the Communists. Pasternak was expelled from the Writers Union and deemed a traitor. Although he was awarded the 1958 **Nobel** and widely translated, his great novel was not published in Russia until 1988.

> The most essential gift for a good writer is a built-in, shock-proof, shit detector. This is the writer's radar and all great writers have had it.
>
> Ernest Hemingway, interview in *Paris Review*, Spring 1958

THE PULITZER PRIZES

fiction

A Death in the Family, James Agee

biography or autobiography

George Washington, Vols. I-VI,
Douglas Southall Freeman
(deceased 1953); *Vol. VII,*
John Alexander Carroll and
Mary Wells Ashworth

poetry

Promises: Poems 1954-1956,
Robert Penn Warren

drama

Look Homeward, Angel, Ketti Frings

Pulitzer Prize winner James Agee

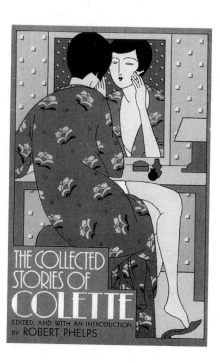

"Lolita" is one of those occasional books which arrive swishing behind them a long tail of opinion and reputation which can knock the unwary reader off his feet . . . Then, as in a fairy tale, his wish comes true, Lolita is its fulfillment. She is the quintessence of the nymphet, discovered by total accident in an Eastern American small town. To get her, Humbert puts himself through a pattern of erotic choreography that would shame a bowerbird. He is grotesque and horrible and unbearably funny, and he knows it.

Elizabeth Janeway, review of
Lolita by Vladimir Nabokov,
NY Times Book Review,
August 17, 1958

[*119*]

write: his play **The Blacks** (1958) uncompromisingly articulated the psychology of racial hatred and caused a sensation in Europe and the United States. After 1961, though, Genet wrote little, devoting himself to controversial political causes, such as support of the PLO and the Black Panthers.

> *Fear tastes like a rusty knife and do not let her into your house. Courage tastes of blood. Stand up straight. Admire the world. Relish the love of a gentle woman. Trust in the Lord.*
>
> John Cheever, last lines of *The Wapshot Chronicle* (1957; 1958 National Book Award)

JEAN GENET (1910–1986) never knew his mother or father, and spent his youth in French state institutions or wandering Europe in abject poverty. He first achieved notoriety as a criminal who on stolen prison paper wrote highly aesthetic and pornographic tracts. On reading his first poem, Jean Cocteau proclaimed him a literary genius and secured him a presidential pardon, after which Genet executed two fantastical prison novels, including *Miracle de la Rose* (1946). Another early admirer was Sartre, who wrote a book on Genet, establishing him as a model Existentialist and heroic outcast. This literary canonization haunted Genet, for he had done much to cultivate his criminal image and greatly feared literary sterility. But he continued to

THE NEWBERY MEDAL
Rifles for Watie, Harold Keith

THE CALDECOTT MEDAL
Time of Wonder, Robert McCloskey

THE NATIONAL BOOK AWARDS

fiction
John Cheever,
The Wapshot Chronicle

nonfiction
Catherine Drinker Bowen,
The Lion and the Throne

poetry
Robert Penn Warren,
Promises: Poems, 1954-1956

1959

HARDCOVER BESTSELLERS

fiction

Exodus, Leon Uris

Doctor Zhivago, Boris Pasternak

nonfiction

'Twixt Twelve and Twenty, Pat Boone

Folk Medicine, D. C. Jarvis

THE ALFRED B. NOBEL PRIZE FOR LITERATURE

Salvatore Quasimodo, Italy

THE PULITZER PRIZES

fiction

The Travels of Jaimie McPheeters, Robert Lewis Taylor

biography or autobiography

Woodrow Wilson: American Prophet, Arthur Walworth

poetry

Selected Poems 1928-1958, Stanley Kunitz

drama

J. B.: A Play in Verse, Archibald MacLeish

DEATH

Raymond Chandler

WILLIAM S. BURROUGHS (1914-1997), the eldest son of the Beat movement, was born in St. Louis, the grandson of the inventor of the adding machine. At Harvard and later Columbia, he met Jack Kerouac and Allen Ginsberg, to whom he introduced the lurid world of New York drug addicts and small-time criminals. Burrough's second and most famous novel, *Naked Lunch* (**Paris,** 1959), compiled from thousands of notes during his years of heroin addiction and withdrawal, was deemed obscene and did not see

legal U.S. publication until 1966. It did, however, cement his reputation as America's most experimental and outrageous writer. In 1951, he shot his wife in a bizarre accident in which she placed a highball glass on her head and due to her husband's bad aim ended up dead, an event that Burroughs said freed him to become a writer. Burroughs has worked as an exterminator, store detective, and marijuana farmer. He is said to be a notorious drug addict and pederast, and despite his wife's shooting remains a ferocious devotee of weapons. In the 1980s, he became a painter, cashing in on the "punk" art movement. In 1997, Burroughs died of a heart attack in Lawrence, KS.

[121]

THE NEWBERY MEDAL

The Witch of Blackbird Pond,
Elizabeth George Speare

THE CALDECOTT MEDAL

Chanticleer and the Fox,
Barbara Clooney

THE NATIONAL BOOK AWARDS

fiction

The Magic Barrel, Bernard Malamud

nonfiction

Mistress to an Age: A Life of Madame De Staël, J. Christopher Herold

poetry

Words for the Wind,
Theodore Roethke

> *You can declare at the very start that it's impossible to write a novel nowadays, but then, behind your back, so to speak, give birth to a whopper, a novel to end all novels.*
>
> Günter Grass, *The Tin Drum*, (1959)

RAYMOND CHANDLER (1888–1959), the famous detective novelist, was born in Chicago and reared in England. He had a late start as a writer, first attempting jobs as a clerk at the English Admiralty, a newspaper reporter ("I was a complete flop, the worst they ever had," he admitted), a soldier in the Canadian army, and a Los Angeles oil company executive (a position from which he was eventually fired). After a bout of depression and boozing, Chandler began writing detective stories for pulp magazines, which secured his literary fame. His tough sleuth character, Philip Marlowe, has become a cult figure, and many of his novels depicting the seedy side of L.A., such as *The Big Sleep* (1939) and *The Long Goodbye* (1954), are hallmarks of detective fiction and the bases of classic Hollywood films.

John
Berryman
The
Dream
Songs

The only complete one-volume edition of
77 Dream Songs [PULITZER PRIZE] and
His Toy, His Dream, His Rest [NATIONAL BOOK AWARD]

Marguerite Duras

MARGUERITE DURAS (1914–), France's most celebrated female writer of the twentieth century, was born and brought up in Indochina, where her parents were both schoolteachers. At four, her father died, leaving her frail mother to fend for her four children alone. Unsurprisingly, Indochina, poverty, and familial instability figure heavily in Duras's work. In 1932, she left to study law and political science at the Paris Sorbonne, participated in the Resistance at great risk (she is Jewish), and published her first semi-autobiographical novels, notably, *La Douleur* (1945). Duras wrote in many styles; her next mode was linguistic minimalism, captured in **Hiroshima Mon Amour** (1959), the famous film for which she wrote the script, and the novel *The Lover* (1984). To date, she has produced over fifty novels, plays, and films, each coming closer to erasing the boundaries between genres and thus, for Duras, escaping the confines of artistic classification.

[*123*]

> *The sleek, expensive girls I teach,*
> *Younger and pinker every year,*
> *Bloom gradually out of reach.*
>
> W. D. Snodgrass,
> "April Inventory" (1959)

1960

ALBERT CAMUS (1913–1960) was born and raised in a working-class milieu in Algeria, the son of a French laborer. At seventeen, he came down with tuberculosis and was beset with it for the rest of his life. Camus's works, as a result, are often concerned with the bleakness of the human condition and the fragility of life. In his early years, he worked at menial jobs, then becoming a theater director, producing his play *Caligula,* and later a reporter for a radical Algiers newspaper. In 1942, his novel *The Stranger* and essay "The Myth of Sisyphus" were published, establishing his reputation as a philosopher-writer of the absurd. In the 1940s, Camus's bad health brought him to Paris, where he served as editor-in-chief of the newspaper *Combat* and became a leading French intellectual, writing on topics as varied as revolt, political and colonial oppression, and Western hypocrisy. He was awarded the 1957 Nobel Prize for Literature.

DEATHS
Albert Camus
Ian Fleming
J. P. Marquand
Boris Pasternak
Richard Wright

RICHARD WRIGHT (1908–1960) was born on a plantation in Mississippi. At five, his father abandoned him, and his mother, having suffered a stroke, placed him in the care of his impoverished relatives. Wright quit school at fifteen,

but proceeded to educate himself (he illicitly used the library, presenting himself as a "nigger boy" fetching a white person's books). In 1932, he moved to Chicago and joined the Communist Party and the Federal Writers' Project, and then went to New York to report for left-wing papers. His first book, *Uncle Tom's Children*, was published to great acclaim in 1938, but it wasn't until his novels, *Native Son* (1940) and *Black Boy* (1945), revealing the depths of racial oppression, that Wright jolted the literary scene and became an influential American and black writer. He settled in France in 1947, became involved in the African independence movement, and after weathering the McCarthy witch hunts and the waning of his popularity, died in poverty in Paris.

> The greatest game of politics is played in Allen Drury's "Advise and Consent" for the ultimate stakes of life and death. This is the best novel about Washington I have ever read.
>
> Charles Poore, review of
> *Advise and Consent*
> by Allan Drury,
> *NY Times Book Review,*
> August 11, 1959
> (1960 Pulitzer Prize winner)

> [A] moving and often brilliant novel.
>
> David Boroff, review of
> *Rabbit, Run* by John Updike,
> *NY Times Book Review*,
> November 6, 1960

National Book Award winner for poetry,
Robert Lowell

THE NATIONAL BOOK AWARDS

fiction

Goodbye, Columbus, Philip Roth

nonfiction

James Joyce, Richard Ellmann

poetry

Life Studies, Robert Lowell

James A. Michener's new novel, "Hawaii," may never make literary history, but for some time it has been making publishing history. It is a selection of both the Book-of-the-Month and Reader's Digest condensed book clubs. It has been sold to a motion picture company for a reputed price of $600,000 . . . It is unfortunate that in order to hold his reader's interest in so many aspects of Hawaii's story Mr. Michener has thought it necessary to crowd his book with scores of brutal, sordid and sensational scenes of sexual violence. They may help with sales, but "Hawaii" would have been popular without them.

> Orville Prescott, review of
> *Hawaii*
> by James Michener,
> *NY Times Book Review*,
> November 20, 1959
> (Bestselling novel 1960)

1961

HARDCOVER BESTSELLERS

fiction

The Agony and the Ecstasy,
Irving Stone

Franny and Zooey, J. D. Salinger

nonfiction

The New English Bible:
The New Testament

The Rise and Fall of the Third Reich,
William Shirer

THE ALFRED B. NOBEL PRIZE FOR LITERATURE

Ivo Andric, Yugoslavia

THE PULITZER PRIZES

fiction

To Kill a Mockingbird, Harper Lee

biography or autobiography

Charles Sumner and the Coming of the Civil War, David Donald

poetry

Times Three: Selected Verse from Three Decades, Phyllis McGinley

drama

All the Way Home, Tad Mosel

THE NEWBERY MEDAL

Island of the Blue Dolphins,
Scott O'Dell

THE CALDECOTT MEDAL

Baboushka and the Three Kings,
Ruth Robbins,
Illustrated by Nicolas Sidjakov

THE NATIONAL BOOK AWARDS

fiction

The Waters of Kronos, Conrad Richter

nonfiction

The Rise and Fall of the Third Reich,
William Shirer

poetry

The Woman at the Washington Zoo,
Randall Jarrell

ERNEST HEMINGWAY (1899–1961) was born in a middle-class suburb of Chicago, the son of a doctor and keen sportsman who introduced him to the masculine pleasures of hunting, shooting, and fishing. In 1917, he joined the *Kansas City Star* as a cub reporter and then volunteered as an ambulance driver on the Italian front, where he was badly wounded but fell in love with an American nurse, an experience he captured in his novel *A Farewell to Arms* (1929). In the 1930s and 1940s, Hemingway worked as a foreign correspondent in Europe and continued to build his reputation as a gifted novelist—most notably for *The Sun Also Rises* (1926) and *For Whom the Bell Tolls* (1940). He also became known for his bullying egotism and alcoholism,

[*127*]

which earned him as many friends as enemies. Despite winning the 1954 Nobel Prize, he spent his last years away from the center of events—mostly in Cuba—and in 1961 killed himself with a shotgun. Hemingway's simple yet immensely evocative style has had a profound influence on the development of American fiction writing.

James Thurber

[*128*]

JAMES THURBER (1894-1961) was born in Columbus, Ohio, the son of a minor politician. Due to a childhood eye injury, he was assigned to desk duty during World War I, where he became interested in journalism, first working in Paris for the *Chicago Tribune*. His entree to *The New Yorker* was perhaps typical for his times: upon being introduced to the magazine's editor by E. B. White, he was offered the position of managing editor, though he lacked administrative experience or ability. Thurber's relationship with *The New Yorker* was to be lifelong, and the subject of much gossip (he had his assistant Truman Capote escort him to lunch-hour trysts, a duty that involved helping him redress). It also was where most of his brilliant comic short stories and essays were published. Thurber additionally wrote novels, plays, and children's stories, but was best known for his humorous nonfiction collections with titles such as *Is Sex Necessary?* (1929, with E. B. White) and *The Beast in Me and Other Animals* (1948).

> *He knows all about art, but he doesn't know what he likes.*
>
> James Thurber (1894-1961), caption for cartoon in *The New Yorker*

JOSEPH HELLER (1923–) was born in Brooklyn, New York, the son of a Russian-Jewish baker. During World War II, he served in the Air Force—an experience that set the seed for his greatest novel—and afterward, taking advantage of the GI bill, attended USC, NYU, and Columbia University, spending a year at Oxford as a Fulbright scholar. He then taught college English and worked in promotion at *Time* and *Look* magazines, while publishing short stories. Heller was lifted from literary anonymity with his first novel, **Catch 22** (1961), a grossly comic satire of heroism and the American military whose title became a catch phrase and whose ironic message became popular among readers of the Vietnam era. His later novels contemplated, often darkly, the fate of a business executive (*Something Happened,* 1974), Jewish family life (*Good as Gold,* 1979), and the paralyzing disease, Guillain-Barré syndrome, that kept him bedridden for most of the 1980s (*No Laughing Matter,* 1986).

Few writers since Joyce would risk such a wealth of words upon events that are purely internal and deeds that are purely talk . . . The Glass saga, as he has sketched it out, potentially contains great fiction. When all reservations have been entered, in the correctly unctuous and apprehensive tone, about the direction he has taken, it remains to acknowledge that it is a direction, and the refusal to rest content, the willingness to risk excess on behalf of one's obsessions, is what distinguishes artists from entertainers, and what makes some artists adventurers on behalf of us all.

John Updike, review of
Franny and Zooey
by J. D. Salinger,
NY Times Book Review,
September 17, 1961

[*129*]

1962

HARDCOVER BESTSELLERS

fiction

Ship of Fools, Katherine Anne Porter

Dearly Beloved,
Anne Morrow Lindbergh

nonfiction

Calories Don't Count,
Dr. Herman Taller

*The New English Bible:
The New Testament*

THE ALFRED B. NOBEL PRIZE FOR LITERATURE

John Steinbeck, U.S.

THE PULITZER PRIZES

fiction

The Edge of Sadness,
Edwin O'Connor

nonfiction

The Making of the President 1960,
Theodore H. White

biography or autobiography

No award

poetry

Poems, Alan Dugan

drama

*How to Succeed in Business Without
Really Trying*, Frank Loesser
and Abe Burrows

WILLIAM FAULKNER (1897-1962) grew up in Oxford, Mississippi, the great-grandson of William C. Falkner [sic], a Civil War colonel and popular author. After a desultory education during which he frequently played truant, he joined the Canadian Royal Air Force because he was too slight for the U.S. requirement. In 1919, Faulkner attended the University of Mississippi, worked odd jobs, drank hard, and began to write poems. His first collection was noticed by Sherwood Anderson, who suggested he try his hand at fiction. The resulting novel, *Soldiers' Pay* (1926), written in six weeks, was soon followed by *The Sound and the Fury* (1929), *As I Lay Dying* (1930), and *Sanctuary* (1931), which established him as a technically innovative writer concerned with race, violence, and the complex history of the American South. Faulkner won the 1949 Nobel Prize for Literature. At sixty-five, he died of a heart attack after falling from a horse.

> "The Golden Note-book" contains several brilliantly described, emotionally powerful episodes. Most of it is dull. Presumably it is a truthful account of British radicals and bohemians—a depressing thought.
>
> Orville Prescott, review of *The Golden Notebook* by Doris Lessing, *NY Times*, June 29, 1962

> George: *Who's afraid of Virginia Woolf . . .*
> Martha: *I . . . am . . .*
> George *. . . I am.*
>
> Edward Albee, *Who's Afraid of Virginia Woolf?* (1962)

DORIS LESSING (1919–) was born in Kermanshah, Iran, where her English-born father worked for the Imperial Bank of Persia. In 1925, he bought a maize farm in Rhodesia, where Lessing spent the remainder of her "hellishly lonely" childhood, reading European and American literature and writing "bad" novels. Between 1937 and 1949, she lived in England, married twice—the second time to the German political activist Gottfried Lessing—and helped to start a nonracialist left-wing party. Her first published novel was *The Grass Is Singing* (1950), a study of the barrenness of white civilization in Africa, which was followed, most famously, by **The Golden Notebook** (1962), now a classic of feminist literature and an exploration of political

[*131*]

assumptions and mental instability. In the 1980s, Lessing provoked a minor storm in the publishing world: she pseudonymously submitted two of her novels to her regular publisher—who soon rejected them—thus demonstrating the difficulties facing unestablished writers.

THE NEWBERY MEDAL

The Bronze Bow,
  Elizabeth George Speare

THE CALDECOTT MEDAL

Once a Mouse, Marcia Brown

THE NATIONAL BOOK AWARDS

fiction

The Moviegoer, Walker Percy

nonfiction

The City in History: Its Origins, Its Transformations and Its Prospects,
  Lewis Mumford

poetry

Poems, Alan Dugan

National Book Award winner
Walker Percy

1963

HARDCOVER BESTSELLERS

fiction

The Shoes of the Fisherman,
Morris L. West

The Group, Mary McCarthy

nonfiction

Happiness Is a Warm Puppy,
Charles M. Schulz

Security Is a Thumb and a Blanket,
Charles M. Schulz

**THE ALFRED B. NOBEL
PRIZE FOR LITERATURE**

Giorgios Seferis (Seferiades), Greece

THE PULITZER PRIZES

fiction

The Reivers, William Faulkner

nonfiction

The Guns of August,
Barbara W. Tuchman

biography or autobiography

*Henry James: Vol. II, The Conquest
of London, 1870-1881; Vol. III,
The Middle Years, 1881-1895,*
Leon Edel

poetry

Pictures from Brueghel,
William Carlos Williams

drama

No award

*Pulitzer Prize winner
William Carlos Williams*

DEATHS
*Jean Cocteau
Robert Frost
Aldous Huxley
Clifford Odets
Sylvia Plath
Theodore Roethke
William Carlos Williams*

[*133*]

ROBERT FROST (1874-1963) was born in
San Francisco, and at ten, after the
death of his father, moved to the New
England farm country with which his
poetry is identified. After briefly
attending Dartmouth, he became a
bobbin-boy in a Massachusetts mill,

and after another short period at Harvard, worked variously, making shoes, teaching, editing a country newspaper, and finally farming. These experiences helped shape his poetry, which he demanded be simple and honest as a hoe. In 1914, he published *North of Boston*, his second collection,

a self-described "book of people," which, with shrewd humor and Yankee understatement, gave brilliant insight into the New England character and established him as a grand American poet. Frost wrote hundreds of poems during the course of his life (and received four Pulitzer Prizes); he was a representative, as John F. Kennedy put it, "of the spirit which informs and controls our strength."

> We haven't the time to take our time.
>
> Eugéne Ionesco,
> *Exit the King*
> (*Le Roi Se Meurt*)
> (1962, 1963)

JEAN COCTEAU (1889-1963), a leading figure of the Parisian avant-garde, was born in Maisons-Laffitte, France, and at an early age entered the fashionable salon world of Anna de Noailles. An experimenter by nature, he took opium, sought salvation through solitude, and sponsored Stravinsky, Picasso, and Chirico, enlivening everything he touched. His most important poetry collections include the Futurist long poem *Le Cap de Bonne Espérance* (1919), the opium-inspired *Opera* (1927), and his masterpiece, *Le Requiem* (1962), in which he pays homage to Homer, Dante, Mallarmé, and others. Cocteau also wrote for the theater and opera, collaborating with such French artists as Satie and Massine, and beginning in the 1930s turned to perhaps his most ideal medium, the cinema, writing and directing the now-classic films *La Belle et la bête* (1945) and *Orphée* (1950).

THE NATIONAL BOOK AWARDS

fiction

Morte D'Urban, J. F. Powers

nonfiction

Henry James, Vol. II: The Conquest of London; Henry James, Vol. III: The Middle Years, Leon Edel

poetry

Traveling Through the Dark, William Stafford

THE NEWBERY MEDAL

A Wrinkle in Time, Madeleine L'Engle

THE CALDECOTT MEDAL

The Snowy Day, Ezra Jack Keats

Pynchon is in his early twenties; he writes in Mexico City—a recluse. It is hard to find out anything more about him. At least there is at hand a testament—this first novel "V."—which suggests that no matter what his circumstances, or where he's doing it, there is at work a young writer of staggering promise.

George Plimpton, review of *V.* by Thomas Pynchon, *NY Times Book Review*, April 4, 1963

Jessica Mitford revives muckraking journalism with The American Way of Death, *a merciless exposé of the funeral industry.*

[*135*]

SYLVIA PLATH (1932–1963) was born in Boston, the daughter of a German-born professor of biology, and educated at Smith College, where, suffering from serious depression, she attempted suicide. While in college, she began publishing poetry and upon graduation, was awarded a Fulbright scholarship, which took her to Cambridge University. There she met and married the poet Ted Hughes, with whom she had two children. Plath published her first volume of poetry in 1960, and three years later issued her first and only novel, *The Bell Jar*, now a feminist classic, documenting her earlier nervous breakdown. In 1963, at her artistic height, Plath succeeded in killing herself. She left behind two collections of visionary, highly intense and personal poetry, *Ariel* and *Winter Trees*, which Hughes published shortly after her death. Her *Collected Poems* was awarded the 1982 Pulitzer Prize.

1963 Newbery Medalist
A Wrinkle in Time
by Madeleine L'Engle.
This cover appeared in 1979.

1964

HARDCOVER BESTSELLERS

fiction

The Spy Who Came in From the Cold, John le Carré

Candy, Terry Southern and Mason Hoffenberg

nonfiction

Four Days, American Heritage and United Press International

I Need All the Friends I Can Get, Charles M. Schulz

THE PULITZER PRIZES

fiction

No award

nonfiction

Anti-Intellectualism in American Life, Richard Hofstadter

biography or autobiography

John Keats, Walter Jackson Bate

poetry

At the End of the Open Road, Louis Simpson

drama

No award

THE ALFRED B. NOBEL PRIZE FOR LITERATURE

Jean Paul Sartre, France (declined)

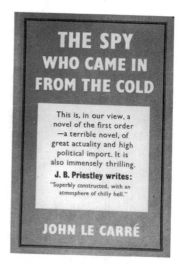

THE SPY WHO CAME IN FROM THE COLD

This is, in our view, a novel of the first order —a terrible novel, of great actuality and high political import. It is also immensely thrilling.

J. B. Priestley writes:
"Superbly constructed, with an atmosphere of chilly hell."

JOHN LE CARRÉ

A great writer is, so to speak, a second government in his country. And for that reason no regime has ever loved great writers, only minor ones.

Aleksandr Solzhenitsyn, *The First Circle* (1964)

THE AUTOBIOGRAPHY OF MALCOLM X

> *All the same, they [books]
> do serve some purpose.
> Culture doesn't save any-
> thing or anyone, it doesn't
> justify. But it's a product of
> man: he projects himself into
> it, he recognizes himself in
> it; that critical mirror alone
> offers him his image.*
>
> Jean Paul Sartre,
> *Les Mots*
> (*The Words*) (1964)

nent of atheistic existentialism, which found expression in *Transcendence of Ego* (1936) and *Being and Nothingness* (1943). Until his death in 1980, Sartre stayed visible as a political activist and wrote novels, plays, and essays, which together influenced the moral and sociopolitical issues of the day. He was awarded but declined to accept the 1964 **Nobel Prize**.

JEAN PAUL SARTRE (1905-1980) was born in Paris and studied at the Sorbonne, where he met his lifelong companion, Simone de Beauvoir. After graduation, he taught philosophy in Le Havre, Paris, and Berlin, until in 1939 he was conscripted into the Army and subsequently taken prisoner, escaping in 1941. It was this war-time experience that led Sartre to his left-wing political commitments. Returning to Paris, he became a member of the Resistance, and in 1946 founded and edited with Beauvoir the avant-garde monthly *Modern Times*. A disciple of Heidegger, he became the most prominent expo-

THE NEWBERY MEDAL
It's Like This, Cat, Emily Neville

THE CALDECOTT MEDAL
Where the Wild Things Are,
Maurice Sendak

THE NATIONAL BOOK AWARDS

fiction
The Centaur, John Updike

arts and letters
John Keats: The Making of a Poet,
Aileen Ward

history and biography
The Rise of the West: A History of the Human Community,
William H. McNeill

science, philosophy and religion

Man-Made America,
Christopher Tunnard and
Boris Pushkarev

poetry
Selected Poems, John Crowe Ransom

KEN KESEY (1935-) was born in La Junta, Colorado, the son of a creamery farmer, and raised in Eugene, Oregon. At University of Oregon, he developed an interest in creative writing and after graduation won a scholarship to Stanford University, but soon dropped out to embrace the alternative lifestyle of drugs and counter-conventions that was flourishing in San Francisco. During that time, he volunteered to undergo army-financed experiments with LSD, and this and the experience of working in a psychiatric hospital served to inspire his first novel, *One Flew Over the Cuckoo's Nest* (1962), which was embraced as a devious critique of American conservatism. Though Kesey's second novel, ***Sometimes a Great Notion*** (1964), was equally well received, in the sixties he gave up writing and turned to further experiments with LSD, forming the group the Merry Pranksters, who toured America by bus dispensing his

favorite hallucinogenic. Kesey quickly became the guru of 1960s hippie drug culture, but as the decade wore thin he returned to writing fiction, which like the radical culture he championed mellowed with age.

> Over the past 10 or 11 years, Jewish writers—Bernard Malamud, J. D. Salinger, Norman Mailer, Philip Roth, inter alia—have emerged as a dominant movement in our literature. "Herzog," in several senses, is the great pay-off book of that movement.
>
> Julian Moynahan,
> review of *Herzog*
> by Saul Bellow,
> *NY Times Book Review*,
> September 20, 1964

FLANNERY O'CONNOR (1924–1964) was born in Savannah, Georgia, in the "Christ-haunted" Bible Belt of the Southern United States. She attended the University of Georgia and in 1947 received a masters degree from the University of Iowa's Writers' Workshop. Her first two novels, *Wise Blood* (1952) and *The Violent Bear It Away* (1960), which deal with religious vocation and portray often freakish, lonely Southern charac-

[*139*]

ters, were well received, but it wasn't until her short story collections, especially *A Good Man Is Hard to Find* (1955), which she called "nine stories about original sin," that she earned her title as a great Southern American writer. O'Connor's life was outwardly uneventful; though she lectured often and was considered a lively, humorous woman, she was often immobilized by lupus, which kept her close to home and at forty killed her.

Caldecott winner Maurice Sendak

DEATHS

Brendan Behan
Rachel Carson
Sean O'Casey
Flannery O'Connor
E. J. Pratt
T. H. White

Brendan Behan

Never eat at any place called "Mom's." And never, ever, no matter what else you do in your life, never sleep with anyone whose troubles are worse than your own.

Nelson Algren,
from *Conversations with Nelson Algren*
by H. E. F. Donohue
(1964)

•   •   •

When will indifference come.

John Berryman
"His Toy, His Dream,
His Rest" (1964)

1965

HARDCOVER BESTSELLERS

fiction

The Source, James A. Michener

Up the Down Staircase, Bel Kaufman

nonfiction

How to Be a Jewish Mother,
Dan Greenburg

A Gift of Prophecy,
Ruth Montgomery

THE ALFRED B. NOBEL PRIZE FOR LITERATURE

Mikhail Sholokhov, U.S.S.R.

THE PULITZER PRIZES

fiction

The Keepers of the House,
Shirley Ann Grau

nonfiction

O Strange New World,
Howard Mumford Jones

biography or autobiography

Henry Adams, Ernest Samuels

poetry

77 Dream Songs, John Berryman

drama

The Subject Was Roses,
Frank D. Gilroy

W. SOMERSET MAUGHAM (1874–1965) was born in Paris, the son of a legal adviser to the English embassy, and lived in France until 1884 when both his parents died and he was sent to England to live with his uncle. At sixteen, while studying in Heidelberg, he experienced his first homosexual affair, which formed the basis of his most popular novel, *Of Human Bondage*. He then studied medicine in London, but after publishing his first novel (1897) and inheriting two legacies he decided to devote himself to writing. Maugham first gained attention as the author of successfully staged West End plays, but his world-weary novels and story collections, such as

[*141*]

Cakes and Ale (1930) and *The Trembling of a Leaf* (1921), were what solidified his reputation. After World War I—where he served as a secret agent—Maugham traveled widely, accompanied by his male lovers-cum-secretaries, and wrote prodigiously. He died at ninety-one, after undergoing bizarre medical treatments to stave off old age.

SIR WINSTON SPENCER CHURCHILL (1874-1965) was born the eldest son of Lord Randolph Churchill, son of the seventh duke of Marlborough, and entered the Army in 1895. He served in Cuba, India, Egypt, and Sudan, worked as a war correspondent, and in 1916 became a lieutenant colonel. Churchill evinced an early brilliance for strategy, diplomacy, and political tact, and was duly rewarded. He served as undersecretary of state for the colonies (1906-1908); president of the board of trade (1908-1910); home secretary (1910-1911); first lord of the Admiralty (1911-1915); secretary of state for war (1918-1921); for the colonies (1921-1922); chancellor of the exchequer (1924-1929); and twice as prime minister (1940-1945, 1951-1955). By the end of his life, he had become England's most powerful and influential statesman. He left behind a large body of important nonfiction work, including *My African Journey* (1909), *The World Crisis* (4 vols, 1923-1929), and *The Second World War* (6 vols, 1958-1954), for which he was awarded the 1953 Nobel Prize.

THE NEWBERY MEDAL

Shadow of a Bull,
Maia Wojciechowska

THE CALDECOTT MEDAL

May I Bring a Friend? Beatrice Schenk de Regniers, Illustrated by Beni Montresor

THE NATIONAL BOOK AWARDS

fiction

Herzog, Saul Bellow

arts and letters

Oysters of Locmariaquer,
Eleanor Clark

history and biography

The Life of Lenin, Louis Fischer

science, philosophy and religion

*God and Golem, Inc: A Comment on
Certain Points Where Cybernetics
Impinges on Religion,*
Norbert Wiener

poetry

The Far Field, Theodore Roethke

HAROLD PINTER
The Homecoming

The book is new
and classic, and its publication now, after the past
terrible year, suggests
that things are looking
up for America and
its civilization.

Julia Moynahan, review of
Herzog
by Saul Bellow,
NY Times Book Review,
September 20, 1964
(1965 National Book Award)

•   •   •

After reading "Up the
Down Staircase" one
understands why public-
school teachers rate
higher salaries, why knif-
ings and riots are
frequent actualities . . .
and why education is an
urgent item of President
Johnson's Great Society.
Miss Kaufman's heroine
is Sylvia Barrett, a new
English teacher, and she
is very willing and very
eager to teach. The
reasons she is not always
able to are what this
book (which the pub-
lishers have billed as a
"novel") is all about.

Beverly Grunwald, review of
Up The Down Staircase
by Bel Kaufman,
NY Times Book Review,
February 14, 1965

[*143*]

1966

*Pulitzer Prize winner
Katherine Anne Porter*

ANDRÉ BRETON (1896-1966), the poet
and leader of the Surrealist movement,
was born in Tinchebray, France. His
early biography is a mercurial one: he
abandoned his medical studies in favor
of poetry, paid a visit to Freud during
his honeymoon, briefly became a
member of the Communist Party
(1927), met Trotsky in Mexico (1938),
and spent most of World War II in the
United States. In 1920, he cowrote the
first text of Surrealism, the revolutionary Paris-based art movement of
which he became the "pope." Breton
and his fellow Surrealists made art in
reaction to realism, reason, and the idea
of progress, an anti-nineteenth-century
philosophy initially inspired by the

carnage of the World War I and later by the futility of twentieth-century technology. He also worked to radicalize the novel genre in books such as *Nadja* (1924), and wrote extensively on the visual branch of Surrealism, led by Miró, Magritte, Man Ray, and Dali.

DEATHS
André Breton
C. S. Forester
Evelyn Waugh

THE NEWBERY MEDAL

I, Juan de Pareja,
Elizabeth Borton de Trevino

THE CALDECOTT MEDAL

Always Room for One More,
Sorche Nic Leodhas,
Illustrated by Nonny Hogrogian

THE NATIONAL BOOK AWARDS

fiction

The Collected Stories of Katherine Anne Porter,
Katherine Anne Porter

arts and letters

Paris Journal, 1944-65, Janet Flanner

history and biography

A Thousand Days,
Arthur M. Schlesinger, Jr.

science, philosophy and religion

No award

poetry

Buckdancer's Choice: Poems,
James Dickey

I didn't want to harm the man. I thought he was a very nice gentleman. Soft-spoken. I thought so right up to the moment I cut his throat.

Truman Capote,
In Cold Blood
(1966)

• • •

At a time when the external happening has become largely meaningless and our reaction to it brutalized, when we shout "Jump" to the man on the ledge, Mr. Capote has restored dignity to the event. His book is also a grieving testament of faith in what used to be called the soul.

Conrad Knickerbocker,
review of *In Cold Blood*
by Truman Capote,
NY Times Book Review,
January 16, 1966

[*145*]

1967

HARDCOVER BESTSELLERS

fiction

The Arrangement, Elia Kazan

Tie:

The Confessions of Nat Turner,
William Styron

The Chosen, Chaim Potok

nonfiction

Death of a President,
William Manchester

Misery Is a Blind Date,
Johnny Carson

THE ALFRED B. NOBEL PRIZE FOR LITERATURE

Miguel Angel Asturias, Guatemala

[But] if the book fails by default, as a novel, it does succeed in many places as a kind of historical tone poem ... Styron has nothing new to say about Negro motives ... But he does have something to say about the physical situation of slavery, the way that America looked and sounded and smelled from underneath ... Styron has performed a signal, non-literary service in writing this book.

Wilfrid Sheed, review of
*The Confessions of
Nat Turner*
by William Styron,
NY Times Book Review,
October 8, 1967

Bestselling author William Manchester

ROBERT BLY (1926-) Born in Minnesota and educated at Harvard, Bly emerged in the 1960s as one of the most critically independent poets of his generation. Although his first collection focused on rural themes, in his second collection, *Light Around the Body* (1967), Bly moved his subject into the political and social arena, claiming poetry deserved a larger frame of experience than the poet's personal interests. During the Vietnam War, he became a dominating spokesman for antiwar groups, staging readings around the country and compiling an anthology of poetic protests. He won the **1968 National Book Award for Poetry** and donated the money to an antidraft organization. In the 1970s, Bly became interested in poetry reflecting the supernatural and supralogical nature of human existence, and translated important writers from German, Spanish, Swedish, and Hindu. His book, *Iron John* (1990), spawned a flurry of discussion on what it means to be a modern male and became an instant bestseller.

EDWARD ALBEE (1928–) grew up in a Westchester County mansion, the adopted son of millionaires. A spoiled, precocious, and unhappy child, he never took to discipline or the pomposities of upper-class life; and after moving from school to school (often after expulsion) and a brief stint at Trinity College, he ended his formal education and took a job at WNYC radio. Albee's first play, *The Zoo Story* (1958), about the lack of communication in modern society, won him instant praise and soon was followed by *The American Dream* (1959-1960), and the Tony Award–winning *Who's Afraid of Virginia Woolf?* (1962), both of which parodied the habits and mores of the American bourgeoisie. In **1967**, he also won a **Pulitzer Prize** for his ironic play *A Delicate Balance*. Though still active in the theater world (he won a Pulitzer in 1994 for *Three Tall Women*), Albee is usually associated with the 1960s renaissance in American drama and largely remembered for his plays of that period.

[*147*]

THE PULITZER PRIZES

fiction
The Fixer, Bernard Malamud

nonfiction
The Problem of Slavery in Western Culture, David Brion Davis

biography or autobiography
Mr. Clemens and Mark Twain, Justin Kaplan

poetry
Live or Die, Anne Sexton

drama
A Delicate Balance, Edward Albee

THE NEWBERY MEDAL
Up a Road Slowly, Irene Hunt

THE CALDECOTT MEDAL
Sam, Bangs & Moonshine, Evaline Ness

> *We have all been in rooms*
> *We cannot die in.*
>
> James Dickey,
> "Adultery" (1967)

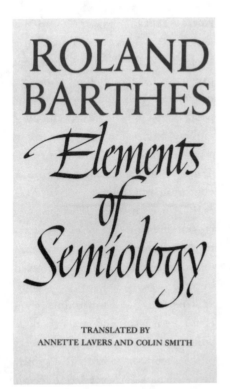

ROLAND
BARTHES
Elements of Semiology

TRANSLATED BY
ANNETTE LAVERS AND COLIN SMITH

people, particularly through his character Jesse B. Semple and in his ironic short story collection *The Ways of White Folks* (1934). In 1932 he traveled again, this time to Russia and Asia, and when he returned founded black theater groups in Chicago, L.A., and Harlem. Hughes is responsible for restoring the rhythmical language of Africa into black writing and remains perhaps the most significant black writer of the century.

[*148*]

LANGSTON HUGHES (1902-1967) was born in Joplin, Missouri, and before he was twelve had lived in five U.S. states. His nomadic life continued through his twenties: in 1923, he attended Columbia University but—distracted by the Harlem Renaissance—departed for West Africa and then a brief exploration of Europe. He began his prolific literary career with *The Weary Blues* (1926), poems on black themes in jazz rhythms and idioms that he declared should be "crooned, shouted and sung." Hughes then sought to depict ordinary black

Knut Hamsun

HUNGER

A new translation by Robert Bly
with an introduction by Isaac Bashevis Singer

CARSON MCCULLERS (1917–1967) was born Lulu Carson Smith in the small town of Columbus, Georgia. A gifted musician, she was sent to study piano at New York's Julliard School at seventeen, but in rather murky circumstances lost her tuition money and ended up working menial jobs while studying creative writing at Columbia and New York universities. In 1937, she married Reeves McCullers, moved to North Carolina, and began to write *The Heart Is a Lonely Hunter* (1940), which brought her great critical prominence. McCullers's marriage was often troubled, sometimes violent, and further complicated by homosexual liaisons; in 1940 it ended, when she moved in with George Davis, the editor of *Harper's Bazaar*. Her most productive years were her most tortuous ones, however. Between 1945 when McCullers remarried Reeves and 1953 when he committed suicide, she wrote *The Member of the Wedding* (1946) and *The Ballad of the Sad Café* (1951), compassionate, psychologically convincing fictional works in the Southern Gothic tradition. She died in New York after many years of ill health.

DEATHS
Langston Hughes
Carson McCullers
John Masefield
Dorothy Parker
Carl Sandburg

[*149*]

1968

HARDCOVER BESTSELLERS

fiction

Airport, Arthur Hailey

Couples, John Updike

nonfiction

Better Homes and Gardens New Cook Book

The Random House Dictionary of the English Language: College Edition, Laurence Urdang, Editor-in-Chief

THE ALFRED B. NOBEL PRIZE FOR LITERATURE

Yasunari Kawabata, Japan

JOHN STEINBECK (1902–1968) was born in Salinas, California, of German-Irish ancestry. His early years were uneasy: he attended Stanford University intermittently; worked in New York as a journalist until he was fired; and supported himself through a series of menial jobs, including apprentice painter, surveyor, and fruit picker. His first three novels made very little impact and less money. But in 1935, his *Tortilla Flat*, a spirited tale of California paisanos, earned him popular attention. Steinbeck continued to write compassionately of America's rural dispossessed in such novels as *Of Mice and Men* (1937) and *The Grapes of Wrath* (1939), the latter of which had a transformative effect on America's social conscience not unlike Harriet Beecher Stowe's *Uncle Tom's Cabin* (1852). Though famous, Steinbeck remained a controversial figure in the United States for his support of the rural poor, and criticism of his later books reflected that sentiment. In 1962, he became the seventh American-born author to win a Nobel Prize.

DEATHS

Edna Ferber

Helen Keller

Martin Luther King, Jr.

Upton Sinclair

John Steinbeck

THE PULITZER PRIZES

fiction
The Confessions of Nat Turner,
William Styron

nonfiction
Rousseau and Revolution,
Will and Ariel Durant

biography or autobiography
Memoirs: 1925-1950,
George F. Kennan

poetry
The Hard Hours, Anthony Hecht

drama
No award

THE NEWBERY MEDAL

*From the Mixed-Up Files of Mrs. Basil
E. Frankweiler,* E. L. Konigsburg

THE CALDECOTT MEDAL

Drummer Hoff, Adapted by
Barbara Emberley,
Illustrated by Ed Emberley

THE NATIONAL BOOK AWARDS

fiction
The Eighth Day, Thornton Wilder

arts and letters
Selected Essays, William Troy

history and biography
Memoirs: 1925-1950,
George F. Kennan

science, philosophy and religion
Death at an Early Age,
Jonathan Kozol

poetry
The Light Around the Body,
Robert Bly

translation
*Soren Kierkegaard's Journals and
Papers,* Howard and Edna Hong

> The best American writers in the 19th century talked about themselves all the time . . . "Armies of the Night" is just as brilliant a personal testimony as Whitman's diary of the Civil War, "Specimen Days," . . . Mailer's intuition in this book is that the times demand a new form. He has found it.
>
> Alfred Kazin, review of
> *The Armies of the Night*
> by Norman Mailer,
> *NY Times Book Review,*
> May 5, 1968

NIKKI GIOVANNI (1943-), hailed as "the Princess of Black Poetry," was born in Knoxville, Tennessee, into an educated middle-class family. She attended Fisk University and did graduate work at the University of Pennsylvania and

Columbia, after which she taught writing at CUNY and Rutgers. Politically active from an early age, Giovanni was involved in the Student Nonviolent Coordinating Committee in the 1960s, and after the publication of her first poetry collection, **Black Feeling, Black Talk** (1968), became the most impassioned female voice of the emerging black literary revolution. Though somewhat mellowed with age, Giovanni continues to stir up political and literary debate. Her recent book, *Sacred Cows and Other Edibles* (1988), has challenged commonly cherished assumptions among black feminists, activists, and intellectuals alike.

> *Writers are always selling somebody out.*
>
> Joan Didion,
> *Slouching Towards Bethlehem (1968)*

EDITOR'S CHOICE
the new york times best books of the year

The Collected Essays, Journalism and Letters of George Orwell, Sonia Orwell and Ian Angus, eds.

The Armies of the Night, Norman Mailer

His Toy, His Dream, His Rest, John Berryman

Confessions of a Disloyal European, Jan Myrdal

Soul on Ice, Eldridge Cleaver

The Double Helix, James D. Watson

Lytton Strachey: A Critical Biography, Michael Holroyd

A Cab at the Door, V. S. Pritchett

The First Circle, Aleksandr Solzhenitsyn

Anti-Memoirs, André Malraux

Slouching Towards Bethlehem *(1968)*
by Joan Didion.
This jacket was reissued in 1990.

> *We are condemned
> to kill time:
> Thus we die
> bit by bit*
>
> Octavio Paz,
> "Cuento de los Jardines"
> (1968)

1969

HARDCOVER BESTSELLERS

fiction

Portnoy's Complaint, Philip Roth

The Godfather, Mario Puzo

nonfiction

The Money Game, Adam Smith

Jennie, Ralph G. Martin

THE ALFRED B. NOBEL PRIZE FOR LITERATURE

Samuel Beckett, Ireland

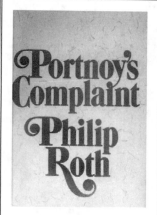

A Jewish man with parents alive is a fifteen-year-old boy, and will remain a fifteen-year-old boy till they die!

Philip Roth,
Portnoy's Complaint (1969)

• • •

If . . . it is the very novel that every American-Jewish writer has been trying to write in one guise or another since the end of World War II—then it may very well be what is called a masterpiece—but so what? It could still also be nothing more than a cul-de-sac.

Josh Greenfeld, review of
Portnoy's Complaint
by Philip Roth,
NY Times Book Review,
February 23, 1969

Philip Roth

Norman Mailer announcing that he will use his Pulitzer Prize money as "the first contribution" in his bid for the Democratic nomination for mayor of New York City.

THE PULITZER PRIZES

fiction

House Made of Dawn,
N. Scott Momaday

nonfiction

The Armies of the Night,
Norman Mailer

*So Human an Animal: How We Are
Shaped by Surroundings and Events,*
Rene Jules Dubos

biography or autobiography

*The Man from New York: John Quinn
and His Friends,* B. L. Reid

poetry

Of Being Numerous, George Oppen

THE NEWBERRY MEDAL

The High King, Lloyd Alexander

THE CALDECOTT MEDAL

*The Fool of the World and the Flying
Ship,* Retold by Arthur
Ransome, Illustrated by Uri
Shulevitz

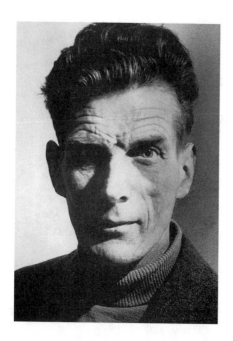

European drama. In the 1960s and early 1970s, Beckett published plays and focused on theater, as before, testing its artistic boundaries. He was awarded the 1969 **Nobel Prize.**

SAMUEL BECKETT (1909-1986) was born at Foxrock, Ireland, and educated at Dublin's Trinity College, where he met and formed a lasting relationship with James Joyce. In 1930, he became a lecturer at Trinity, but resigned four years later to embark on five productive but peripatetic years through Germany, France, Ireland, and England. During that time and afterward, he published a study of Proust, short stories, and several blackly comic novels. Beckett achieved public acclaim with the 1953 Paris performance of *Waiting for Godot,* a bleakly symbolic play about the human condition. From that time, he was associated with the Theatre of the Absurd, whose use of the stage and of dramatic narrative revolutionized

---

THE NATIONAL BOOK AWARDS

fiction
Steps, Jerzy Kosinski

nonfiction (arts and letters)
The Armies of the Night,
Norman Mailer

history and biography
White Over Black: American Attitudes Toward the Negro, 1550-1812,
Winthrop D. Jordan

poetry
His Toy, His Dream, His Rest,
John Berryman

DEATH
Jack Kerouac

[*155*]

JACK KEROUAC (1922-1969) was born in Lowell, Massachusetts, the third child of working-class French–Canadian émigrés. In 1939, he attended Columbia on a football scholarship, but in the first season broke his leg, dropped out, and became a Merchant Marine. Hanging around the Columbia

campus in 1944, he met William Burroughs and Allen Ginsberg, whose Bohemian lifestyle, though appealing, often got him into trouble: during those years, he was arrested for murder and hospitalized for excessive use of Benzedrine, the drug he would use, with alcohol, the rest of his life. Kerouac began writing in the mid-1940s, but it was not until 1957, with the publication of *On the Road*, a semiautobiographical road book written in spontaneous prose, that he became "King of the Beats," though paradoxically he spent his later years as a recluse, in the home of his mother. At forty-seven, he died in his mother's bathroom from an abdominal hemorrhage induced by vomiting.

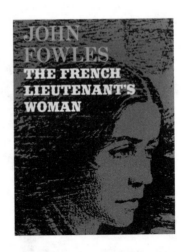

> We had forgotten that wars were fought by babies. When I saw those freshly shaved faces, it was a shock. "My God, my God—" I said to myself, "it's the Children's Crusade."
>
> Kurt Vonnegut, Jr.
> Slaughterhouse Five
> (1969)

EDITOR'S CHOICE
the new york times best books of the year

Present at the Creation: My Years at the State Department, Dean Acheson

Sherwood Anderson's Memoirs, Ray Lewis White, ed.

Akenfield: A Portrait of an English Village, Ronald Blythe

Castle to Castle, Louis-Ferdinand Céline

Gandhi's Truth: The Origins of Militant Nonviolence, Erik H. Erikson

The Enlightenment, Peter Gay [volume two]

them, Joyce Carol Oates

Portnoy's Complaint, Philip Roth

The Collected Stories of Jean Stafford

The Collected Stories of Peter Taylor

Slaughterhouse Five or The Children's Crusade, Kurt Vonnegut, Jr.

Huey Long, T. Harry Williams

1970

HARDCOVER BESTSELLERS

fiction

Love Story, Erich Segal

The French Lieutenant's Woman, John Fowles

nonfiction

Everything You Wanted to Know about Sex but Were Afraid to Ask, David Reuben, M. D.

The New English Bible

THE ALFRED B. NOBEL PRIZE FOR LITERATURE

Aleksandr Solzhenitsyn, U.S.S.R.

Aleksandr Solzhenitsyn

ALEKSANDR SOLZHENITSYN (1918–) was born in Kislovodsk, Russia, and brought up in Rostov, where he earned degrees in mathematics and physics. After distinguished service with the Red Army in World War II, he was arrested and sentenced to eight years in a Siberian labor camp for criticizing Stalin's conduct in the war. In 1962, his first novel, *One Day in the Life of Ivan Denisovich*, was published to great acclaim, but by 1967, he again fell afoul of the authorities for denouncing Soviet censorship. His later novels, *The Cancer Ward* (1968) and *The Gulag Archipelago* (1975), were banned in Russia though closely read in the West.

And in 1974, four years after winning the Nobel Prize, he was arrested and forced into exile. For the next two decades, Solzhenitsyn lived reclusively in Vermont, writing essays and an historical epic, but in 1994, he surprised many by returning to Russia to participate—as talk show host, political commentator, and national writer—in his homeland's quest for reform.

[*157*]

DEATHS

E. M. Forster
Erle Stanley Gardner
François Mauriac
Yukio Mishima
John O'Hara
John Dos Passos
Erich Maria Remarque

MAYA ANGELOU (1928–) was born Marguerite Johnson in St. Louis, Missouri, and educated in Arkansas and California public schools. She studied dance under Martha Graham, and in her long and varied career has been hailed as an author, playwright, journalist, teacher, actress, and singer. She is best known for her autobiographical work, *I Know Why the Caged Bird Sings* (1970), the story of a black girl growing up in a repressive system, which generated a wealth of critical literature and established Angelou as a major African-American writer. Since the 1970s, she has published over a dozen books, including six collections of poems, and *I Wouldn't Take Nothing for My Journey Now* (1987), a memoir concerned with spirituality, sensuality, and healing. Angelou read "On the Pulse of Morning" at President Bill Clinton's inauguration on January 20, 1993.

Kate Millet's book on "sexual politics" is thus a rare achievement. Its measure of detachment is earned by learning, reason and love, its measure of involvement is frankly set out. It is a piece of passionate thinking on a life-and-death aspect of our public and private lives.

Barbara Hardy, review of
Sexual Politics
by Kate Millett,
NY Times Book Review,
September 6, 1970

THE NATIONAL BOOK AWARDS

fiction
Joyce Carol Oates, *them*

arts and letters
Lillian Hellman, *An Unfinished Woman: A Memoir*

children's books
Isaac Bashevis Singer, *A Day of Pleasure: Stories of a Boy Growing Up in Warsaw*

history and biography
T. Harry Williams, *Huey Long*

philosophy and religion
Erik H. Erikson, *Gandhi's Truth: On the Origins of Militant Nonviolence*

translation
Ralph Manheim, *Céline's Castle to Castle*

poetry
Elizabeth Bishop, *The Complete Poems*

YUKIO MISHIMA (1925–1970) was born in Tokyo and began his adult life as a civil servant, before embarking on a prolific writing career. Though he was a modern novelist—his first work, *Confessions of a Mask* (1949, 1958), dealt with his homosexuality—Mishima combined elements of both Eastern and Western literature, and was passionately interested in the chivalrous traditions of Imperial Japan. In 1968, in expression of his conservative, mili-

taristic views, he founded the Shield Society, a group of one hundred youths dedicated to the revival of the Samurai knightly code of honor. Two years later, the day he finished his great tetralogy, *The Sea of Fertility* (1965–1970), he committed suicide in hari-kiri fashion after a staged attempt to convince Japan to return to its prewar nationalist views. Mishima once said that his life's obsession was "my heart's leaning toward Death and Night and Blood," an aphorism he proved to be absolutely true.

EDITOR'S CHOICE

the new york times best books of the year

City Life, Donald Barthelme

Roosevelt: The Soldier of Freedom, James MacGregor Burns

The Coming Crisis of Western Sociology, Alvin Gouldner

Jefferson the President: First Term, 1801–1805, Dumas Malone

One Hundred Years of Solitude, Gabriel García Márquez

Zelda: A Biography, Nancy Milford

Sexual Politics, Kate Millett

Crisis in the Classroom: The Remaking of American Education, Charles E. Silberman

Inside the Third Reich, Albert Speer

Cocteau: A Biography, Francis Steegmuller

Bech: A Book, John Updike

Losing Battles, Eudora Welty

reporter, working first for Pennsylvania papers, then *Time* maga- zine, and after 1932 as a regular con- tributor for *The New Yorker*. The next year, he began writing his first novel, *Appointment in Samarra* (1934), an account of the last three days in the life of Julian English, which was widely applauded, and then segued to work as a Hollywood scriptwriter. O'Hara wrote eighteen novels and 374 stories in his lifetime, the most famous of which are the 1935 novel *Butterfield 8* and the 1940 story collection *Pal Joey*. Most of his books were written about the aspirations of middle-class materi- alistic Americans, which the critics found tiresome, but one remarked: "If future generations seek an American Balzac to lay bare life in the United States from 1900 to 1970, they will find John O'Hara the most complete, the most accurate, and the most readable chronicler."

JOHN O'HARA (1905-1970) was born in the small town of Pottsville, Pennsylvania, the oldest son of a pros- perous Irish-American doctor. Unable to afford Yale after his father's death, he became a newspaper

1971

HARDCOVER BESTSELLERS

fiction
Wheels, Arthur Hailey
The Exorcist, William P. Blatty

nonfiction
The Sensuous Man, "M"
Bury My Heart at Wounded Knee, Dee Brown

THE ALFRED B. NOBEL PRIZE FOR LITERATURE

Pablo Neruda, Chile

PABLO NERUDA (1904-1973) was born in Southern Chile, the son of a train driver, and educated in Santiago, where he began writing poetry. In the 1930s, he became a fervent proponent of populism in art and politics, joined the Communist Party, and between 1927 and 1943 held diplomatic posts in East Asia, Spain (during the civil war), and Mexico. It was in Mexico that Neruda visited the Inca city that would inspire one of his greatest poems, *The Heights of Macchu Picchu* (1945). Once back in Chile, he was elected to the senate, but when the Communist Party was outlawed in 1948, Neruda was forced to flee. For the next four years, he traveled throughout the U.S.S.R., China, and Eastern Europe, finally returning to his homeland in 1952. From 1961, he spent much of his time writing on Isla Negra, which he willed to the copper workers of Chile. He was honored with the **1971 Nobel Prize for literature**.

THE PULITZER PRIZES

fiction
No award

nonfiction
The Rising Sun, John Toland

biography or autobiography
Robert Frost: The Years of Triumph, 1915-1938, Lawrence Thompson

poetry
The Carrier of Ladders, William S. Merwin

drama
The Effect of Gamma Rays on Man-in-the-Moon Marigolds, Paul Zindel

THE BOOKER PRIZE
In a Free State, V. S. Naipaul

THE NEWBERY MEDAL
Summer of the Swans, Betsy Byars

THE CALDECOTT MEDAL
A Story A Story, Gail E. Haley

THE NATIONAL BOOK AWARDS

fiction
Saul Bellow, *Mr. Sammler's Planet*

arts and letters
Francis Steegmuller,
  Cocteau: A Biography

children's books
Lloyd Alexander, *The Marvelous Misadventures of Sebastian*

history and biography
James MacGregor Burns,
  Roosevelt: The Soldier of Freedom

the sciences
Raymond Phineas Sterns, *Science in the British Colonies of America*

translation
Frank Jones,
  Brecht's Saint Joan of the Stockyards

Edward G. Seidensticker,
  Yasunari Kawabata's The Sound of the Mountain

poetry
Mona Van Duyn, *To See, To Take*

V. S. NAIPAUL (1932–) was born in Trinidad, the son of a journalist of Indian Brahman origin. Schooled in Port of Spain, in 1950 he was selected as a recipient of one of the four annual "island scholarships" to attend Oxford University. Naipaul remained in England after his studies, working as a broadcaster for the BBC's *Caribbean Voices* and a fiction reviewer for the *New Statesman*. His first novel, *Mystic Masseur* (1957), and subsequent two fictions were satires of life in Trinidad; however, in his fourth novel, *A House for Mr Biswas* (1961), Naipaul turned to the theme that would preoccupy his latter novels: the sense of dislocation and alienation in the postcolonial "third world." His next few novels, such as *Mimic Men* (1967) and ***In a Free State*** **(1971)**, established Naipaul as a major writer and the leading novelist representing the English-speaking Caribbean. Although he has been criticized for his unflattering portraits of colonial society, Naipaul has more often been praised for his technical mastery, his authenticity, and his ability to depict the complexities of the late-twentieth-century world.

DEATH
Ogden Nash

FLANNERY
O'CONNOR

THE COMPLETE STORIES

... brilliantly written ...
It is Greer's fundamental
insight that women have
been systematically
robbed of productive
energy by society's insis-
tence on confining them
to a passive sexual role.

Sally Kempton, review of
The Female Eunuch
by Germaine Greer,
NY Times Book Review,
April 25, 1971

EDITOR'S CHOICE

the new york times best books of the year

The Gift Relationship: From Human
Blood to Social Policy,
Richard M. Titmuss

The Waste Land: A Facsimile and
Transcript of the Original Drafts
Including the Annotations of Ezra
Pound, T. S. Eliot

The European Discovery of America:
The Northern Voyages A.D. 500–
1600, Samuel Eliot Morison

Rabbit Redux, John Updike

Eleanor and Franklin: The Story of
Their Relationship Based on
Eleanor Roosevelt's Private Papers,
Joseph P. Lash

Upstate: Records and Recollections of
Northern New York,
Edmund Wilson

Bound to Violence, Yambo
Ouologuem, Translated from the
French by Ralph Manheim

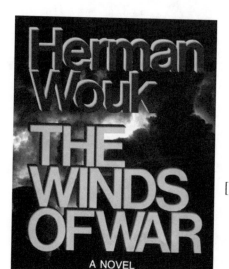

Herman
Wouk

THE
WINDS
OF WAR

A NOVEL

[*163*]

1972

HARDCOVER BESTSELLERS

fiction
Jonathan Livingston Seagull,
Richard Bach
August 1914,
Aleksandr Solzhenitsyn

nonfiction
The Living Bible, Kenneth Taylor
I'm O.K., You're O.K,
Thomas Harris

THE ALFRED B. NOBEL PRIZE FOR LITERATURE
Heinrich Böll, Germany

THE PULITZER PRIZES

fiction
Angle of Repose, Wallace Stegner

nonfiction
Stilwell and the American Experience in China, 1911-1945,
Barbara W. Tuchman

biography or autobiography
Eleanor and Franklin, Joseph P. Lash

poetry
Collected Poems, James Wright

drama
No award

EZRA POUND (1885-1972) was born in Idaho, raised in Philadelphia, and educated at the University of Pennsylvania and Hamilton College. In 1907, he lost his teaching job at Indiana's Wabash College for entertaining an actress in his rooms, and the next year sailed for Europe, where he became a champion of the London/Paris literary scene and published criticism and poetry, including his lifelong project, the *Cantos* (1926-1968). Beginning in 1924, Pound resided in Italy, flirted with Fascism, met Mussolini, and during the war years became an antidemocracy broadcaster. With the arrival of the Partisans in 1945, however, Pound was escorted back to the United States and indicted for treason, but adjudged insane and placed in an asylum. In 1958, he was released and moved back to Italy, where he lived until his death. His influence on modern poetry and criticism continues to be enormous.

> *Writing is nothing more than a guided dream.*
>
> Jorge Luis Borges, *Doctor Brodie's Report* (1972)

THE BOOKER PRIZE
G, John Berger

THE NEWBERY MEDAL
Mrs. Frisby and the Rats of NIMH,
Robert C. O'Brien

THE CALDECOTT MEDAL
One Fine Day, Nonny Hogrogian

MARIANNE MOORE (1887–1972) was
born in Kirkwood, Missouri, the
daughter of a psychologically unstable
engineer-inventor, and educated at
Bryn Mawr College. In 1915, her first
two poems were published, and shortly thereafter she began visiting a group
of New York-based poets, among them
William Carlos Williams and Wallace
Stevens, who convinced her to move to
Manhattan. Moore came to prominence in 1921 with the publication of
Observations, after winning an award
from the prestigious literary journal
Dial, which she later edited. Her poetic concerns were always varied and passionate, encompassing her interests in
natural history, the arts, and contemporary affairs. T. S. Eliot described her as
"one of the few who have done the
language some service in my lifetime."
In 1951, Moore's *Collected Poems* won
virtually every literary honor America
had created, and by the end of her lifetime she was recognized as one of the
leading voices of American poetry.

EDITOR'S CHOICE

the new york times best books of the year

*The Children of Pride: A True Story of
Georgia and the Civil War*,
Robert Manson Myers, ed.

Henry James: The Master, 1901–1916,
Leon Edel

*Fire in the Lake: The Vietnamese and
the Americans in Vietnam*,
Frances FitzGerald

The Coming of Age,
Simone de Beauvoir,
Translated by Patrick O'Brien

A Theory of Justice, John Rawls

[*165*]

> *Not only is there no God,*
> *but try getting a plumber*
> *on weekends.*
>
> Woody Allen, *Getting Even*
> (1972)

translation

Austryn Wainhouse, *Jacques Monod's Chance and Necessity*

poetry

Howard Moss, *Selected Poems*

Frank O'Hara, *The Collected Poems of Frank O'Hara*

THE NATIONAL BOOK AWARDS

fiction

Flannery O'Connor, *The Complete Stories of Flannery O'Connor*

arts and letters

Charles Rosen, *The Classical Style: Haydn, Mozart, Beethoven*

biography

Joseph P. Lash, *Eleanor and Franklin*

children's books

Donald Barthelme, *The Slightly Irregular Fire Engine or the Hithering Thithering Djinn*

contemporary affairs

Steward Brand, ed., *The Last Whole Earth Catalog*

history

Allan Nevins, *Ordeal of the Union, Vols. VII and VIII: The Organized War, 1863-1864* and *The Organized War to Victory*

philosophy and religion

Martin E. Marty, *Righteous Empire: The Protestant Experience in America*

the sciences

George L. Small, *The Blue Whale*

DEATHS

Ezra Pound
Edmund Wilson
John Berryman
Marianne Moore
Jean Garrigue

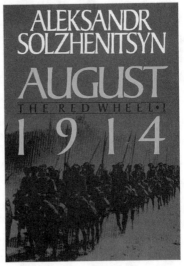

Bestselling novel

1973

HARDCOVER BESTSELLERS

fiction

Jonathan Livingston Seagull,
Richard Bach

Once Is Not Enough,
Jacqueline Susann

nonfiction

The Living Bible, Kenneth Taylor

Dr. Atkins' Diet Revolution,
Robert C. Atkins

THE ALFRED B. NOBEL PRIZE FOR LITERATURE

Patrick White, Australia

W. H. AUDEN (1907–**1973**) Born in York, England, the youngest son of a doctor, Auden began to be taken seriously as a poet while a student at Christ Church, Oxford. In the 1930s, he wrote passionately on social problems from a left-wing perspective, and T. S. Eliot identified him as the most talented voice of his generation. In 1937, he went to Spain as a civilian in support of the Republicans, which resulted in the volume *Spain,* cowritten with Christopher Isherwood. He then emigrated to New York, where he met Chester Kallman, his lifelong companion, and worked as a university professor, continuing to publish important works, including *The Age of Anxiety: A Baroque Eclogue,* which won the 1948 Pulitzer Prize, and the poetry collection *The Shield of Achilles* (1955). Today Auden is considered one of the most influential poets of the century, comparable in influence to a British poet of the previous generation, William Butler Yeats.

[167]

> *So we think of Marilyn who was every man's love affair with America . . . She was our angel, the sweet angel of sex, and the sugar of sex came up from her like a resonance of sound in the clearest grain of a violin.*
>
> Norman Mailer, *Marilyn*
> (1973)

PEARL S. BUCK (1892-1973) was born in West Virginia and reared in Chinkiang on China's Yangtse River by her parents, who were missionaries. Schooled in Shanghai, at eighteen she returned for the first time to the United States to attend college. In 1917, she married an agricultural missionary and accompanied him to China, where she taught English at several universities. But in 1924 she returned to America to raise her retarded daughter, who became the subject of her first book, *The Child Who Never Grows.* In 1935, Buck divorced her first husband, married her second (her publisher), and moved to Pennsylvania, where she bore one child and adopted a further nine. Her second novel, *The Good Earth,* about rural life in China, achieved enormous popular and critical success, selling 1.8 million copies in its first year and winning the 1932 Pulitzer Prize. It was followed by two related novels and two books on her parents, which the Nobel committee, who gave her the 1938 prize—the first ever to an American woman—called "masterpieces of biography." In her later years, she worked for the mentally handicapped and established the Pearl S. Buck Foundation to assist Asian children.

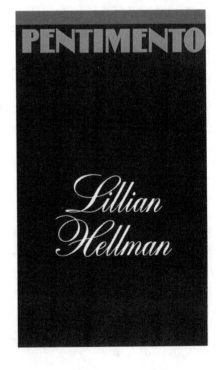

PENTIMENTO

Lillian Hellman

THE NATIONAL BOOK AWARDS

fiction

John Barth, *Chimera*

John Williams, *Augustus*

arts and letters

Arthur M. Wilson, *Diderot*

biography

James Thomas Flexner, *George Washington, Vol. IV: Anguish and Farewell, 1793–1799*

children's books

Ursula K. LeGuin, *The Farthest Shore*

contemporary affairs

Frances FitzGerald, *Fire in the Lake: The Vietnamese and the Americans in Vietnam*

history

Robert Manson Myers, *The Children of Pride*

Isaiah Trunk, *Judenrat*

philosophy and religion

Sydney E. Ahlstrom, *A Religious History of the American People*

the sciences

George B. Schaller, *The Serengeti Lion: A Study of Predator-Prey Relations*

translation

Allen Mandelbaum, *The Aeneid of Virgil*

poetry

A. R. Ammons, *Collected Poems, 1951–1971*

EDITOR'S CHOICE

the new york times best books of the year

Gravity's Rainbow, Thomas Pynchon

The Summer Before the Dark, Doris Lessing

Macaulay: The Making of a Historian, John Clive

Yet who can presume to say what the war wants, so vast and aloof it is . . . so absentee.

Thomas Pynchon,
Gravity's Rainbow (1973)

DEATHS

W. H. Auden
Pearl S. Buck
Pablo Neruda
Conrad Aiken
Arna Bontemps
J. R. R. Tolkien

[*169*]

1974

HARDCOVER BESTSELLERS

fiction

Centennial, James A. Michener

Watership Down, Richard Adams

nonfiction

The Total Woman, Marabel Morgan

All the President's Men,
Carl Bernstein and
Bob Woodward

THE ALFRED B. NOBEL PRIZE FOR LITERATURE

Eyvind Johnson, Sweden

Harry Edmund Martinson, Sweden

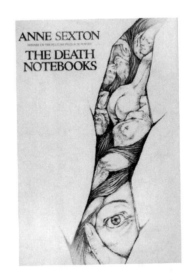

ANNE SEXTON
THE DEATH
NOTEBOOKS

ANNE (HARVEY) SEXTON (1928-1974) was born in Newton, Massachusetts, to a family descending from William Brewster, a Mayflower voyager. Sexton may have had a normal childhood or one quite bizarre, for she once claimed that she was locked in a room until she was five. Either way, her adulthood was marred by mental instability. At nineteen, she eloped with a wool company executive, and in the mid-1950s, after having two daughters, she suffered a nervous breakdown. "As I came out of it," Sexton later wrote, "I started to write poems"—about herself, depression, and mental illness, which were influenced by her teacher Robert Lowell and fellow poet Sylvia Plath. Sexton was awarded a Pulitzer Prize for *Live or Die* (1966) and became a professor at Boston University, but her sadness was overwhelming. At forty-six, she committed suicide. She was thrust back into the limelight in 1991 when a controversial biography appeared based on Sexton's tape-recorded discussions with her therapist.

> *Poetry is an act of peace.*
> *Peace goes into the making*
> *of a poet as flour goes into*
> *the making of bread.*
>
> Pablo Neruda
> *Confieso Que He Vivido:*
> *Memorias (Memoirs)* (1974)

THE PULITZER PRIZES

fiction

No award

nonfiction

The Denial of Death, Ernest Becker

biography or autobiography

O'Neill, Son and Artist,
  Louis Sheaffer

poetry

No award

drama

No award

THE BOOKER PRIZE

The Conservationist,
  Nadine Gordimer

Holiday, Stanley Middleton

THE NEWBERY MEDAL

The Slave Dancer, Paula Fox

THE CALDECOTT MEDAL

Duffy and the Devil,
  Retold by Harve Zemach
  Pictures by Margot Zemach

Caldecott Medalist

Other people can talk about how to expand the destiny of mankind. I just want to talk about how to fix a motorcycle. I think that what I have to say has more lasting value.

Robert Maynard Pirsig,
Zen and the Art of Motorcycle Maintenance
(1974)

• • •

I had been my whole life a bell, and never knew it until at that moment I was lifted and struck.

Annie Dillard,
Pilgrim at Tinker Creek
(1974)

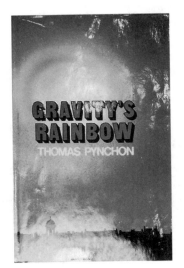

National Book Award winner

THE NATIONAL BOOK AWARDS

fiction

Thomas Pynchon, *Gravity's Rainbow*

Isaac Bashevis Singer, *A Crown of Feathers and Other Stories*

arts and letters

Pauline Kael, *Deeper into the Movies*

biography

John Clive, *Macaulay: The Shaping of the Historian*
(Also Won History Award)

Douglas Day, *Malcolm Lowry: A Biography*

children's books

Eleanor Cameron, *The Court of the Stone Children*

contemporary affairs

Murray Kempton, *The Briar Patch*

history

John Clive, *Macaulay: The Shaping of the Historian*
(Also Won Biography Award)

philosophy and religion

Maurice Natanson, *Edmund Husserl: Philosopher of Infinite Tasks*

the sciences

S. E. Luria, *Life: The Unfinished Experiment*

translation

Karen Brazell, *The Confessions of Lady Nijo*

Helen R. Lane, *Octavio Paz's Alternating Current*

Jackson Mathews, *Paul Valery's Monsieur Teste*

poetry

Allen Ginsberg, *The Fall of America: Poems of These States*

Adrienne Rich, *Diving into the Wreck: Poems 1971-1972*

National Book Award winner Allen Ginsberg

he published his first book, *Call for the Dead* (1961), which in depicting the futility of diplomacy and espionage adumbrated his later spy novels. Although many critics have accused le Carré of being thematically repetitive and structurally formulaic, he is by far the most outstanding writer of his genre. His most popular thrillers—*The Spy Who Came In From the Cold* (1963), **Tinker, Tailor, Soldier, Spy (1974)**, and *Smiley's People* (1980)—have sold millions and been extolled by all breeds of fiction readers.

JOHN LE CARRÉ (1931–) was born Davis John Moore Cornwell in Dorset, England, the son of a shady businessman who engaged in several million-pound scams and was imprisoned for fraud. Unsurprisingly, le Carré has named his father as a primary reason for his interest in duplicity and deceit. Educated at Berne University in Switzerland and—after military service in Austria—at Oxford, le Carré first worked as master at Eton. Within two years, though, he tired of the scholarly life and joined the Foreign Service, serving in Germany and later Hamburg, during which time he sleuthed for England's M15. In 1961,

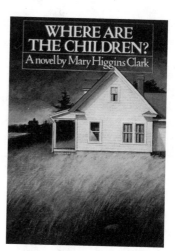

Where are the Children?
by Mary Higgins Clark

[*173*]

1975

HARDCOVER BESTSELLERS

fiction

Ragtime, E. L. Doctorow

The Moneychangers, Arthur Hailey

nonfiction

Angels: God's Secret Agents,
Billy Graham

Winning through Intimidation,
Robert Ringer

THE ALFRED B. NOBEL PRIZE FOR LITERATURE

Eugenio Montale, Italy

works have included a bestselling
memoir, *An American Childhood* (1987);
a nonfictional account of her occupation, *The Writing Life* (1989); and a celebrated historical novel set in the
Pacific Northwest, *The Living* (1992).

THE PULITZER PRIZES

fiction

The Killer Angels, Michael Shaara

nonfiction

Pilgrim at Tinker Creek,
Annie Dillard

biography or autobiography

*The Power Broker: Robert Moses and
the Fall of New York*,
Robert A. Caro

poetry

Turtle Island, Gary Snyder

drama

Seascape, Edward Albee

ANNIE DILLARD (1945–) was born in
Pittsburgh, Pennsylvania, into a
wealthy idiosyncratic family, and educated at Hollins College. She began
her literary career on Tinker Creek in
Virginia's Roanoke Valley, which
inspired her most famous nonfiction
book, *Pilgrim at Tinker Creek* (1974),
which won a **1975 Pulitzer Prize** and
has been compared to Thoreau's
Walden Pond for its metaphysical
insights. The same year, Dillard gained
recognition as a poet for *Tickets for a
Prayer Wheel*, which also explores the
rhythmic variations of the natural
world. A versatile writer, Dillard's

DEATHS

Hannah Arendt
Thornton Wilder
P. G. Wodehouse
Rex Stout
Carlo Levi

Rex Stout

HANNAH ARENDT (1906–1975) was prominent among the German-Jewish refugee scholars who contributed to America's postwar intellectual life. Born in Hanover, raised in Königsberg, Arendt earned her doctorate from the University of Heidelberg. In 1933, she fled the rising Nazi regime and settled in Paris. There she married Heinrich Blücher, a professor of philosophy, and moved with him in the early 1940s to the United States, where she headed various Jewish cultural organizations and worked as chief editor of Schocken Books. Her first and most famous book, *The Origins of Totalitarianism* (1951), sought to locate the roots of Nazism and anti-Semitism and probably is the most influential book ever written on the theme. Beginning in 1960, Arendt served as a professor at the University of Chicago, Princeton, and later at the New School for Social Research. Her correspondence with Mary McCarthy was published in 1994.

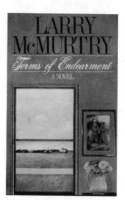

Terms of Endearment
by Larry McMurtry

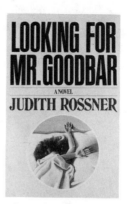

Looking for Mr. Goodbar
by Judith Rossner

[*175*]

THE BOOKER PRIZE

Heat and Dust, Puth Prawer Jhabvala

THE NEWBERY MEDAL

M. C. Higgins, the Great,
  Virginia Hamilton

THE CALDECOTT MEDAL

Arrow to the Sun,
  Gerald McDermott

THE NATIONAL BOOK AWARDS

fiction

Robert Stone, *Dog Soldiers*

Thomas Williams,
  The Hair of Harold Roux

arts and letters

Roger Shattuck, *Marcel Proust*

Lewis Thomas, *The Lives of a Cell:
  Notes of a Biology Watcher* (Also
  Won The Sciences Award)

biography

Richard B. Sewall,
  The Life of Emily Dickinson

children's books

Virginia Hamilton,
  M. C. Higgins the Great

contemporary affairs

Theodore Rosengarten, *All God's
  Dangers: The Life of Nate Shaw*

history

Bernard Bailyn, *The Ordeal of
  Thomas Hutchinson*

the sciences

Silvano Arieti,
  Interpretation of Schizophrenia

Lewis Thomas, *The Lives of a Cell:
  Notes of a Biology Watcher* (Also
  Won Arts and Letters Award)

translation

Anthony Kerrigan, *Miguel
  DeUnamuno's The Agony of
  Christianity and Essays on Faith*

poetry

Marilyn Hacker, *Presentation Piece*

DAVID MAMET (1947-), the son of a semantics-obsessed lawyer, grew up in Chicago, which he calls his earliest dramatic muse. He began his study of American dialects as a comedy cabaret busboy, and all his dramatic work has since focused on "bring[ing] out the poetry in plain everyday language" and depicting a country as rootless and shifting as its tongue. After studying at Goddard College, Mamet worked variously as a cab driver, fast-food cook, window washer, office cleaner, and drama teacher to support his playwriting habit. In **1975**, he gained national attention when a joint production of his **Sexual Perversity in Chicago** and *Duck Variations* moved from his hometown to off-Broadway and was named by *Time* magazine as one the top ten plays of the year. Since then, Mamet has been viewed as a leading American dramatist; among his award-winning plays are *American Buffalo* (1977) and *Glengarry Glen Ross* (1984). He has also written popular Hollywood screenplays such as *The Postman Always Rings Twice* and *The Untouchables*.

EDITOR'S CHOICE

the new york times best books of the year

The Dead Father, Donald Barthelme

Humboldt's Gift, Saul Bellow

Against Our Will: Men, Women and Rape, Susan Brownmiller

The Problem of Slavery in the Age of Revolution: 1770-1823, David Brion Davis

The War Against the Jews 1933-1945, Lucy S. Dawidowicz

Ragtime, E. L. Doctorow

A Sorrow Beyond Dreams, Peter Handke

Edith Wharton, R. W. B. Lewis

Far Tortuga, Peter Matthiessen

I Would Have Saved Them If I Could, Leonard Michaels

Guerrillas, V. S. Naipaul

The Gulag Archipelago, Aleksandr Solzhenitsyn

The Great Railway Bazaar, Paul Theroux

WOODY ALLEN (ALLEN STEWART KONIGSBERG) (1935–) was born in Brooklyn, New York, and began his career writing comic articles for a *New York Post* columnist while still in high school. After briefly attending New York University and City College, he appeared as a stand-up comedian in clubs and on the *Ed Sullivan Show* and *Tonight Show*. In 1965, he wrote and acted in *What's New Pussycat?*, and, in 1969, directed his first complete feature film, *Take the Money and Run*. Since then, he has written and directed over twenty award-winning films, including *Manhattan* (1979), *Radio Days* (1987), and *Husbands and Wives* (1992), usually casting himself as a wry, self-deprecating New York Jew with artistic sensibilities. His humorous sketches have also been published in two collections, *Getting Even* (1971) and **Without Feathers (1975)**. In 1993, Allen was embroiled in a highly public custody dispute with his estranged companion, the actress Mia Farrow.

THE NATIONAL BOOK CRITICS CIRCLE AWARDS

fiction
Ragtime, E. L. Doctorow

nonfiction
Edith Wharton, R. W. B. Lewis

poetry
Self-Portrait in a Convex Mirror, John Ashbery

criticism
The Great War and Modern Memory, Paul Fussell

1976

THE ALFRED B. NOBEL PRIZE FOR LITERATURE

Saul Bellow, U.S.

*Bestselling authors
Carl Bernstein and Bob Woodward*

AGATHA CHRISTIE (1890-1976). Born in Torquay, England, Christie had a conventional late Victorian upbringing, was educated at home, and at sixteen was sent to Paris to study music. She married Col. Archibald Christie in 1914 and during World War I worked as a volunteer nurse, which gave her a knowledge of poisons later to prove useful in her work. In 1926, her marriage broke up, and in 1930 she married the archeologist Max Mallowan, whom she accompanied on his excavations in Syria and Iraq. Her first detective novel, *The Mysterious Affair at Styles* (1920), introduced the Belgian detective Hercule Poirot. In *Murder at the Vicarage* (1930) she introduced the elderly spinster detective, Jane Marple. In the next fifty-six years, Christie wrote sixty-six detective novels, including *Murder on the Orient Express* (1934) and *Death on the Nile* (1937), in which she displayed genius plotting and sustained spell-binding suspense, talents for which she was dubbed "the Queen of Crime."

DEATHS

*Agatha Christie
Lionel Trilling
André Malraux
Martin Heidegger*

*Nobel and Pulitzer Prize winner
Saul Bellow*

SAUL BELLOW (1915-) Born in Quebec to Russian-Jewish parents, reared in Chicago, and educated at the University of Chicago and Northwestern, Bellow is one of America's most distinguished postwar novelists. His first two books, *Dangling Man* (1944) and *The Victim* (1947), established him as a disciplined intellect, influenced by Flaubert. But in his next novel, *The Adventures of Augie March* (1953), which won the National Book Award, Bellow emerged as a vital, eccentric stylist and a rebel against the Anglo-Saxon hold on American literature. Through the next three decades, he published important, provocative novels, in particular: *Herzog* (1964), depicting the inner life of a Jewish intellectual driven to insanity by his wife's adultery; *Dr. Sammler's Planet* (1969), a fictive critique on modern society; and *Humboldt's Gift* (1976 Pulitzer Prize), featuring a cunning, comic character beset by a crisis of the self. Bellow was awarded the **1976 Nobel Prize**.

THE PULITZER PRIZES

fiction
Humboldt's Gift, Saul Bellow

nonfiction
Why Survive? Being Old in America, Robert N. Butler

biography or autobiography
Edith Wharton: A Biography, R. W. B. Lewis

poetry
Self-Portrait in a Convex Mirror, John Ashbery

drama
A Chorus Line, Michael Bennet, James Kirkwood, Nicholas Dante, Marvin Hamlisch, and Edward Kleban

[*179*]

JOHN ASHBERY (1927–) was born in Rochester, New York, attended Harvard College, and studied French literature at Columbia and New York universities. In the 1950s, he became an art and literary critic in France and published his first poems, which were influenced by French Surrealism. His later poems bore relation to another movement in the visual arts: the abstractions of painters such as Jackson Pollock and Robert Motherwell. They have been described as melodious, dreamlike, unconventional, illogical, and sensuously beautiful. His collections include *Self-Portrait in a Convex Mirror*—which received the **1976 National Book Award**, the 1975 National Book Critics' Circle Award, and the **1976 Pulitzer Prize**—and *Flow Chart* (1991), a 216-page poem abstractly detailing the minutiae of everyday life. He has also published a novel and several plays; his most recent poetry collection is *The Stars Were Also Shining* (1995).

THE BOOKER PRIZE
Saville, David Storey

THE NEWBERY MEDAL
The Grey King, Susan Cooper

THE CALDECOTT MEDAL
Why Mosquitoes Buzz in People's Ears, Retold by Verna Aardema
Pictures by Leo and Diane Dillon

THE NATIONAL BOOK AWARDS

fiction
William Gaddis, *JR*

arts and letters
Paul Fussell, *The Great War and Modern Memory*

children's literature
Walter D. Edmonds, *Bert Breen's Barn*

contemporary affairs
Michael J. Arlen, *Passage to Ararat*

history and biography
David Brion Davis, *The Problem of Slavery in the Age of Revolution, 1770-1823*

poetry
John Ashbery, *Self-Portrait in a Convex Mirror*

What we dream up must be lived down, I think.

James Merrill,
"The Book of Ephraim" (1976)

EDITOR'S CHOICE

the new york times best books of the year

Speedboat, Renata Adler

To Jerusalem and Back: A Personal Account, Saul Bellow

The Uses of Enchantment: The Meaning and Importance of Fairy Tales, Bruno Bettelheim

Women of the Shadows, Ann Cornelisen

The Damnable Question: A Study of Anglo-Irish Relations, George Dangerfield

October Light, John Gardner

Roots: The Saga of an American Family, Alex Haley

World of Our Fathers, Irving Howe

Heat and Dust, Ruth Prawer Jhabvala

The Woman Warrior: Memoirs of a Girlhood Among Ghosts, Maxine Hong Kingston

Born on the Fourth of July, Ron Kovic

André Malraux, Jean Lacouture

The Autumn of the Patriarch, Gabriel García Márquez

Details of a Sunset: And Other Stories, Vladimir Nabokov

Hearing Secret Harmonies, Anthony Powell

A Voice from the Chorus, Abram Tertz

The Easter Parade, Richard Yates

THE NATIONAL BOOK CRITICS CIRCLE AWARDS

fiction

October Light, John Gardner

nonfiction

The Woman Warrior: Memoirs of a Girlhood Among Ghosts, Maxine Hong Kingston

poetry

Geography III, Elizabeth Bishop

criticism

The Uses of Enchantment: The Meaning and Importance of Fairy Tales, Bruno Bettelheim

PAT CONROY (1945–) was born in Atlanta, Georgia, the son of a strict Marine Corps pilot who Conroy said "would make John Wayne look like a pansy." After graduation from the Citadel, he refused his father's profession and elected to teach illiterate black children on a small, isolated island off the South Carolina coast, but within a short time was fired for the unorthodoxy of his teaching methods. Unable to continue in his profession, Conroy turned to writing, completing in 1971 *The Water Is Wide*, his first semiautobiographical novel. His second book, **The Great Santini (1976)**, shed further light on his dual obsessions—oppressive father figures and the South—and made him into a best selling novelist. Conroy has since successfully depicted the vicissitudes of white Southern family life; his later novels, particularly *The Lords of Discipline* (1980) and *The Prince of Tides* (1986), teem with disciplinarians, misfits, eccentrics, liars, and braggarts.

[*181*]

1977

HARDCOVER BESTSELLERS

fiction

The Silmarillion, J. R. R. Tolkien;
Christopher Tolkien, ed.

The Thorn Birds,
Colleen McCullough

nonfiction

Roots, Alex Haley

Looking Out for #1,
Robert Ringer

PAPERBACK BESTSELLERS

mass market

Elvis: What Happened? Red West,
Sonny West and Dave Hebler,
as told to Steve Dunleavy

Star Wars, George Lucas

trade

Shanna, Kathleen E. Woodiwiss

The Illustrated Elvis,
W. A. Harbinson

THE ALFRED B. NOBEL PRIZE FOR LITERATURE

Vicente Aleixandre, Spain

DEATHS

Robert Lowell
Vladimir Nabokov

Bestselling author J. R. R. Tolkien

---

*You're going to learn that
one of the most brutal
things in the world is your
average nineteen-year-old
American boy.*

Philip Joseph Caputo,
A Rumor of War

• • •

"Dispatches" is the best
book to have been writ-
ten about the Vietnam
War . . . nothing else so
far has even come close
to conveying how differ-
ent this war was from
any we fought—or how
utterly different were the
methods and the men
who fought for us.

C. D. B. Bryan, review of
Dispatches by Michael Herr,
NY Times Book Review,
November 11, 1977

VLADIMIR NABOKOV (1899–1977) was born in St. Petersburg, and spent his childhood among the Russian elite until the Bolshevik Revolution forced his family to emigrate. Trilingual, with literary aspirations, he took refuge in studies at Cambridge, and between 1922 and 1937 lived in Berlin, where he wrote and supported his wife and son as a tutor, tennis coach, and chess problem composer. His first nine novels—suffused with nostalgia, loss, and linguistic brilliance—were written in Russian. But in 1937, having abandoned Nazi Germany for Paris, he completed the first of his nine English-language novels, becoming one of the few twentieth-century writers to successfully make this transition. In 1940, he moved to the United States, where he became famous for his scandalous novel *Lolita* (1955),

an amoral tale of a man's erotic obsession with a pubescent "nymphet," at once a metaphor for his love for English and his abhorrence of America's cultural landscape. He died in Switzerland, a devoted lepidopterist and writer of dazzling linguistic ingenuity.

THE PULITZER PRIZES

fiction
No award

nonfiction
Beautiful Swimmers,
William W. Warner

biography or autobiography
*A Prince of Our Disorder: The Life of
T. E. Lawrence,* John E. Mack

poetry
Divine Comedies, James Merrill

drama
The Shadow Box, Michael Cristofer

THE BOOKER PRIZE
Staying On, Paul Scott

THE NEWBERY MEDAL
Roll of Thunder, Hear My Cry,
Mildred D. Taylor

THE CALDECOTT MEDAL
Ashanti to Zulu, Margaret
Musgrove, Pictures by
Leo and Diane Dillon

[*183*]

ANAÏS NIN (1903-1977) was born in Paris to parents of mixed Spanish-Cuban descent. At twenty, she married Hugh Guiler, a Parisian banker, who fell far from meeting her bohemian cravings. They soon, however, were fulfilled by a number of amorous liaisons—with her psychologist Otto Rank and, triangularly, with Henry Miller (whom she collaborated with, supported, and inspired) and June, his wife. Nin is best known for her elaborately written and sexually explicit journals, the unexpurgated 1993 volume of which documents her father's sexual abuse of her as a child and her seduction of him later in life, among other startling erotic events. In the 1940s, Nin lived in New York, California, and Mexico, where she wrote a sequence of novels entitled *Cities of the Interior* and was embraced by American feminists.

THE NATIONAL BOOK AWARDS

fiction
Wallace Stegner, *The Spectator Bird*

biography and autobiography
W. A. Swanberg, *Norman Thomas: The Last Idealist*

children's literature
Katherine Paterson, *The Master Puppeteer*

contemporary thought
Bruno Bettelheim, *The Uses of Enchantment: The Meaning and Importance of Fairy Tales*

history
Irving Howe, *World of Our Fathers*

translation
Li-Li Ch'en, *Master Tung's Western Chamber Romance*

poetry
Richard Eberhart, *Collected Poems, 1930-1976*

THE NATIONAL BOOK CRITICS CIRCLE AWARDS

fiction
Song of Solomon, Toni Morrison

nonfiction
Samuel Johnson, W. Jackson Bate

poetry
Day by Day, Robert Lowell

criticism
On Photography, Susan Sontag

"Song of Solomon" easily lifts above them on the wide slow wings of human sympathy, well-informed wit and the rare plain power to speak wisdom to other human beings. A long story, then, and better than good. Toni Morrison has earned attention and praise. Few Americans know, and can say, more than she has in this wise and spacious novel.

Reynolds Price, review of
Song of Solomon
by Toni Morrison,
NY Times Book Review,
September 11, 1977

Every Child's Birthright: In Defense of Mothering, Selma Fraiberg

Dispatches, Michael Herr

Chinese Shadows, Simon Leys

Day by Day, Robert Lowell

Song of Solomon, Toni Morrison

The Path Between the Seas: The Creation of the Panama Canal, 1870-1914, David McCullough

Coming into the Country, John McPhee

India: A Wounded Civilization, V. S. Naipaul

Robert Frost: The Work of Knowing, Richard Poirier

The Gentle Barbarian: The Life and Work of Turgenev, V. S. Pritchett

Staying On, Paul Scott

On Photography, Susan Sontag

Letters on Literature and Politics: 1912-1972, Edmund Wilson

EDITOR'S CHOICE

the new york times best books of the year

Delmore Schwartz: The Life of an American Poet, James Atlas

Samuel Johnson, W. Jackson Bate

Falconer, John Cheever

Afterimages, Arlene Croce

Gates of Eden: American Culture in the Sixties, Morris Dickstein

A Book of Common Prayer, Joan Didion

[*185*]

1978

HARDCOVER BESTSELLERS

fiction

Chesapeake, James A. Michener

War and Remembrance,
Herman Wouk

nonfiction

*If Life Is a Bowl of Cherries—What
Am I Doing in the Pits?*
Erma Bombeck

Gnomes, Wil Huygen,
Illustrated by Rien Poortvliet

PAPERBACK BESTSELLERS

mass market

The Thorn Birds,
Colleen McCullough

The Other Side of Midnight,
Sidney Sheldon

trade

The Crowd Pleasers,
Rosemary Rogers

Shanna, Kathleen E. Woodiwiss

> *Everyone who is born
> holds dual citizenship, in
> the kingdom of the well
> and in the kingdom of
> the sick.*
>
> Susan Sontag, *Illness as
> Metaphor* (1978)

DEATHS

Hugh MacDiarmid
Margaret Mead
Norman Rockwell

JOHN IRVING (1942-) was born in Exeter, New Hampshire, where his stepfather was a teacher of Russian history and his mother a social worker. He attended his hometown's prestigious prep school, Exeter Academy, and between 1961 and 1967 studied at the universities of Pennsylvania, Vienna (where he looked after a bear), New Hampshire, and Iowa. In 1969, Irving published his first novel, *Setting Free the Bears*, which enabled him to get a teaching job at Mount Holyoke College and support his family. He then taught at the University of Iowa until his fourth novel, *The World According to Garp* (1978), became a huge success—spending a phenomenal six months on the bestseller lists—and moved Irving into the ranks of leading American authors. He has since published several top-selling novels, including *The Hotel New Hampshire* (1981) and *The Cider House Rules* (1985), which are often set in the Northeast and touch on—in an entertaining and often light-hearted way—contemporary moral issues.

1950, and was followed by humorous and mystical short stories, reflections on traditional Poland, children's tales, and novels on modern America, including *Enemies: A Love Story* (1970, 1972). Singer was awarded the **1978 Nobel Prize**, and when asked of his recreation, replied: "walking in the bad air of New York City."

> *In a figurative way,
> Yiddish is the wise and
> humble language of us all,
> the idiom of a frightened
> and hopeful humanity.*
>
> Isaac Bashevis Singer,
> Nobel lecture,
> December 8, 1978

ISAAC BASHEVIS SINGER (1904–1991) was born in Radzymin, Poland, the son and grandson of Hasidic rabbis and the brother of the novelists Joshua Singer and Esther Kreitman. He spent his youth in Warsaw and Bilgoray, a Jewish shtetl, and worked first as a proofreader and translator. In 1935, he emigrated to the United States, and under the influence of his brother, became a journalist for New York's *Jewish Daily Forward*. Singer started writing in Hebrew but soon turned to Yiddish; he is the last great Yiddish author. His autobiographical novel, *The Family Moskat*, was published in

THE PULITZER PRIZES
fiction
Elbow Room, James Alan McPherson

nonfiction
The Dragons of Eden, Carl Sagan

biography or autobiography
Samuel Johnson, W. Jackson Bate

poetry
Collected Poems, Howard Nemerov

drama
The Gin Game, Donald L. Coburn

THE BOOKER PRIZE

The Sea, The Sea, Iris Murdoch

THE NEWBERY MEDAL

Bridge to Terabithia,
Katherine Paterson

THE CALDECOTT MEDAL

Noah's Ark, Peter Spier

THE NATIONAL BOOK AWARDS

fiction

Mary Lee Settle, *Blood Ties*

biography and autobiography

W. Jackson Bate, *Samuel Johnson*

children's literature

Judith Kohl and Herbert Kohl,
The View from the Oak

contemporary thought

Gloria Emerson, *Winners & Losers*

history

David McCullough, *The Path
Between the Seas: The Creation of
the Panama Canal 1870-1914*

translation

Richard Winston and Clara
Winston, *Uwe George's In the
Deserts of This Earth*

poetry

Howard Nemerov, *The Collected
Poems of Howard Nemerov*

Pulitzer Prize winner James McPherson

Booker Prize winner Iris Murdoch

THE NATIONAL BOOK CRITICS CIRCLE AWARDS

fiction

The Stories of John Cheever,
John Cheever

nonfiction

Tie:
   Facts of Life, Maureen
   Howard

*Inventing America: Jefferson's
Declaration of Independence*,
Garry Wills

poetry

*Hello, Darkness: The Collected Poems
of L. E. Sissman*, Peter Davison

criticism

*Modern Art: 19th and 20th Centuries,
Selected Papers*, Meyer Schapiro

EDITOR'S CHOICE

the new york times best books of the year

In Patagonia, Bruce Chatwin

The Stories of John Cheever,
John Cheever

*Discipline and Punish: The Birth of the
Prison*, Michel Foucault

E. M. Forster: A Life, P. N. Furbank

Final Payments, Mary Gordon

The Flounder, Günter Grass

*A Savage War of Peace: Algeria
1954-1962*, Alistair Horne

Facts of Life, Maureen Howard

Leon Trotsky, Irving Howe

The World According to Garp,
John Irving

Lying Low, Diane Johnson

Stories, Doris Lessing

Wrinkles, Charles Simmons

The Coup, John Updike

*The Eye of the Story: Selected Essays
and Reviews,* Eudora Welty

*Inventing America: Jefferson's
Declaration of Independence,*
Garry Wills

1979

HARDCOVER BESTSELLERS

fiction

The Matarese Circle,
Robert Ludlum

Sophie's Choice, William Styron

nonfiction

Aunt Erma's Cope Book,
Erma Bombeck

The Complete Scarsdale Medical Diet,
Herman Tarnower, M.D., and
Samm Sinclair Baker

PAPERBACK BESTSELLERS

mass market

The Thorn Birds,
Colleen McCullough

The Amityville Horror, Jay Anson

trade

Ashes in the Wind,
Kathleen Woodiwiss

Mary Ellen's Best of Helpful Hints,
Mary Ellen Pinkham and
Pearl Higginbotham

Pulitzer Prize winner Sam Shepard

THE ALFRED B. NOBEL PRIZE FOR LITERATURE

Odysseus Elytis, Greece

THE PULITZER PRIZES

fiction

The Stories of John Cheever,
John Cheever

nonfiction

On Human Nature,
Edward O. Wilson

biography or autobiography

*Days of Sorrow and Pain: Leo Baeck
and the Berlin Jews,* Leonard Baker

poetry

Now and Then: Poems 1976-1978,
Robert Penn Warren

drama

Buried Child, Sam Shepard

DEATHS

*Elizabeth Bishop
James T. Farrell
S. J. Perelman
Jean Stafford*

ELIZABETH BISHOP (1911-1979) was born in Worcester, Massachusetts, and endured a difficult childhood: when she was one, her father died, and

when she was seven, her mother was committed to a mental institution and never seen by her daughter again. Bishop was educated at Vassar, where she met Marianne Moore, her mentor and lifelong friend, who encouraged her to write poetry. In 1955, she received a Pulitzer Prize for her first two collections, *North and South* (1946) and *Cold Spring* (1955), which afforded her the time and money to travel. While in South America, she met and fell in love with Maria Soares (Lota), with whom she lived in Brazil for over ten years, producing fine poems and short stories, as well as translations from Spanish and Portuguese. But in the 1960s, Lota committed suicide and Bishop moved back to the States and taught at Harvard. Though a recognized poet— she also received the 1970 National Book Award for her *Collected Poems*— Bishop's importance became appreciated only after her death.

THE BOOKER PRIZE
Offshore, Penelope Fitzgerald

THE NEWBERY MEDAL
The Westing Game, Ellen Raskin

THE CALDECOTT MEDAL
The Girl Who Loved Wild Horses, Paul Goble

THE NATIONAL BOOK AWARDS

fiction
Tim O'Brien, *Going After Cacciato*

biography and autobiography
Arthur M. Schlesinger, Jr., *Robert Kennedy and His Times*

children's literature
Katherine Paterson, *The Great Gilly Hopkins*

contemporary thought
Peter Matthiessen, *The Snow Leopard*

history
Richard Beale Davis, *Intellectual Life in the Colonial South, 1585-1763*

translation
Clayton Eshleman and Jose Rubia Barcia, *Cesar Vallejo's The Complete Posthumous*

poetry
James Merrill, *Mirabell: Book of Numbers*

[*191*]

MILAN KUNDERA (1929-) was born in Brno, Czechoslvokia, the son of a pianist. He studied at Prague's Charles University and Academy of Music and Arts, and then worked as a rural laborer, jazz pianist, and professor of film. In 1962, he began writing his first novel, *The Joke*, which was hesitantly published in 1967. Kundera became a cultural leader of the Prague Spring, but after its crushing by the Soviets in 1968, was labeled a state enemy. His novel was banned, and in 1975 he was permitted to take a teaching position in France. Four years later, with the publication of perhaps his greatest novel, **The Book of Laughter and Forgetting (1979, 1980)**, his citizenship was revoked. Kundera has lived in France since, and has come to be seen not just as an important Czech writer but also as one of one America and Europe's finest novelists, whose concerns stretch from power and memory to love, sex, and the ironies of life.

[*192*]

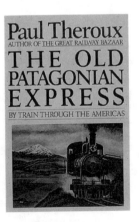

I think no one but Mailer could have dared this book. The authentic Western voice, the voice heard in "The Executioner's Song," is one heard often in life but only rarely in literature, the reason being that to truly know the West is to lack all will to write it down. The very subject of "The Executioner's Song" is that vast emptiness at the center of the Western experience, a nihilism antithetical not only to literature but to most other forms of human endeavor, a dread so close to zero that human voices fade out, trail off, like skywriting ... [This is] an absolutely astonishing book.

Joan Didion, review of
The Executioner's Song
by Norman Mailer,
NY Times Book Review,
October 7, 1979

• • •

The idea was to prove at every foot of the way up that you were one of the elected and anointed ones who has the right stuff...

Tom Wolfe,
The Right Stuff (1979)

EDITOR'S CHOICE

the new york times best books of the year

The White Album, Joan Didion

King of the Jews, Leslie Epstein

Sleepless Nights, Elizabeth Hardwick

Gödel, Escher, Bach: An Eternal Golden Braid, Douglas R. Hofstadter

Eighth Day of Creation: Makers of the Revolution in Biology, Horace Freeland Judson

The Nabokov-Wilson Letters: Correspondence Between Vladimir Nabokov and Edmund Wilson, 1940-1971

White House Years, Henry Kissinger

The Culture of Narcissism: American Life in an Age of Diminishing Expectations, Christopher Lasch

The Executioner's Song, Norman Mailer

The Rise of Theodore Roosevelt, Edmund Morris

A Bend in the River, V. S. Naipaul

The Habit of Being, Flannery O'Connor, Edited by Sally Fitzgerald

The Boer War, Thomas Pakenham

The Man Who Kept the Secrets: Richard Helms and the CIA, Thomas Powers

The Ghost Writer, Philip Roth

Sideshow: Kissinger, Nixon and the Destruction of Cambodia, William Shawcross

Too Far to Go: The Maples Stories, John Updike

[*193*]

1980

quently teach abroad. Barthes did not have a conventional academic career. It was only in 1960, after years of research, writing, and journalism, that he gained a university post. He is best known for his passionate concern for language, signs, and literature, which led to the creation of a new science of signs—semiology—that aims to describe the signifying systems that structure our world. His books—*Writing Degree Zero* (1953) and *Mythologies* (1957), for example—have left an indelible mark on literary criticism. He died in a street accident outside the Collège de France.

DEATHS

Roland Barthes
Henry Miller
Katherine Anne Porter
Jean Paul Sartre

ROLAND BARTHES (1915-1980), the French semiotician and leader of the Structuralist movement, was born into the Bayonne bourgeoisie, the son of a naval officer. In youth, he suffered from tuberculosis, which prevented him from going to war but allowed him to read the classics and subse-

Henry Miller 1891-1980

Norman Mailer

NORMAN MAILER (1923–) was born in New Jersey and raised in Brooklyn, "the most secure Jewish community in the world." After Harvard, he served as a front-line Intelligence and Reconnaissance infantryman in World War II, gathering material for his first novel, *The Naked and the Dead* (1948), which became a bestseller and allowed him to "lobotomize the past" and to begin the process of reinventing himself. After flirting with anarchism and living in Paris, Mailer moved to Greenwich Village and helped found *The Village Voice.* He soon gained a reputation as a multiply divorced bar brawler, actor, filmmaker, and would-be politician (he ran twice for New York's mayoralty, on the platform that the city secede from the state and that juvenile delinquency be alleviated by gladiatorial combat). His *Armies of the Night* (1969), an exhibitionist memoir about the 1967 protest march on the Pentagon, and **The Executioner's Song (1979)**, about the life and execution of Gary Gilmore, are considered his finest books and have won Pulitzer Prizes.

[*195*]

> *Every word she [Lillian Hellman] writes is a lie, including "and" and "the."*
>
> Mary McCarthy,
> television interview, 1980

THE BOOKER PRIZE
Rites of Passage, William Golding

THE NEWBERY MEDAL
A Gathering of Days, Joan W. Blos

THE CALDECOTT MEDAL
Ox-Cart Man, Donald Hall,
Illustrated by Barbara Cooney

> The only reason people want to be masters of the future is to change the past.
>
> Milan Kundera,
> *The Book of Laughter and Forgetting* (1980)

THE NATIONAL BOOK AWARDS

fiction (hardcover)
William Styron, *Sophie's Choice*

fiction (paperback)
John Irving,
The World According to Garp

first novel
William Wharton, *Birdy*

mystery (hardcover)
John D. MacDonald,
The Green Ripper

mystery (paperback)
William F. Buckley, Jr., *Stained Glass*

science fiction (hardcover)
Frederick Pohl, *Jem*

science fiction (paperback)
Walter Wangerin, Jr.,
The Book of the Dun Cow

western
Louis L'Amour, *Bendigo Shafter*

autobiography (hardcover)
Lauren Bacall,
Lauren Bacall by Myself

autobiography (paperback)
Malcolm Cowley, *And I Worked at the Writer's Trade: Chapters of Literary History 1918-1978*

biography (hardcover)
Edmund Morris,
The Rise of Theodore Roosevelt

biography (paperback)
A. Scott Berg, *Max Perkins: Editor of Genius*

children's books (hardcover)
Joan W. Blos, *A Gathering of Days: A New England Girl's Journal*

children's books (paperback)
Madeleine L'Engle,
A Swiftly Tilting Planet

current interest (hardcover)
Julia Child,
Julia Child and More Company

current interest (paperback)
Christopher Lasch,
The Culture of Narcissism

general nonfiction (hardcover)

Tom Wolfe, *The Right Stuff*

general nonfiction (paperback)

Peter Matthiessen, *The Snow Leopard*

general reference books (hardcover)

Elder Witt, ed., *Congressional Quarterly's Guide to the U.S. Supreme Court*

general reference books (paperback)

Tim Brooks and Earle Marsh, *The Complete Directory of Prime Time Network TV Shows: 1946-Present*

history (hardcover)

Henry A. Kissinger, *The White House Years*

history (paperback)

Barbara W. Tuchman, *A Distant Mirror: The Calamitous 14th Century*

religion/inspiration (hardcover)

Elaine Pagels, *The Gnostic Gospels*

religion/inspiration (paperback)

Sheldon Vanauken, *A Severe Mercy*

science (hardcover)

Douglas Hofstadter, *Gödel, Escher, Bach: An Eternal Golden Braid*

science (paperback)

Gary Zukav, *The Dancing Wu Li Masters: An Overview of the New Physics*

translation

William Arrowsmith, *Cesare Pavese's Hard Labor*

Jane Gary Harris and Constance Link, *Osip E. Mandelstam's Complete Critical Prose and Letters*

poetry

Philip Levine, *Ashes*

THE NATIONAL BOOK CRITICS CIRCLE AWARDS

fiction

The Transit of Venus, Shirley Hazzard

nonfiction

Walter Lippmann and the American Century, Ronald Steel

poetry

Sunrise, Frederick Seidel

criticism

Part of Nature, Part of Us: Modern American Poets, Helen Vendler

EDITOR'S CHOICE

the new york times best books of the year

Falling in Place, Ann Beattie

Christianity, Social Tolerance, and Homosexuality, John Boswell

Italian Folktales, Italo Calvino

Loon Lake, E. L. Doctorow

Man in the Holocene, Max Frisch

Walt Whitman, Justin Kaplan

China Men, Maxine Hong Kingston

The Cost of Good Intentions, Charles R. Morris

Nature and Culture, Barbara Novak

Conrad in the Nineteenth Century, Ian Watt

The Collected Stories of Eudora Welty, Eudora Welty

[*197*]

1981

as a migrant worker. His career as a writer of realistic novels began with *Somebody in Boots* (1935) and *Never Come Morning* (1942), both of which center on class division and social protest. His most famous novel, *The Man with the Golden Arm* (1949), depicts the life of a dope addict who commits suicide. Algren continued to explore themes of violence and underground life in his next few novels, but in his later years turned to softer subjects and other genres: short stories, travel essays, and poetry. He had a transatlantic love affair with Simone de Beauvoir, which is described in her famous novel *The Mandarins*.

DEATHS

Nelson Algren
Anita Loos
William Saroyan

NELSON ALGREN (1909–1981). Born in Detroit and reared in the Chicago slums, Algren grew up poor in a Jewish family with the name William Algren Abraham. At the University of Illinois, he trained as a journalist, but during the Depression earned his way

Some of us are becoming the men we wanted to marry.

Gloria Steinem,
speech at Yale University,
September 1981

THE PULITZER PRIZES

fiction

A Confederacy of Dunces,
John Kennedy Toole

nonfiction

Fin-de-Siècle Vienna: Politics and Culture, Carl E. Schorske

biography or autobiography

Peter the Great: His Life and World,
Robert K. Massie

poetry

The Morning of the Poem,
James Schuyler

drama

Crimes of the Heart, Beth Henley

THE PEN/FAULKNER AWARD

How German Is It?, Walter Abish

THE BOOKER PRIZE

Midnight's Children, Salman Rushdie

THE NEWBERY MEDAL

Jacob Have I Loved,
Katherine Paterson

THE CALDECOTT MEDAL

Fables, Arnold Lobel

SALMAN RUSHDIE (1947–) was born in Bombay two months before Indian independence to a Muslim family who spoke Urdu and English. In 1961, he was sent to England's Rugby School, and in 1964, his family made the reluctant move to Pakistan as part of the Muslim exodus. Cultural dislocation, conflicting religious views, and divided loyalties are a large part of Rushdie's work. In 1975, after graduating from Cambridge and a brief career as a advertising copywriter, he published his first novel, *Grimus*. Though it was little read, it showed his story-writing ability and the influence of the magical realists and writers such as Joyce and Grass. Rushdie became well known with his second novel, ***Midnight's Children (1981)***, a comic allegory about Indian history, but it wasn't until *The Satanic Verses* (1988), a hyperbolic meditation on Islam, that he achieved international notoriety, for Iran's Ayatollah Khomeini issued a fatwah against Rushdie, forcing him into permanent hiding.

THE NATIONAL BOOK AWARDS

fiction (hardcover)
Wright Morris, *Plains Song*

fiction (paperback)
John Cheever,
  The Stories of John Cheever

first novel
Ann Arensberg, *Sister Wolf*

children's books, fiction (hardcover)
Betsy Byars, *The Night Swimmers*

children's books, fiction (paperback)
Beverly Cleary,
  Ramona and Her Mother

autobiography/biography (hardcover)
Justin Kaplan, *Walt Whitman*

autobiography/biography (paperback)
Deirdre Bair, *Samuel Beckett*

children's books, nonfiction (hardcover)
Alison Cragin Herzig and Jane
  Lawrence Mali, *Oh Boy! Babies*

general nonfiction (hardcover)
Maxine Hong Kingston, *China Men*

general nonfiction (paperback)
Jane Kramer, *The Last Cowboy*

history (hardcover)
John Boswell, *Christianity, Social
  Tolerance and Homosexuality*

history (paperback)
Leon F. Litwak, *Been in the Storm
  So Long: The Aftermath of Slavery*

science (hardcover)
Stephen Jay Gould,
  *The Panda's Thumb: More
  Reflections in Natural History*

science (paperback)
Lewis Thomas,
  The Medusa and the Snail

translation
Francis Steegmuller,
  The Letters of Gustave Flaubert

John E. Woods, *Arno Schmidt's
  Evening Edged in Gold*

poetry
Lisel Mueller, *The Need to Hold Still*

THE NATIONAL BOOK CRITICS CIRCLE AWARDS

fiction
Rabbit Is Rich, John Updike

nonfiction
The Mismeasure of Man,
  Stephen Jay Gould

poetry
A Coast of Trees, A. R. Ammons

criticism
A Virgil Thomson Reader,
  Virgil Thomson

EDITOR'S CHOICE

the new york times best books of the year

The Chaneysville Incident,
  David Bradley

Bad Blood, James H. Jones

Haydn: Chronicle and Works,
  H. C. Robbins Landon

Philosophical Explanations,
  Robert Nozick

Old Glory, Jonathan Raban

Housekeeping, Marilynne Robinson

Midnight's Children, Salman Rushdie

The Gate of Heavenly Peace,
  Jonathan Spence

A Flag for Sunrise, Robert Stone

The White Hotel, D. M. Thomas

*Prisoner Without a Name, Cell
  Without a Number*,
  Jacobo Timerman

Rabbit Is Rich, John Updike

*Some writers take to drink,
others take to audiences.*

Gore Vidal,
interview in *Paris Review*,
1981

Nadine Gordimer has always been an admirable writer, combining skill with social conscience; but here she has outdone herself. "July's People" demonstrates with breathtaking clarity the tensions and complex interdependencies between whites and blacks in South Africa. It is so flawlessly written that every one of its events seems chillingly, ominously possible.

Anne Tyler, review of
July's People
by Nadine Gordimer,
NY Times Book Review,
July 7, 1981

William Saroyan (1905-1981)

[201]

1982

DEATHS

John Cheever
John Gardner
Ayn Rand

GABRIEL GARCÍA MÁRQUEZ (1928-) was born in Aracataca, Colombia, and studied law and journalism in Bogotá. During the 1950s, he worked as a left-leaning newspaper reporter, and in 1954, while a foreign correspondent in Europe, began writing creatively. Since 1961, he has lived in Barcelona and Mexico, directing films and writing fiction. García Márquez is Latin America's most important contemporary novelist, celebrated as a genius of the poetic imagination and a virtuoso of magical realism. He won the **1982 Nobel Prize** for literature, and is largely responsible for the increasing visibility and popularity of writers of Spanish. His masterpiece, *One Hundred Years of Solitude* (1967, 1970), is a vast novel charting the history of one Colombian family, house, and town, from mythic genesis through centuries of history, war, and politics. He has also written *The Autumn of the Patriarch* (1975, 1976) and *Chronicle of a Death Foretold* (1981, 1982).

JOHN CHEEVER (1912–1982) was born in Quincy, Massachussetts, where his father was a prosperous shoe manufacturer who lost his fortune in the 1929 stock-market collapse. His formal education ended at seventeen when he was expelled from Thayer Academy, an incident he made fiction-worthy in his story "Expelled," which the *New Republic* bought and published in 1930. For the next few years, Cheever sup-

ported himself by writing synopses for MGM and by selling his stories to various magazines. More than any writer, he developed the genre that became known as "the *New Yorker* story." Cheever was married in 1941 and served for four years in the U.S. Army, during which his first collection of stories, *The Way Some People Live* (1943), was published. His first novel, *The Wapshot Chronicle*, earned him the 1958 National Book Award, and along with *Bullet Park* (1969) and his Pulitzer Prize-winning short stories, established his reputation as an ironic chronicler of the suburbs. The posthumous publication of Cheever's letters and diaries served to reveal much about his personal life, including his promiscuous bisexuality and addiction to alcohol.

THE NATIONAL BOOK AWARDS

fiction (hardcover)
John Updike, *Rabbit Is Rich*

fiction (paperback)
William Maxwell,
So Long, See You Tomorrow

first novel
Robb Forman Dew,
Dale Loves Sophie to Death

children's books, fiction (hardcover)
Lloyd Alexander, *Westmark*

children's books, fiction (paperback)
Ouida Sebestyen, *Words by Heart*

autobiography/biography (hardcover)
David McCullough,
Mornings on Horseback

autobiography/biography (paperback)
Ronald Steel, *Walter Lippmann and the American Century*

children's books, nonfiction
Susan Bonners, *A Penguin Year*

children's books, picture books (hardcover)
Maurice Sendak, *Outside Over There*

children's books, picture books (paperback)
Peter Spier, *Noah's Ark*

general nonfiction (hardcover)
Tracy Kidder,
The Soul of a New Machine

general nonfiction (paperback)
Victor S. Navasky, *Naming Names*

history (hardcover)
Father Peter John Powell, *People of the Sacred Mountain: A History of the Northern Cheyenne Chiefs and Warrior Societies, 1830-1879*

history (paperback)
Robert Wohl,
The Generation of 1914

science (hardcover)
Donald C. Johanson and
Maitland A. Edey, *Lucy: The Beginnings of Humankind*

science (paperback)
Fred Alan Wolf, *Taking the Quantum Leap: The New Physics for Nonscientists*

translation
Robert Lyons Danly, *Higuchi Ichiyo's In the Shade of Spring Leaves*

Ian Hideo Levy, *The Ten Thousand Leaves: A Translation of the Man'Yoshu, Japan's Premier Anthology of Classical Poetry*

poetry
William Bronk, *Life Supports: New and Collected Poems*

THE NATIONAL BOOK CRITICS CIRCLE AWARDS

fiction

George Mills, Stanley Elkin

nonfiction

The Path to Power: The Years of Lyndon Johnson, Robert A. Caro

poetry

Antarctic Traveler, Katha Pollitt

criticism

The Second American Revolution and Other Essays, 1976-82, Gore Vidal

EDITOR'S CHOICE

the new york times best books of the year

The Burning House, Ann Beattie

Waiting for the Barbarians, J. M. Coetzee

Tumultuous Years, Robert J. Donovan

Schindler's List, Thomas Keneally

Years of Upheaval, Henry A. Kissinger

The Fate of the Earth, Jonathan Schell

Bronx Primitive, Kate Simon

Aké, Wole Soyinka

Isak Dinesen, Judith Thurman

Dinner at the Homesick Restaurant, Anne Tyler

Bech Is Back, John Updike

Aunt Julia and the Scriptwriter, Mario Vargas Llosa

Is there a writer anywhere more exasperating or whom we read with more delight and dismay than Stanley Elkin? . . . No writer I know of is so consistently undone by the unrestrained exercise of his own inherent gifts.

Leslie Epstein, review of *George Mills* by Stanley Elkin, *NY Times Book Review*, October 31, 1982

• • •

No one is better at the plangent detail, at evoking the floating, unreal ambiance of grief . . . If Miss Beattie were a ballerina you could sell tickets to her warm-ups.

Margaret Atwood, review of *The Burning House* by Ann Beattie, *NY Times Book Review*, September 26, 1982

• • •

Her command of her art is sure and her right to trust her feelings for the complications both of our nature and of our nurturing arrangements stands beyond question.

Benjamin DeMott, review of *Dinner at the Homesick Restaurant* by Anne Tyler, *NY Times Book Review*,

[205]

1983

HARDCOVER BESTSELLERS

fiction

The Little Drummer Girl,
John le Carré

Christine, Stephen King

nonfiction

Megatrends, John Naisbitt

In Search of Excellence,
Thomas J. Peters and
Robert H. Waterman, Jr.

PAPERBACK BESTSELLERS

mass market

Truly Tasteless Jokes, Blanche Knott

*When Bad Things Happen to Good
People,* Harold S. Kushner

trade

Color Me Beautiful, Carole Jackson

Living, Loving and Learning,
Leo Buscaglia

THE ALFRED B. NOBEL PRIZE FOR LITERATURE

William Golding, England

TENNESSEE WILLIAMS (1911-1983) was born in Columbus, Mississippi, the son of a traveling salesman, whose increasingly diminishing circumstances exacerbated his sister and mother's instability and led young Tennessee to exorcise these tensions through writing. After graduating from the University of Iowa, he wrote plays and worked menial jobs until his agent managed to negotiate a six-month Hollywood screenwriting contract. Williams's first success was *The Glass Menagerie* (1944), an autobiographical play about a young woman's sexual obsessions. Then came the Pulitzer Prize–winning *A Streetcar Named Desire* (1947), which was made into a hit movie starring Marlon Brando and secured Williams's position as a leading American playwright. In the 1960s, Williams remained popular and prolific but became increasingly dependent on drink and drugs. He died in a New York hotel room by choking on the cap of a bottle of barbiturates.

THE PULITZER PRIZES

fiction
The Color Purple, Alice Walker

nonfiction
Is There No Place on Earth for Me?,
Susan Sheehan

biography or autobiography
Growing Up, Russell Baker

poetry
Selected Poems, Galway Kinnell

drama
'night, Mother, Marsha Norman

> *I think it pisses God off*
> *if you walk by the color*
> *purple in a field some-*
> *where and don't notice it.*
>
> Alice Walker,
> *The Color Purple* (1982)

ALICE WALKER (1944–) was born the youngest of eight children in Eatonton, Georgia, to a poor farming family. Her father, active in the civil rights movement, defied death threats to cast the first black vote in the county. In 1961, Walker enrolled in Spelman College, and upon graduating won a scholarship to Sarah Lawrence College. In 1964, she traveled around Africa and wrote a series of interrelated poems collected in *Once* (1968). Inspired by the civil rights movement, Walker relocated to Mississippi in 1966 to register voters and met her husband, the civil rights activist Melvyn Leventhal. Her first novel, *The Third Life of Grange Copeland*, was published in 1970, and was followed, most notably, by *The Color Purple* (1982), the story of two sisters in the cruel, segregated world of the interwar Deep South, which won the **1983 Pulitzer Prize** and became a groundbreaking Hollywood movie.

THE PEN/FAULKNER AWARD
Seaview, Toby Olson

THE BOOKER PRIZE
Life and Times of Michael K.,
J. M. Coetzee

THE NEWBERY MEDAL
Dicey's Song, Cynthia Voigt

THE CALDECOTT MEDAL
Shadow, Blaise Cendrars, Translated and illustrated by Marcia Brown

[207]

THE NATIONAL BOOK AWARDS

fiction (hardcover)
Alice Walker, *The Color Purple*

fiction (paperback)
Eudora Welty,
Collected Stories of Eudora Welty

first novel
Gloria Naylor,
The Women of Brewster Place

children's fiction (hardcover)

Jean Fritz,
Homesick: My Own Story

children's fiction (paperback)

Paula Fox, *A Place Apart*

Joyce Carol Thomas, *Market by Fire*

**autobiography/biography
(hardcover)**

Judith Thurman, *Isak Dinesen: The
Life of a Storyteller*

**autobiography/biography
(paperback)**

James R. Mellow, *Nathaniel
Hawthorne in His Time*

children's books, nonfiction

James Cross Giblin, *Chimney Sweeps*

**children's picture books
(hardcover)**

Barbara Cooney, *Miss Rumphius*

William Steig, *Doctor De Soto*

**children's picture books
(paperback)**

Mary Ann Hoberman; Betty Fraser,
ill., *A House Is a House for Me*

general nonfiction (hardcover)

Fox Butterfield,
China: Alive in the Bitter Sea

general nonfiction (paperback)

James Fallows, *National Defense*

history (hardcover)

Alan Brinkley, *Voices of Protest:
Huey Long, Father Coughlin and
the Great Depression*

history (paperback)

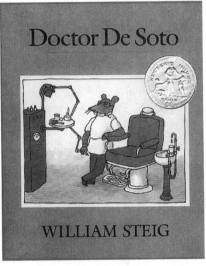

Doctor De Soto

WILLIAM STEIG

National Book Award winner

Frank E. Manuel and Fritzie P.
Manual, *Utopian Thought in the
Western World*

original paperback

Lisa Goldstein, *The Red Magician*

science (hardcover)

Abraham Pais,
*"Subtle Is the Lord . . .": The Science
and Life of Albert Einstein*

science (paperback)

Philip J. Davis and Reuben Hersh,
The Mathematical Experience

translation

Richard Howard, *Charles
Baudelaire's Les Fleurs du Mal*

poetry

Galway Kinnell, *Selected Poems*

Charles Wright, *Country Music:
Selected Early Poems*

AMIRI BARAKA [LEROI JONES] (1934–). Born into a middle-class family in Newark, New Jersey, Baraka attended Rutgers and Howard universities, served in the Strategic Air Command, and studied philosophy and German literature at Columbia and the New School for Social Research before becoming a revolutionary spokesman for his people. In 1957, he settled in Greenwich Village, consorted with members of the Beat Movement, and wrote poetry and jazz criticism. His first collection was *Preface to a Twenty-Volume Suicide Note* (1961). In 1965, Baraka renounced much of this life: he divorced his white wife, took the name Imamu Amiri Baraka, and founded a black community center in Newark,

Spirit House. There he wrote influential poems, essays, and plays, in which he lashed out at the gross inequities of the American system. In **1983**, he published *The Autobiography of LeRoi Jones*, and began teaching on the African-American Studies faculty of SUNY, Stony Brook.

THE NATIONAL BOOK CRITICS CIRCLE AWARDS

fiction
Ironweed, William Kennedy

nonfiction
The Price of Power: Kissinger in the Nixon White House, Seymour M. Hersh

biography or autobiography
Minor Characters, Joyce Johnson

poetry
The Changing Light at Sandover, James Merrill

criticism
Hugging the Shore: Essays and Criticism, John Updike

[*209*]

DEATHS

Kenneth Clark
Owen Dodson
Temple Hornaday Fielding
Ezra Jack Keats
Arthur Koestler
Ross Macdonald
Rebecca West
Tennessee Williams

[I think] Mr. Carver is showing us at least part of the truth about a segment of American experience few of our writers trouble to notice . . . at his best he is probing, as many American writers have done before, the waste and destructiveness that prevail beneath the affluence of American life.

Irving Howe, review of
Cathedral
by Raymond Carver,
NY Times Book Review,
September 11, 1983

•   •   •

Throughout her career Bishop aimed to bring morality and invention together in a single thought . . . Elizabeth Bishop alone now seems secure beyond the disputation of schools or the sway of period loyalties. Like all great poets, she was less a maker of poems than a maker of feelings.

David Bromwich, review of
The Complete Poems:
1927-1979
by Elizabeth Bishop,
NY Times Book Review,
February 27, 1983

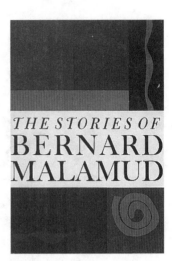

THE STORIES OF
BERNARD
MALAMUD

EDITOR'S CHOICE

the new york times best books of the year

Cathedral, Raymond Carver

During the Reign of the Queen of Persia, Joan Chase

The Name of the Rose, Umberto Eco

Attlee, Kenneth Harris

The Price of Power, Seymour M. Hersh

Modern Times, Paul Johnson

Ironweed, William Kennedy

Chronicle of a Death Foretold, Gabriel García Márquez

The Moons of Jupiter, Alice Munro

The Rosenberg File, Ronald Radosh and Joyce Milton

The Anatomy Lesson, Philip Roth

The Social Transformation of American Medicine, Paul Starr

Hugging the Shore, John Updike

1984

HARDCOVER BESTSELLERS

fiction

The Aquitaine Progression,
Robert Ludlum

" . . .and ladies of the club,"
Helen Hooven Santmyer

nonfiction

Motherhood: The Second Oldest Profession, Erma Bombeck

Nothing Down, Robert Allen

PAPERBACK BESTSELLERS

mass market

Megatrends: Ten New Directions Transforming Our Lives,
John Naisbitt

Out on a Limb, Shirley MacLaine

trade

The One Minute Manager,
Kenneth Blanchard and
Spencer Johnson

The Color Purple, Alice Walker

Truman Capote hosts a party at the Plaza.

TRUMAN CAPOTE (1924-1984) Born in New Orleans, the only child of an irresponsible steamboat clerk and his much younger wife, Capote spent his odd youth in Monroeville, Alabama, and started writing fiction at age eight. With his early wild creativity he became the model for Dill in *To Kill a Mockingbird* (1960), written by his childhood friend Harper Lee. At seventeen, he left home and began work at *The New Yorker. Other Voices, Other Rooms* (1948), his first novel, about a homosexually inclined boy groping toward maturity, won him critical acclaim, and was followed by *Breakfast at Tiffany's* (1958), a camp metropolitan comedy, which became a successful movie. In 1959, he read about the murder of a wealthy family in Holcomb, Kansas, and with sponsorship from *The New Yorker,* set off to interview the townspeople. The result was *In Cold Blood* (1966), a highly detailed re-creation of the murderers and their victims, a nonfiction novel, as Capote called it, which made him into a national figure.

[*211*]

THE ALFRED B. NOBEL PRIZE FOR LITERATURE

Jaroslav Seifert, Czechoslovakia

THE PULITZER PRIZES

fiction
Ironweed, William Kennedy

nonfiction
Social Transformation of American Medicine, Paul Starr

biography or autobiography
Booker T. Washington,
Louis R. Harlan

poetry
American Primitive, Mary Oliver

drama
Glengarry Glen Ross, David Mamet

THE PEN/FAULKNER AWARD

Sent for You Yesterday,
John Edgar Wideman

THE BOOKER PRIZE

Hotel du Lac, Anita Brookner

THE NEWBERY MEDAL

Dear Mr. Henshaw, Beverly Cleary

THE CALDECOTT MEDAL

The Glorious Flight: Across the Channel with Louis Blériot,
Alice and Martin Provensen

THE NATIONAL BOOK AWARDS

fiction
Ellen Gilchrist, *Victory Over Japan: A Book of Stories*

first work of fiction
Harriet Doerr, *Stones for Ibarra*

nonfiction
Robert V. Remini, *Andrew Jackson & the Course of American Democracy, 1833-1845*

---

*You lose more of yourself
than you redeem
Doing the decent thing.*

Seamus Heaney,
Station Island (1984)

DEATHS

*Ansel Adams
Leonard S. Baker
Basil Blackwell
Truman Capote
Margaret Farrar
Lillian Hellman
Chester Himes
Alfred A. Knopf
James Reid Parker
J. B. Priestly
Ellen Raskin
Irwin Shaw*

her story "The World's Greatest Fisherman," which became the first chapter of **Love Medicine (1984)**, winner of the National Book Critics Circle Award and also the first novel in a tetralogy that includes *The Beet Queen* (1986), *Tracks* (1988), *Bingo Palace* (1994) and *Tales of Burning Love* (1996).

> *I was in love with the whole world and all that lived in its rainy arms.*
>
> Louise Erdrich,
> Love Medicine (1984)

LOUISE ERDRICH (1954–), of Chippewa and German descent, was raised in North Dakota, where her parents worked for the Wahpeton Indian School. In 1972, she entered Dartmouth College's first coeducational class through the Native American Studies program, where she met her future husband and collaborator, Michael Dorris, the program's director. After graduation, Erdrich held a variety of jobs and in 1979 earned a Master's degree from the Johns Hopkins Creative Writing Program, becoming a writer in residence. In 1982, she won a fiction competition for

THE NATIONAL BOOK CRITICS CIRCLE AWARDS

fiction
Love Medicine, Louise Erdrich

nonfiction
Weapons of Hope, Freeman Dyson

biography or autobiography
Dostoevsky: The Years of Ordeal, 1850-1859, Joseph Frank

poetry
The Dead and the Living, Sharon Olds

criticism
Twentieth Century Pleasures: Prose on Poetry, Robert Hass

EDITOR'S CHOICE

the new york times best books of the year

The Bourgeois Experience: Victoria to Freud, Volume One: Education of the Senses, Peter Gay

Brothers and Keepers, John Edgar Wideman

Dawn to the West: Japanese Literature in the Modern Era, Donald Keene

Deadly Gambits: The Reagan Administration and the Stalemate in Nuclear Arms Control, Strobe Talbott

Him with His Foot in His Mouth and Other Stories, Saul Bellow

In Her Own Right: The Life of Elizabeth Cady Stanton, Elizabeth Griffin

Life and Times of Michael K., J. M. Coetzee

Lives of the Poets: Six Stories and a Novella, E. L. Doctorow

Machine Dreams, Jayne Anne Phillips

The Memory Palace of Matteo Ricci, Jonathan Spence

The Quality of Mercy: Cambodia, Holocaust and Modern Conscience, William Shawcross

The Unbearable Lightness of Being, Milan Kundera

Walt Whitman: The Making of a Poet, Paul Zweig

The War of the End of the World, Mario Vargas Llosa

With a Daughter's Eye: A Memoir of Margaret Mead and Gregory Bateson, Mary Catherine Bateson

1985

HARDCOVER BESTSELLERS
fiction
If Tomorrow Comes, Sidney Sheldon

The Hunt for Red October,
Tom Clancy

nonfiction
Iacocca: An Autobiography,
Lee Iococca with William Novak

The Frugal Gourmet, Jeff Smith

PAPERBACK BESTSELLERS
mass market
" . . . and ladies of the club,"
Helen Hooven Santmyer

Full Circle, Danielle Steel

trade
Tie:

The One Minute Manager,
Kenneth Blanchard and
Spencer Johnson

*In Search of Excellence: Lessons from
America's Best-Run Companies*,
Thomas J. Peters and
Robert J. Waterman, Jr.

The Road Less Traveled,
M. Scott Peck, M.D.

THE ALFRED B. NOBEL PRIZE FOR LITERATURE
Claude Simon, France

Pulitzer Prize winner Alison Lurie

THE PULITZER PRIZES
fiction
Foreign Affairs, Alison Lurie

nonfiction
The Good War, Studs Terkel

biography or autobiography
The Life and Times of Cotton Mather,
Kenneth Silverman

Poetry
Yin, Carolyn Kizer

drama
Sunday in the Park with George,
Stephen Sondheim and
James Lapine

[*215*]

STUDS TERKEL (1912-) was born Louis Terkel in New York City, and after being trained as a lawyer, worked as a Chicago stage actor and radio host. By the 1950s, he commanded his own TV show, but when the House Un-American

Activities Committee interpreted his liberal politics as a cover for Communist sympathies he left television and devoted himself to the freer realms of local radio. There he developed the interview technique that served as the basis for his popular books. Terkel has traveled to practically every corner of the United States to record Americans' opinions on topics ranging from World War II and the Depression to the American Dream, race, and the widening economic gap. These oral histories, collected in *Division Street: America* (1967), *American Dreams: Lost and Found* (1980), *The Great Divide* (1988), and the **1985 Pulitzer Prize winner, *The Good War***, among other books, have won Terkel a unique place in American letters. His greatest contribution, as he put it, has been to "celebrate the uncelebrated," and thus render a broad swath of American sensibility and sentiment.

THE PEN/FAULKNER AWARD
The Barracks Thief, Tobias Wolff

THE BOOKER PRIZE
The Bone People, Keri Hulme

THE NEWBERY MEDAL
The Hero and the Crown,
 Robin McKinley

THE CALDECOTT MEDAL
Saint George and the Dragon,
 Retold by Margaret Hodges,
 Illustrated by Trina Schart Hyman

DEATHS
Heinrich Boll
Italo Calvino
Robert Graves
Orson Welles
E. B. White

THE NATIONAL BOOK AWARDS

fiction
Don DeLillo, *White Noise*

first work of fiction
Bob Shacochis, *Easy in the Islands*

nonfiction
J. Anthony Lukas, *Common Ground: A Turbulent Decade in the Lives of Three American Families*

THE NATIONAL BOOK CRITICS CIRCLE AWARD

fiction

The Accidental Tourist, Anne Tyler

nonfiction

Common Ground: A Turbulent Decade in the Lives of Three American Families, J. Anthony Lukas

biography or autobiography

Henry James: A Life, Leon Edel

poetry

The Triumph of Achilles, Louise Gluck

criticism

Habitations of the Word: Essays, William Gass

EDITOR'S CHOICE

the new york times best books of the year

The Abandonment of the Jews: America and the Holocaust, 1941-1945, David S. Wyman

All Fall Down: America's Tragic Encounter with Iran, Gary Sick

Common Ground: A Turbulent Decade in the Lives of Three American Families, J. Anthony Lukas

Flaubert's Parrot, Julian Barnes

Footsteps: Adventures of a Romantic Biographer, Richard Holmes

House, Tracy Kidder

Love Medicine, Louise Erdrich

Mr. Palomar, Italo Calvino, Translated by William Weaver

Move Your Shadow: South Africa, Black and White, Joseph Lelyveld

The Old Forest and Other Stories, Peter Taylor

The Periodic Table, Primo Levi, Translated by Raymond Rosenthal

DON DELILLO (1936–) was raised by Italian immigrants in the Bronx and educated at Fordham University. After quitting his loathsome job as an advertising copywriter at Ogilvy & Mather in New York, he started his first novel, *Americana,* which he wrote amidst a series of temporary jobs and saw published in 1971. DeLillo's subsequent novels are biting black satires on contemporary America, comparable to the work of Thomas Pynchon and William Gaddis, and include **White Noise (1985)**, the story of a suburban professor's attempts to save his family from airborne industrial waste, which won the American Book Award, and *Libra* (1988), a recreation of Oswald's shooting of J.F.K., which won the first International Fiction Prize. DeLillo publishes short stories in *The New Yorker, Esquire,* and *Atlantic,* and lives a quiet life (he avoids conversations with the press) in Westchester County with his wife.

[217]

1986

HARDCOVER BESTSELLERS

fiction

The Mammoth Hunters,
Jean M. Auel

The Bourne Supremacy,
Robert Ludlum

nonfiction

Fit for Life, Harvey and
Marilyn Diamond

*Callanetics: 10 Years Younger in
10 Hours,* Callan Pinckney

PAPERBACK BESTSELLERS

mass market

Women Who Love Too Much,
Robin Norwood

The Hunt for Red October,
Tom Clancy

trade

The Road Less Traveled,
M. Scott Peck

Rand McNally Road Atlas 1986

THE ALFRED B. NOBEL PRIZE FOR LITERATURE

Wole Soyinka, Nigeria

DEATHS

*Simone de Beauvoir
Jorge Luis Borges
Jean Genet
Christopher Isherwood
Bernard Malamud*

SIMONE DE BEAUVOIR (1908-1986) grew up in Paris in what she described as a typical Catholic girlhood. She developed an early interest in the humanities, politics, and her own individual freedom, and in 1929 became the ninth woman in France to pass the prestigious *agrégation* exam in philosophy, coming second only to Jean-Paul Sartre, her lover. With the existentialist notion of freedom as her departure, Beauvoir focused on the problem of reconciling women's need for social and economic independence with her need for love and sexual fulfillment, themes she developed triumphantly in *The Second Sex* (1949, 1953) a series of essays on women that made her world-famous. On publication in France, the book was greeted with outrage: Beauvoir was classified as "unsatisfied, cold, priapic, nymphomaniac, [and a] lesbian." But the first volume sold twenty thousand copies in two weeks, and today remains a founding text of Western feminism.

JORGE LUIS BORGES (1899–1986) was born in Buenos Aires, Argentina, and educated in Geneva. In Madrid, he became associated with the Spanish literary movement *ultraismó*, and after his return to Argentina promoted its expressionist cause through the journal *Proa*. His first volume of poetry was published in 1923, followed by verse and essays, but he is best known for his short stories, the first collection of which, *A Universal History of Infamy* (1935), is a landmark of Latin American literature and the first work of magical realism. In these quasi-detective stories, Borges explores the relationship between fiction, identity, and truth, and the nature of violence. Later stories collected in *Ficciones* (1945) and *Labyrinths* (1953), which established his reputation abroad, became even more experimental and provocative, addressing, among many modern themes, the cyclical nature of time. Eye trouble and eventually blindness prevented Borges from writing in his later years; his last story collection, *Doctor Brodie's Report*, appeared in English in 1971.

> The Holocaust is a central event in many people's lives, but it has also become a metaphor for our century. There cannot be an end to speaking and writing about it.
>
> Aharon Appelfeld, in the *New York Times*, November 15, 1986

[*219*]

Beet Queen *by Louise Erdrich*

THE NATIONAL BOOK AWARDS

fiction
E. L. Doctorow, *World's Fair*

nonfiction
Barry Lopez, *Arctic Dreams: Imagination and Desire in a Northern Landscape*

THE NATIONAL BOOK CRITICS CIRCLE AWARDS

fiction
Kate Vaiden, Reynolds Price

nonfiction
War Without Mercy: Race and Power in the Pacific War, John W. Dower

biography or autobiography
Tombee: Portrait of a Cotton Planter, Theodore Rosengarten

poetry
Wild Gratitude, Edward Hirsch

criticism
Less Than One: Selected Essays, Joseph Brodsky

EDITOR'S CHOICE
the new york times best books of the year

Arab and Jew: Wounded Spirits in a Promised Land, David K. Shipler

Arctic Dreams: Imagination and Desire in a Northern Landscape, Barry Lopez

Crossing the Line: A Year in the Land of Apartheid, William Finnegan

FDR: The New York Years: 1928-1933, Kenneth S. Davis

FDR: The New Deal Years: 1933-1937, Kenneth S. Davis

The Handmaid's Tale, Margaret Atwood

John Maynard Keynes, Volume One: Hopes Betrayed 1883-1920, Robert Skidelsky

CHRISTOPHER ISHERWOOD (1904-1986) was born in Cheshire and educated at Cambridge University, where he befriended the poets W. H. Auden and Stephen Spender, the three forming a triumvirate that soon exemplified the progressive, left-wing literature of the 1930s. In 1928, his first novel, *The Conspirators*, was published, and the following year he left for Berlin, where he submerged himself in the city's homosexual subculture. Isherwood successfully captured the mood of pre-Hitler Berlin in *Mr. Norris Changes Trains* (1935) and *Goodbye to Berlin* (1939), before leaving to collaborate with Auden on experimental plays in Europe and a book researched in China on the Japanese invasion. Isherwood then decided to move to California, where he wrote novels, worked for MGM, and met and became disciple to Swami Prabhavananda, whom he assisted in the translation of Hindu texts. He died in Santa Monica, a figurehead of the emergent gay liberation movement.

[*221*]

1987

HARDCOVER BESTSELLERS

fiction

Windmills of the Gods,
  Sidney Sheldon

The Prince of Tides, Pat Conroy

nonfiction

Tie:

A Day in the Life of America,
  Rick Smolen and David Cohen

Love, Medicine & Miracles,
  Bernie S. Siegel

Tie:

Communion, Whitley Strieber

The Closing of the American Mind,
  Allan Bloom

PAPERBACK BESTSELLERS

mass market

Women Who Love Too Much,
  Robin Norwood

The Hunt for Red October,
  Tom Clancy

trade

The Road Less Traveled,
  M. Scott Peck, M.D.

Dianetics, Revised Edition,
  L. Ron Hubbard

THE ALFRED B. NOBEL PRIZE FOR LITERATURE

Joseph Brodsky, U.S.

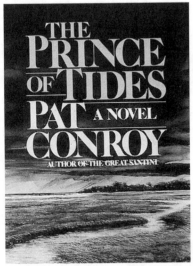

Bestselling novel The Prince of Tides
by Pat Conroy

Nobel Prize winner Joseph Brodsky

THE PULITZER PRIZES

fiction

A Summons to Memphis, Peter Taylor

nonfiction

Arab and Jew, David K. Shipler

biography or autobiography

*Bearing the Cross:
Martin Luther King, Jr. and the
Southern Christian Leadership
Conference,* David J. Garrow

poetry

Thomas and Beulah, Rita Dove

drama

Fences, August Wilson

Pulitzer Prize winner Rita Dove

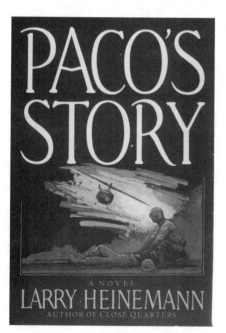

National Book Award winner

THE PEN/FAULKNER AWARD

Soldiers in Hiding, Richard Wiley

THE BOOKER PRIZE

Moon Tiger, Penelope Lively

THE NEWBERY MEDAL

The Whipping Boy, Sid Fleischman

THE CALDECOTT MEDAL

Hey, Al, Arthur Yorinks,
Illustrated by Richard Egielski

THE NATIONAL BOOK AWARDS

fiction

Larry Heinemann, *Paco's Story*

nonfiction

Richard Rhodes,
The Making of the Atom Bomb

[223]

JAMES BALDWIN (1924-1987) was born in Harlem, New York, and brought up by his stepfather, a mean-hearted preacher, who raised his children in an atmosphere of bigotry, fear, and religious fanaticism. At fourteen, he became a Holy Roller preacher, but by seventeen renounced the church, and after his father's death, moved to Greenwich Village, set on a literary career. For the next few years, Baldwin worked odd jobs, writing at night, until in 1945, with the support of his mentor Richard Wright, he received a fellowship, which allowed him to work in Paris. In 1954, *Go Tell It to the Mountain*, a powerful autobiographical first novel, was published, followed by *Notes of a Native Son* (1955), a collection of provocative essays on black-white relationships, and *Giovanni's Room* (1957), in which he turned to the theme of homosexuality. In 1957, Baldwin returned to the United States and became involved in the civil rights movement. He continued to write on race and discrimination in his famous novel *Another Country* (1963) and essay collection *The Fire Next Time* (1963), but after the murder of Martin Luther King, Jr., returned to Europe, certain that the civil rights movement had died with the fallen leader.

THE NATIONAL BOOK CRITICS CIRCLE AWARDS

fiction
The Counterlife, Philip Roth

nonfiction
The Making of the Atomic Bomb,
Richard Rhodes

biography or autobiography
*Chaucer: His Life, His Works,
His World*, Donald Howard

poetry
Flesh and Blood, C. K. Williams

criticism
Dance Writings, Edwin Denby

EDITOR'S CHOICE

the new york times best books of the year

*An Arrow in the Wall: Selected Poetry
and Prose*, Andrei Voznesensky,
William Jay Smith and
F. D. Reeve, eds.

Beloved, Toni Morrison

The Bonfire of the Vanities, Tom Wolfe

Chaos: Making a New Science,
James Gleick

The Counterlife, Philip Roth

*The Embarrassment of Riches: An
Interpretation of Dutch Culture in
the Golden Age*, Simon Schama

*Evelyn Waugh: The Early Years
1903-1939*, Martin Stannard

The Fatal Shore, Robert Hughes

The Ice: A Journey to Antarctica,
Stephen J. Pyne

Life and Death in Shanghai,
Nien Cheng

The Making of the Atomic Bomb,
Richard Rhodes

More Die of Heartbreak, Saul Bellow

Staring at the Sun, Julian Barnes

*The Truly Disadvantaged: The Inner
City, the Underclass, and Public
Policy*, William Julius Wilson

*Veil: The Secret Wars of the CIA
1981-1987*, Bob Woodward

World's End, T. Coraghessan Boyle

In "And the Band Played On," Randy Shilts, a reporter for *The San Francisco Chronicle* who has covered AIDS full time since 1983, takes us almost day by day through the first five years of the unfolding epidemic and the responses—confusion and fear, denial and indifference, courage and determination . . . "And the Band Played On" is about the kind of people we have been for the past seven years. That is its terror, and its strength.

Jack Geiger, review of
And the Band Played On
by Randy Shilts,
NY Times Book Review,
November 8, 1987

[*225*]

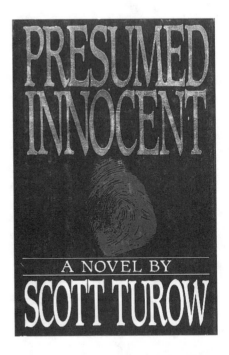

Now comes Tom Wolfe,
aging enfant terrible,
with his first novel, . . . a
big, bitter, funny, craftily
plotted book that grabs
you by the lapels and
won't let go . . . The fun
of the book, and much
of its energy, comes from
watching Mr. Wolfe evis-
cerate one pathetic char-
acter after another . . .
when it turns out that
everyone is pathetic
(except for me and thee,
of course), the fun can
turn sour. Malice is a
powerful spice. Too much
can ruin the stew, and
Mr. Wolfe comes close.

Frank Conroy, review of
The Bonfire of the Vanities
by Tom Wolfe,
NY Times Book Review,
November 1, 1987

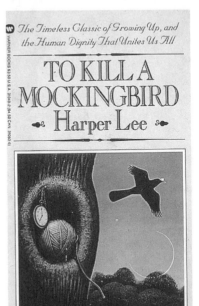

DEATHS

James Baldwin
Erskine Caldwell
Clare Boothe Luce
Howard Moss

ERSKINE CALDWELL (1903–1987). Born in rural Georgia, Caldwell spent his first twenty years traveling widely through the American South with his father, a Presbyterian minister. He was educated on the road by his mother, and at eighteen went briefly to college in South Carolina, before departing for South America on a gun-running boat. Caldwell, like many American writers of his generation, gained his education outside the university, working variously as a poolroom attendant, professional football player, bodyguard, and Hollywood screenwriter. His two most famous novels, *Tobacco Road* (1932) and *God's Little Acre* (1933), depict the lives of poor whites and blacks and were prosecuted for obscenity (Caldwell appeared in court more than any of his contemporaries). From 1938 to 1941, he traveled extensively as a foreign correspondent and later wrote excellent travelogues as well as novels (many semipornographic), essays, autobiography, and hundreds of fine short stories. During his final years, he settled in Scottsdale, Arizona, with his fourth wife.

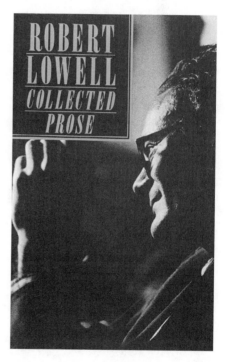

[227]

1988

HARDCOVER BESTSELLERS

fiction

The Bonfire of the Vanities,
Tom Wolfe

Love in the Time of Cholera,
Gabriel García Márquez

nonfiction

The 8-Week Cholesterol Cure,
Robert W. Kowalski

Trump: The Art of the Deal,
Donald J. Trump with
Tony Schwartz

PAPERBACK BESTSELLERS

mass market

The Prince of Tides, Pat Conroy

Presumed Innocent, Scott Turow

trade

The Road Less Traveled,
M. Scott Peck

Calvin & Hobbes, Bill Watterson

THE ALFRED B. NOBEL PRIZE FOR LITERATURE

Naguib Mahfouz, Egypt

Bestselling author Tom Wolfe

TOM WOLFE (1931-) was born in Richmond, Virginia, into a long-established Southern family. He attended Washington and Lee and in 1956 earned a Ph.D. from Yale in American Studies. Wolfe first worked as a reporter on the *Springfied Union,* then transferring to *The Washington Post*, and in 1962—frustrated by what he described as the "pale, beige tone" of journalism—moved to magazine work at *New York* and *Esquire*. In 1963, unable to complete an article about California customized cars, he wrote up his notes in a long, detailed stream-of-consciousness style, which was published untouched as *The Kandy-Kolored Tangerine-Flake Streamline Baby*, giving birth to his signature prose style. Wolfe went on to become a trenchant critic, espousing the need for the "New Journalism." In 1979, he published *The Right Stuff*, which earned a National Book Award, and in **1987**, his first novel, ***The Bonfire of the Vanities***, a testament to the decadent inequities of the 1980s, became a bestseller.

THE PULITZER PRIZES

fiction

Beloved, Toni Morrison

nonfiction

The Making of the Atomic Bomb, Richard Rhodes

biography or autobiography

Look Homeward: A Life of Thomas Wolfe, David Herbert Donald

poetry

Partial Accounts: New and Selected Poems, William Meredith

drama

Driving Miss Daisy, Alfred Uhry

THE PEN/FAULKNER AWARD

World's End, T. Coraghessan Boyle

THE BOOKER PRIZE

Oscar and Lucinda, Peter Carey

THE NEWBERY MEDAL

Lincoln: A Photobiography, Russell Freedman

THE CALDECOTT MEDAL

Owl Moon, Jane Yolen, Illustrated by John Schoenherr

THE NATIONAL BOOK AWARDS

fiction

Pete Dexter, *Paris Trout*

nonfiction

Neil Sheehan, *A Bright Shining Lie: John Paul Vann and America in Vietnam*

Pulitzer Prize winner Toni Morrison

Whoever has come under the sway of Primo Levi's luminous mind and the lovely prose will feel pained at the realization that we shall not be hearing from him again. At a time when the Holocaust, like almost everything else in our culture, has been subjected to the vulgarity of public relations, Primo Levi wrote about this most terrible event with a purity of spirit for which we can only feel grateful. This was man.

Irving Howe, review of *The Drowned and the Saved* by Primo Levi, *NY Times Book Review*, January 10, 1988

[*229*]

THE NATIONAL BOOK CRITICS CIRCLE AWARDS

fiction
The Middleman and Other Stories, Bharati Mukherjee

nonfiction
Parting the Waters: America in the King Years, 1954-63, Taylor Branch

biography or autobiography
Oscar Wilde, Richard Ellman

poetry
The One Day, Donald Hall

criticism
Works and Lives: The Anthropologist as Author, Clifford Geertz

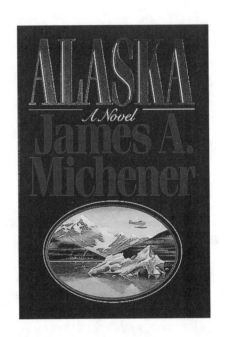

DEATHS
Charles Addams
Paul Cowan
Edward Dodd
Robert Heinlein
Louis L'Amour
William McCarthy
Norman Newhouse
Ursula Nordstrom
Alan Paton
Kim Philby
George Woods

WILHELM GRIMM
MAURICE SENDAK
DEAR MILI

EDITOR'S CHOICE

the new york times best books of the year

Arabesques, Anton Shammas,
Translated by Vivian Eden

*Battle Cry of Freedom: The Civil War
Era,* James M. McPherson

*Bernard Shaw, Volume One,
1856-1898: The Search for Love,*
Michael Holroyd

*A Brief History of Time: From the Big
Bang to Black Holes,*
Stephen W. Hawking

*A Bright Shining Lie: John Paul Vann
and America in Vietnam,*
Neil Sheehan

Coming of Age in the Milky Way,
Timothy Ferris

*Dictionary of the Khazars: A Lexicon
Novel in 100,000 Words,*
Milorad Pavic, Translated by
Christina Pribicevic-Zoric

Libra, Don DeLillo

Love in the Time of Cholera, Gabriel
García Márquez, Translated by
Edith Grossman

The Magic Lantern: An Autobiography,
Ingmar Bergman,
Translated by Joan Tate

*Original Intent and the Framers'
Constitution,* Leonard W. Levy

*Parting the Waters: America in the King
Years, 1954-63,* Taylor Branch

*The Rise and Fall of the Great
Powers: Economic Change and
Military Conflict From 1500 to 2000,*
Paul Kennedy

Stories in an Almost Classical Mode,
Harold Brodkey

The Tenants of Time,
Thomas Flanagan

*Where I'm Calling From: New and
Selected Stories,* Raymond Carver

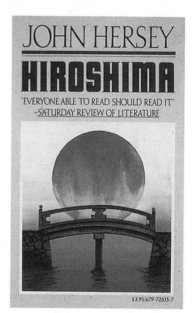

Paperback reissue of the
John Hersey classic, Hiroshima.

1989

HARDCOVER BESTSELLERS

fiction

The Joy Luck Club, Amy Tan

The Satanic Verses, Salman Rushdie

nonfiction

All I Really Need to Know I Learned in Kindergarten, Robert Fulghum

A Brief History of Time, Stephen W. Hawking

PAPERBACK BESTSELLERS

mass market

The Shell Seekers, Rosamunde Pilcher

The Bonfire of the Vanities, Tom Wolfe

trade

Codependent No More, Melody Beattie

The Road Less Traveled, M. Scott Peck

THE ALFRED B. NOBEL PRIZE FOR LITERATURE

Camilo José Cela, Spain

University and then pursued graduate studies in Russian at Columbia. But after the successful publication of her first two novels, *If Morning Ever Comes* (1964) and *The Tin Can Tree* (1965), she decided to give up academia and devote herself full-time to fiction. Her work is largely concerned with the ties of family and the complexity of relationships given individual desires, which she has best explored in her award-winning novels *Dinner at the Homesick Restaurant* (1982), *The Accidental Tourist* (1985), and the **1989 Pulitzer prize winner** ***Breathing Lessons***. Tyler lives in Baltimore with her husband, a child psychologist, and their two children.

THE PULITZER PRIZES

fiction

Breathing Lessons, Anne Tyler

nonfiction

A Bright Shining Lie: John Paul Vann and America in Vietnam, Neil Sheehan

biography or autobiography

Oscar Wilde, Richard Ellmann

poetry

New and Collected Poems, Richard Wilbur

drama

The Heidi Chronicles, Wendy Wasserstein

[*232*]

ANNE TYLER (1941-) was born in Minneapolis, Minnesota, the daughter of an industrial chemist and social worker, and spent her childhood in Quaker communities in the rural South before settling in Raleigh, North Carolina. She earned a B.A. from Duke

"The Satanic Verses" has sparked bitter controversy among Muslims in South Africa . . . Some of the noisiest objections have been raised by people who have never read the book and have no intention of ever reading it. This opposition does little to educate a woefully ignorant and prejudiced Western public about the Islamic faith . . . Talent? Not in question. Big talent. Ambition? Boundless ambition. Salman Rushdie is a story-teller of prodigious powers, able to conjure up whole geographies, causalities, climates, creatures, customs, out of thin air. Yet, in the end, what have we? As a display of narrative energy and wealth of invention, "The Satanic Verses" is impressive. As a sustained exploration of the human condition it flies apart into delirium.

A.G. Mojtabai, review of
The Satanic Verses
by Salman Rushdie,
NY Times Book Review,
January 29, 1989

Bestselling author Salman Rushdie

Bestselling author Amy Tan

[*233*]

THE PEN/FAULKNER AWARD

Dusk, James Salter

THE BOOKER PRIZE

The Remains of the Day,
Kazuo Ishiguro

THE NEWBERY MEDAL

Joyful Noise: Poems for Two Voices,
Paul Fleischman

THE CALDECOTT MEDAL

Song and Dance Man,
Karen Ackerman,
Illustrated by Stephen Gammell

THE NATIONAL BOOK AWARDS

fiction

John Casey, *Spartina*

nonfiction

Thomas L. Friedman,
From Beirut to Jerusalem

THE NATIONAL BOOK CRITICS CIRCLE AWARDS

fiction

Billy Bathgate, E. L. Doctorow

nonfiction

The Broken Cord, Michael Dorris

biography or autobiography

*A First-Class Temperament: The
Emergence of Franklin Roosevelt*,
Geoffrey C. Ward

poetry

Transparent Gestures, Rodney Jones

criticism

*Not by Fact Alone: Essays on the
Reading and Writing of History*,
John Clive

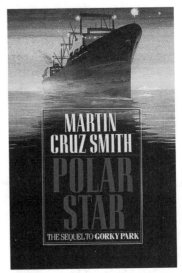

Polar Star
by Martin Cruz Smith

RAYMOND CARVER (1939-1989). Born in Clatskanie, Oregon, where his father was a sawmill worker and his mother a waitress, Carver came to write stories about the characters he grew up with. In 1957, shortly after leaving high school, he married his sixteen-year-old girlfriend, and to support his wife and two children, worked as a gas station attendant, janitor, and salesman. In 1958, Carver took a creative writing course with John Gardner at California's Chico State College, and then attended Humboldt State University, spending his free time writing. His first stories were published in obscure literary magazines, but in 1967, "Will You Be Quiet Please?" appeared in *Best American Short Stories*, leading to a critically acclaimed collection of the same name. His other well-known works include *What We Talk About When We Talk About Love* (1981) and *Cathedral* (1984). Today his reputation continues to grow as the American writer who articulated the lives of the working class and poor.

Mary McCarthy

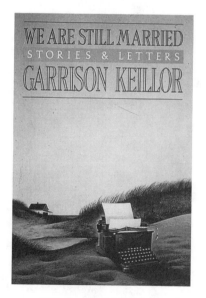

We Are Still Married
by Garrison Keillor

[235]

A History of the World in 10 1/2
  Chapters, Julian Barnes

How War Came: The Immediate
  Origins of the Second World War,
  1938-1939,
  Donald Cameron Watt

If the River Was Whiskey,
  T. Coraghessan Boyle

A Peace to End All Peace: Creating the
  Modern Middle East 1914-1922,
  David Fromkin

The Remains of the Day,
  Kazuo Ishiguro

The Satanic Verses, Salman Rushdie

The Shawl, Cynthia Ozick

EDITOR'S CHOICE

the new york times best books of the year

Billy Bathgate, E. L. Doctorow

Citizens: A Chronicle of the French
  Revolution, Simon Schama

Federico Garcia Lorca: A Life,
  Ian Gibson

Foucault's Pendulum, Umberto Eco

From Beirut to Jerusalem,
  Thomas L. Friedman

Harold Macmillan, Volume One:
  1894-1956, Alistair Horne

Harold Macmillan, Volume Two:
  1957-1986, Alistair Horne

1990

HARDCOVER BESTSELLERS

fiction

Oh, The Places You'll Go!, Dr. Seuss

Clear and Present Danger, Tom Clancy

nonfiction

Wealth Without Risk, Charles Givens

Barbarians at the Gate: The Fall of RJR Nabisco, Bryan Burrough and John Helyar

PAPERBACK BESTSELLERS

mass market

All I Really Need to Know I Learned in Kindergarten, Robert Fulghum

The Joy Luck Club, Amy Tan

trade

Codependent No More, Melody Beattie

The T-Factor Fat Gram Counter, Jamie Pope-Cordle and Martin Katahn

THE ALFRED B. NOBEL PRIZE FOR LITERATURE

Octavio Paz, Mexico

THE PULITZER PRIZES

fiction

The Mambo Kings Play Songs of Love, Oscar Hijuelos

nonfiction

And Their Children After Them, Dale Maharidge and Michael Williamson

biography or autobiography

Machiavelli in Hell, Sebastian de Grazia

poetry

The World Doesn't End, Charles Simic

drama

The Piano Lesson, August Wilson

AUGUST WILSON (1945–) grew up poor in Pittsburgh, Pennsylvania, the son of an interracial working couple. At sixteen, he was wrongly expelled from school but managed to proceed with his education in a local library, while working menial jobs and successfully submitting poetry to black publications. At age twenty-three, he founded—with no prior experience—the Black Horizons Theatre [237] Company in St. Paul, Minnesota, to "try to raise consciousness through theater." Wilson spent years struggling to gain recognition until in 1982 his third play, *Ma Rainey's Black Bottom*, so impressed the director of the Yale Repertory Theatre that he helped usher it to Broadway, where Wilson was heralded as a wonderful new talent. Wilson's next two plays, *Fences* (1985) and *Joe Turner's Come and Gone*

(1986), won him almost every major theatrical award. He has since spent his career exploring the intricate canvas of black America, weaving powerful and often boldly realistic stories about racial problems in America. His 1990 *The Piano Lesson* won him the **Pulitzer Prize**.

> *Literature is the one place in any society where, within the secrecy of our own heads, we can hear voices talking about everything in every possible way.*
>
> Salman Rushdie,
> "Is Nothing Sacred?" (1990)

THE PEN/FAULKNER AWARD
Billy Bathgate, E. L. Doctorow

THE BOOKER PRIZE
Possession: A Romance, A. S. Byatt

THE NEWBERY MEDAL
Number the Stars, Lois Lowry

THE CALDECOTT MEDAL
Lon Po Po, Ed Young

THE NATIONAL BOOK AWARDS
fiction
Charles Johnson, *Middle Passage*

nonfiction
Ron Chernow, *The House of Morgan: An American Banking Dynasty and the Rise of Modern Finance*

THE NATIONAL BOOK CRITICS CIRCLE AWARDS

fiction
Rabbit at Rest, John Updike

nonfiction
The Content of Our Character: A New Vision of Race in America, Shelby Steele

biography or autobiography
Means of Ascent: The Years of Lyndon Johnson, Robert Caro

poetry
Bitter Angel, Amy Gerstler

criticism
Encounters and Reflections: Art in the Historical Present, Arthur Danto

E. L. DOCTOROW (1931-) was born in Brooklyn, New York, where his father owned a record store. After graduating from Ohio's Kenyon College, he took a job in publishing, later becoming editor-in-chief of Dial Press, where he edited notable authors such as James Baldwin and Norman Mailer. In 1971, Doctorow left his successful career to devote himself full-time to writing. His first novel, *Welcome to Hard Times* (1960), a Dakota frontier story, announced the theme that would preoccupy much of his fictional work—the foundations of American progress and its brutalization by commerce and crime. Doctorow today is considered one of the most eloquent, popular, and critically acclaimed writers in postwar America. He received a National Book Critics Circle Award for *Ragtime* (1975), his ode to early-twentieth-century America; the American Book Award for *World's Fair* (1985), a semiautobiographical Bronx boy's tale; and the 1990 **PEN/Faulkner Award** for *Billy Bathgate* (1989), a parable of New York gangsterism.

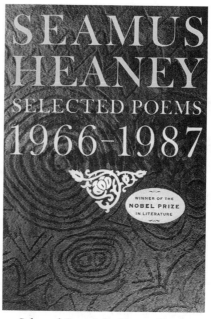

Selected Poems *by Seamus Heaney*

Puss in Boots, *Charles Perrault, with illustrations by Fred Marcellino*

"Rabbit at Rest" is certainly the most brooding, the most demanding, the most concentrated of John Updike's longer novels . . . the Rabbit quartet constitutes a powerful critique of America.

Joyce Carol Oates, review of *Rabbit at Rest* by John Updike, *NY Times Book Review,* September 30, 1990

[*239*]

WALKER PERCY (1916–1990) was born in Birmingham, Alabama. After his father committed suicide and his mother was killed in a car accident, Walker, then thirteen, was raised by his father's cousin, William Alexander Percy, a high-born Mississippi poet, whom he described as a profound influence and beneficent guardian. In 1941, he earned an M.D. from Columbia University, but when forced to spend two years in a tuberculosis sanitarium, decided to become a writer to focus "not on the physiological and pathological problems with man's body but with the problems of man himself, the nature and destiny of man." He wrote several unpublished books and then in 1961 saw the publication of *The Moviegoer*, the story of an alienated New Orleans stockbroker addicted to the cinema, which was awarded a National Book Award and earned Percy a reputation as a philosophical Southern writer. Percy's later novels and nonfiction books strengthened that classification, though he was quick to claim that "My South was always the New South."

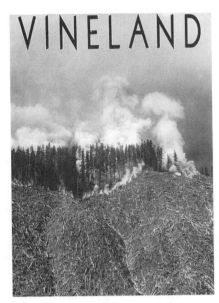

Vineland *by Thomas Pynchon*

DEATHS
Roald Dahl
Lawrence Durrell
Walker Percy
Patrick White

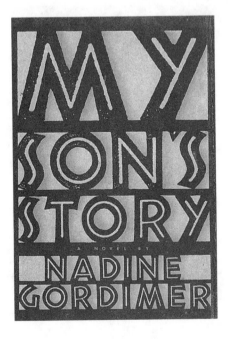

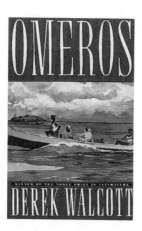

[But] his new epic does not so much tell a story as explain the feelings and reflections of some inhabitants—past, present or, like Mr. Walcott himself, intermittent—of St. Lucia in the Windward Islands . . . Mr. Walcott's epic is a significant and timely reminder that the past is not the property of those who first created it; it always matters to all of us, no matter who we are or where we were born.

Mary Lefkowitz, review of *Omeros* by Derek Walcott, *NY Times Book Review*, October 7, 1990

EDITOR'S CHOICE
the new york times best books of the year

Biting the Grave: The Irish Hunger Strikes and the Politics of Despair, Padraig O'Malley

The Complete Poems of Anna Akhmatova, Roberta Reeder, ed., Translated by Judith Hemschemeyer

Friend of My Youth, Alice Munro

Lawrence of Arabia: The Authorized Biography of T. E. Lawrence, Jeremy Wilson

London Fields, Martin Amis

My Son's Story, Nadine Gordimer

Omeros, Derek Walcott

Possession: A Romance, A. S. Byatt

Rabbit at Rest, John Updike

The Search for Modern China, Jonathan D. Spence

Simone de Beauvoir: A Biography, Deirdre Bair

The Things They Carried, Tim O'Brien

Tropical Gangsters, Robert Klitgaard

Vladimir Nabokov: The Russian Years, Brian Boyd

[*241*]

1991

HARDCOVER BESTSELLERS

fiction

The Firm, John Grisham

Loves Music, Loves to Dance,
Mary Higgins Clark

nonfiction

Iron John: A Book About Men,
Robert Bly

Wealth Without Risk,
Charles J. Givens

PAPERBACK BESTSELLERS

mass market

The Silence of the Lambs,
Thomas Harris

Tie:

The Joy Luck Club, Amy Tan

Dances with Wolves, Michael Blake

trade

7 Habits of Highly Effective People,
Stephen R. Covey

The T-Factor Fat Gram Counter,
Jamie Pope-Cordle and
Martin Katahn

THE ALFRED B. NOBEL PRIZE FOR LITERATURE

Nadine Gordimer, South Africa

NADINE GORDIMER (1923–) was born in the small mining town of Springs, Transvaal, in South Africa, the daughter of a Lithuanian-Jewish watchmaker and an English-born mother. She was educated at a convent and spent a year at Johannesburg's University of Witwatersrand without taking a degree. Gordimer began writing in childhood and as a teenager found what would be her lifelong subject matter: the political situation of her native land and the hypocrisy and impotence of white middle-class liberalism, themes powerfully developed in her prize-winning novels *The Late Bourgeois World* (1966), *The Conservationist* (1977), and *My Son's Story* (1990). Although Gordimer never joined a political party, she became a visible opponent to the apartheid regime and an active campaigner against censorship. She was awarded the 1991 **Nobel Prize in Literature**.

DEATHS

Graham Greene
Jerzy Kosinski
Dr. Seuss
Isaac Bashevis Singer

cartoonist for magazines and advertising agencies and as a writer and animator in Hollywood, and when his first children's book, *And to Think That I Saw It on Mulberry Street* (1937), was published he took the pseudonym Dr. Seuss in a humorous reference to his abandoned academic title. This was followed by many more comic storybooks, and in 1957 by a Random House "Beginner Book" series, starting with *The Cat in the Hat*, which by 1970 sold thirty million copies and revolutionized the juvenile book industry. Dr. Seuss is one of the best-loved children's book writers of our time; his classics, such as *How the Grinch Stole Christmas* (1957) and *Green Eggs and Ham* (1963), are favorites of children and parents alike.

DR. SEUSS (1904–1991) was born Theodor Seuss Geisel in Springfield, Massachusetts, to German-American parents. Educated at Dartmouth, he pursued a doctorate in English at Oxford, but was advised by his fellow student and future wife to be an illustrator. He first worked as a freelance

Pulitzer Prize winner John Updike

[243]

THE NATIONAL BOOK AWARDS

fiction
Norman Rush, *Mating*

nonfiction
Orlando Patterson, *Freedom*

poetry
Philip Levine, *What Work Is*

THE NATIONAL BOOK CRITICS CIRCLE AWARDS

fiction
A Thousand Acres, Jane Smiley

nonfiction
Backlash: The Undeclared War Against American Women, Susan Faludi

biography or autobiography
Patrimony: A True Story, Philip Roth

poetry
Heaven and Earth: A Cosmology, Albert Goldbarth

criticism
Holocaust Testimonies: The Ruins of Memory, Lawrence L. Langer

GRAHAM GREENE (1904–1991) was educated at Berkhamsted School where his father was headmaster. During his troubled adolescence, he poisoned himself, underwent psychoanalysis, and played Russian roulette with his brother's revolver. Greene's first book of verse was published the year he left Balliol College, Oxford. From there, he worked as a subeditor at *The Times*, converted to Roman Catholicism to marry, and published his first novel, *The Man Within* (1929), a tale of nineteenth-century smuggling. Beginning in the 1930s, he traveled widely in dangerous and politically unstable parts of the world, such as Liberia, Mexico, and Sierra Leone, where during the war he joined Kim Philby as an MI6 agent, the basis for his famous novel *The Heart of the Matter* (1948). In the 1940s and 1950s, his roamings brought him to the Far East, Africa, and Latin America, where an attraction to left-wing politics (and a hostility to the United States) was reflected in his friendships with Fidel Castro and Daniel Ortega. Greene died in England a few years after winning the Order of Merit.

This is a book about farming in America, the loss of family farms, the force of the family itself. It is intimate and involving. What, Ms. Smiley asks, is it to be a true daughter? And what is the price to be paid for trying one's whole life to please a proud father ...

Ron Carlson, review of
A Thousand Acres
by Jane Smiley,
NY Times Book Review,
November 3, 1991

Isaac Bashevis Singer
Winner of the Nobel Prize in Literature

Scum

JERZY KOSINSKI (1933-1991) was six when Hitler invaded his native Poland and his Jewish parents placed him in foster care. Thereafter, his early biographical details are unclear. According to his famous novel, *Painted Bird* (1965), he spent five boyhood years wandering the countryside of war-torn Eastern Europe, alone and under ferocious racial attack. The novel was initially read as autobiographical and a Holocaust testament but later regarded as a product of Kosinski's facile imagination. Kosinski once said: "The whole didactic point of my novels is how you redeem yourself if you are threatened by the chances of daily life." He nevertheless was a survivor; while a student in Lodz, he falsified academic sponsorship to "conduct research" on the United States, arriving in New York in 1957, a penniless immigrant. But within a year, he was studying at Columbia and within three had married a fabulously wealthy young widow. His first three books on collective behavior under communism became bestsellers, as were several of his later novels, including *Being There* (1970). Kosinski ended his own life in 1991, many believe because he could not reconcile the horrific events of his childhood.

EDITOR'S CHOICE
the new york times best books of the year

Complete Collected Stories,
V. S. Pritchett

Consciousness Explained,
Daniel C. Dennett

Holocaust Testimonies: The Ruins of Memory, Lawrence L. Langer

The Journals of John Cheever,
John Cheever

A Life of Picasso: Volume One, 1881-1906, John Richardson, with the collaboration of Marilyn McCully

Mating, Norman Rush

Maus, A Survivor's Tale II: And Here My Troubles Began, Art Spiegelman

The Truth About Chernobyl, Grigory Medvedev, Translated by Evelyn Rossiter

Two Lives: "Reading Turgenev" and "My House in Umbria," William Trevor

Wartime Lies, Louis Begley

1992

ALEX HALEY (1921–1992) was born in Ithaca, New York, and raised in Henning, Tennessee, amidst an extended family who exchanged stories about their ancestors—in particular, a man named Kunta Kinte who was kidnapped into slavery in West Africa. Haley first started writing at sea, while working for the U.S. Coast Guard, and over the course of his twenty-year career rose to the rank of the Guard's chief journalist. But by 1959 he had become tired of that life and decided to try his luck as a freelance journalist. It was on one of his early magazine assignments that Haley first met Malcolm X, whom he convinced to write an autobiography. *The Autobiography of Malcolm X* (1965), which Haley authored, stands today as perhaps the most important political memoir in twentieth-century African-American history. It made Haley into a national figure and soon inspired him to conduct his own autobiographical research, the result of which was *Roots* (1976), a riveting historical portrait of Kunta Kinte and his descendants. *Roots* went on to sell eight million copies, was awarded Spingarn and Pulitzer prizes as well as the National Book Award, and became the basis for a groundbreaking mini-series of the same name.

DEATHS

John E. Alcorn
Isaac Asimov
Red Barber
Angela Carter
M. F. K. Fisher
Alex Haley
S. I. Hayakawa
Ben Maddow
Ralph Manheim
James Marshall
Richard Yates

Isaac Asimov

THE ALFRED B. NOBEL PRIZE FOR LITERATURE

Derek Walcott, Trinidad

THE PULITZER PRIZES

fiction

A Thousand Acres, Jane Smiley

nonfiction

The Prize: The Epic Quest for Oil, Daniel Yergin

biography or autobiography

Fortunate Son: The Healing of a Vietnam Vet, Lewis B. Puller, Jr.

poetry

Selected Poems, James Tate

drama

The Kentucky Cycle, Robert Schenkkan

THE PEN/FAULKNER AWARD

Mao II, Don DeLillo

THE BOOKER PRIZE

The English Patient, Michael Ondaatje

Sacred Hunger, Barry Unsworth

THE NEWBERY MEDAL

Shiloh, Phyllis Reynolds Naylor

THE CALDECOTT MEDAL

Tuesday, David Wiesner

[*247*]

THE NATIONAL BOOK AWARDS

fiction

Cormac McCarthy,
All the Pretty Horses

nonfiction

Paul Monette,
Becoming a Man: Half a Life Story

poetry

Mary Oliver, *New and Selected Poems*

THE NATIONAL BOOK CRITICS CIRCLE AWARDS

fiction

All the Pretty Horses,
Cormac McCarthy

nonfiction

Young Men and Fire,
Norman Maclean

biography or autobiography

Writing Dangerously: Mary McCarthy and Her World, Carol Brightman

poetry

Collected Poems, 1946-1991,
Hayden Carruth

eventually earned her Ph.D. and today teaches. Her early short stories were published in the *Atlantic* and *Mademoiselle,* and she first gained attention with her story "Lily," which was given an O. Henry Award and published along with the novella *The Age of Grief* (1987). Smiley gained further acclamation for *A Thousand Acres*, a modern reworking of *King Lear* depicting a dysfunctional Midwestern farming family. The novel was awarded a 1992 **Pulitzer Prize** and the 1991 National Book Critics Circle Award, and since has won her a following of devoted readers concerned with rural themes and the fracturing of the American family.

EDITOR'S CHOICE
the new york times best books of the year

The Ant and the Peacock: Altruism and Sexual Selection from Darwin to Today, Helena Cronin

The English Patient,
Michael Ondaatje

Jazz, Toni Morrison

Kissinger: A Biography,
Walter Isaacson

Lincoln at Gettysburg: The Words That Remade America, Garry Wills

The Lost Upland, W. S. Merwin

Outerbridge Reach, Robert Stone

Regeneration, Pat Barker

Young Men and Fire,
Norman Maclean

JANE SMILEY (1952–) was born in Los Angeles, but grew up in St. Louis, Missouri. After graduating from Vassar College and spending a year in England digging on an archeological site, she moved with her first husband to Iowa where she worked in a toy factory. Smiley began her literary career at the Writers' Workshop at the University of Iowa, where she

The doomed 18th-century love affair of Lady Hamilton and Lord Nelson seems an improbable subject for Susan Sontag, famed explicator of the avant-garde . . . In fact, one thing that makes "The Volcano Lover" such a delight to read is the way it throws off ideas and intellectual sparks like a Roman candle.

Michiko Kakutani, review of
The Volcano Lover
by Susan Sontag,
NY Times Book Review,
March 24, 1992

CORMAC MCCARTHY (1933–) was born in Providence, Rhode Island, but grew up in the South, where all of his novels are set. After graduating from high school in Knoxville, Tennessee, he matriculated at the University of Tennessee, but stayed only a year. Little is known about McCarthy—his views on fiction or his personal life—because he rarely gives interviews and will not lecture. Perhaps this is why he is something of a cult figure. His novels, with the exception of the award-winning *All the Pretty Horses* (1992), however, are not widely read, considered difficult, and stigmatized as "writer's writing." Nonetheless, he often is compared to the great Southern American authors William Faulkner, Flannery O'Connor, and Carson McCullers, and is continually cited as "the best undiscovered novelist of his generation." He lives in El Paso, Texas, where he is working on the third volume of his Border Trilogy, the second book of which was *The Crossing* (1994).

[*249*]

An unforgettable journey: part literary, part adventure, part romance, part dream.

Herbert Mitgang, review of
All The Pretty Horses
by Cormac McCarthy,
NY Times Book Review,
May 27, 1992

1993

HARDCOVER BESTSELLERS

fiction

The Bridges of Madison County,
Robert James Waller

The Client, John Grisham

nonfiction

Women Who Run with the Wolves,
Clarissa Pinkola Estés

The Way Things Ought to Be,
Rush Limbaugh

PAPERBACK BESTSELLERS

mass market

A Time to Kill, John Grisham

The Pelican Brief, John Grisham

trade

7 Habits of Highly Effective People,
Stephen R. Covey

Life's Little Instruction Book,
Stephen H. Jackson Brown, Jr.

THE ALFRED B. NOBEL PRIZE FOR LITERATURE

Toni Morrison, U.S.

THE PULITZER PRIZES

fiction

*A Good Scent from a Strange
Mountain*, Robert Olen Butler

nonfiction

Lincoln at Gettysburg, Garry Willis

biography or autobiography

Truman, David McCullough

poetry

The Wild Iris, Louise Glück

drama

*Angels in America: Millennium
Approaches*, Tony Kushner

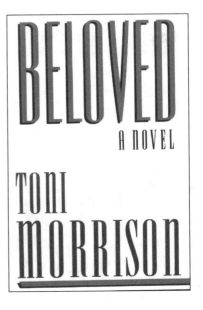

TONI MORRISON (1931–) was born
Chloe Anthony Wafford in an Ohio
steel mill town, the daughter of black
sharecroppers from the South who had
lost their land and moved to work in
the North's mills and mines. She read
voraciously as a child, and in 1949
went to Howard University where,
after a course at Cornell, she returned
to teach English. After the breakup of

her marriage, Morrison began writing, which resulted in her first book, *The Bluest Eye* (1970). From there she moved to New York, and, while supporting two sons and writing fiction, became a senior editor at Random House, where she furthered the careers of other female black writers. Morrison, who won the 1993 **Nobel Prize**, the first awarded to an African-American woman, has been hailed for her courage of subject matter and extraordinary, lyrical language, comparable to the blues, black folk rhythms, Joyce, and Faulkner. Her fifth novel, *Beloved*, which deals with slavery and infanticide, was awarded the 1988 Pulitzer Prize.

THE PEN/FAULKNER AWARD
Postcards, E. Annie Proulx

THE BOOKER PRIZE
Paddy Clarke Ha Ha Ha,
Roddy Doyle

THE NEWBERY MEDAL
Missing May, Cynthia Rylant

THE CALDECOTT MEDAL
Mirette on the High Wire,
Emily Arnold McCully

THE NATIONAL BOOK AWARDS
fiction
E. Annie Proulx, *The Shipping News*

nonfiction
Gore Vidal,
United States: Essays 1952-1992

poetry
A. R. Ammons, *Garbage*

THE NATIONAL BOOK CRITICS CIRCLE AWARDS
fiction
A Lesson Before Dying,
Ernest J. Gaines

nonfiction
Land Where Blues Began,
Alan Lomax

biography or autobiography
Genet, Edmund White

poetry
My Alexandria, Mark Doty

criticism
Opera in America, John Dizikes

GORE VIDAL (1925–) was born in West Point, New York, but was raised in Washington, D.C., in the home of his scholarly, witty grandfather, Senator Thomas Gore. After an undistinguished education at Philips Exeter Academy, Vidal joined the U.S. Army, which gave him material for his first novel, *Williwaw* (1946), written when he was nineteen. Though unsuccessful, the novel prompted Vidal to write more novels, including *The City and the Pillar* (1948), the shocking story of a homosexual boy (Vidal claimed it was the first of its genre), and *Myra*

[*251*]

Breckinridge (1968), also an attack on sexual norms, and work for television in the hopes of making a quick fortune. In 1960, Vidal came extremely close to winning a New York State congressional seat, the loss of which convinced him to remain a novelist and political commentator. He is best known for his work as a dissenting insider and an unconventional Democrat; his books *Burr* (1974), *Creation* (1981), *Lincoln* (1984), and recent autobiography *Palimpsest* (1995) have all been bestsellers. *United States: Essays 1952-1992* won the 1993 **National Book Award**.

Bestselling author Howard Stern announces his candidacy for governor of New York.

DEATHS
Anthony Burgess
William Golding
John Hersey
William Shirer
Wallace Stegner

Pulitzer Prize winner, Truman *by David McCullough*

EDITOR'S CHOICE
the new york times best books of the year

Across the Bridge: Stories, Mavis Gallant

Balkan Ghosts: A Journey Through History, Robert D. Kaplan

Before Night Falls, Reinoldo Arenas

The Collected Stories, William Trevor

The Fate of the Elephant, Douglas H. Chadwick

The Island: Three Tales, Gustaw Herling

Jesus' Son: Stories, Denis Johnson

Judge on Trial, Ivan Klíma

The Last Panda, George B. Schaller

Lenin's Tomb: The Last Days of the Soviet Empire, David Remnick

Mazurka for Two Dead Men, Camilo José Cela

A Moment of War: A Memoir of the Spanish War, Laurie Lee

Shylock: A Legend and Its Legacy, John Gross

Travels with Lizbeth, Lars Eighner

1994

HARDCOVER BESTSELLERS

fiction

The Bridges of Madison County,
Robert James Waller

The Celestine Prophecy,
James Redfield

nonfiction

Men Are from Mars, Women Are from Venus, John Gray

The Book of Virtues,
William J. Bennett

PAPERBACK BESTSELLERS

mass market

The Client, John Grisham

Without Remorse, Tom Clancy

trade

The Road Less Traveled,
M. Scott Peck, M.D.

7 Habits of Highly Effective People,
Stephen R. Covey

THE ALFRED B. NOBEL PRIZE FOR LITERATURE

Kenzaburo Oe, Japan

THE PULITZER PRIZES

fiction

The Shipping News, E. Annie Proulx

nonfiction

Lenin's Tomb: The Last Days of the Soviet Empire, David Remnick

biography or autobiography

W. E. B. Du Bois: Biography of a Race, 1868-1919, David Levering Lewis

poetry

Neon Vernacular, Yusef Komunyakaa

drama

Three Tall Women, Edward Albee

KENZABURO OE (1935-) was born in Ehime, Shikoku, and came of age during twentieth-century Japan's most politically unstable period. August 15, 1945, was a pivotal day in his life, for it was then he realized that Emperor Hirohito was no living god but an "ordinary" human. Oe has been politically active since his student days; he has fiercely opposed war, nuclear weapons, racism, and the "Emperor system." (In 1994, he refused the government-awarded Order of Culture). Although he has offended many Japanese with his unveiled rebellion against traditional values and his unconventional writing style, Oe is one of Japan's most widely read authors, "touted," as his translator John Nathan explains, "as their answer to Mailer, their send-up on Sartre, their oriental version of Henry Miller." Oe's novels, notably *A Personal Matter* (1964, 1968) and *The Pinch Runner Memorandum* (1976, 1995), have been

[*253*]

strongly influenced by his son Hikari, who was born brain damaged. Through Hikari, he has examined Japanese notions of shame and trauma, especially as experienced by the events of World War II. Since winning the 1994 **Nobel Prize**, Oe's work has been translated into English and is slowly gaining an international readership.

THE PEN/FAULKNER AWARD

Operation Shylock, Philip Roth

THE BOOKER PRIZE

How Late It Was, How Late, James Kelman

THE NEWBERY MEDAL

The Giver, Lois Lowry

THE CALDECOTT MEDAL

Grandfather's Journey, Allen Say

THE NATIONAL BOOK AWARDS

fiction
William Gaddis, *A Frolic of His Own*

nonfiction
Sherwin B. Nuland, *How We Die: Reflections on Life's Final Chapter*

poetry
James Tate, *Worshipful Company of Fletchers*

THE NATIONAL BOOK CRITICS CIRCLE AWARDS

fiction
The Stone Diaries, Carol Shields

nonfiction
The Rape of Europa: The Fate of Europe's Treasures in the Third Reich and the Second World War, Lynn H. Nicholas

biography or autobiography
Shot in the Heart, Mikal Gilmore

poetry
Rider, Mark Rudman

criticism
The Culture of Bruising: Essays on Prizefighting, Literature and Modern American Culture, Gerald Early

RALPH ELLISON (1914–1994) was born in Oklahoma City, the grandson of slaves. When he was three, his father died and his mother found work as a maid for a white family, whose discarded magazines and records served as Ellison's first cultural inspirations. Ellison studied music at Tuskegee Institute in Alabama, but, short of funds, left college and went north to New York City. There he met the black writers Richard Wright and Langston Hughes and worked on the Federal Writers' Project. A fellowship received after he returned from World War II allowed Ellison to write his only novel, *Invisible Man* (1952), which won a National Book Award and is perhaps the most influential mid-century novel written about the African-American experience. Though revered as a great author and embraced by academia, Ellison eventually disappointed many readers by not publishing more fiction. Two volumes of essays were published in his lifetime, and a posthumous collection of early, mostly disappointing, short stories appeared in 1996.

EDITOR'S CHOICE
the new york times best books of the year

Balzac: A Life, Graham Robb

Conquest: Montezuma, Cortés, and the Fall of Old Mexico, Hugh Thomas

A Frolic of His Own, William Gaddis

In the Lake of the Woods, Tim O'Brien

The Language Instinct, Steven Pinker

The Moral Animal: Evolutionary Psychology and Everyday Life, Robert Wright

Naturalist, Edward O. Wilson

Open Secrets: Stories, Alice Munro

Stalin and the Bomb: The Soviet Union and Atomic Energy, 1939-1956, David Holloway

A Way in the World, V. S. Naipaul

W. E. B. Du Bois: Biography of a Race, 1868-1919, David Levering Lewis

---

In E. Annie Proulx's vigorous, quirky novel "The Shipping News," set in present-day Newfoundland, there are indeed a lot of drownings. The main characters are plagued by dangerous undercurrents, both in the physical world and in their own minds . . . Throughout "The Shipping News" the sinuousness of her prose seems to correspond physically with the textures of the weather and the sea . . . while the novel displays Ms. Proulx's surreal humor and her zest for the strange foibles of humanity.

Howard Norman, review of
The Shipping News
by E. Annie Proulx,
NY Times Book Review,
April 13, 1993
(1994 Pulitzer Prize winner)

[*255*]

DEATHS
Pierre Boulle
James Clavell
Ralph Ellison
Eugéne Ionesco
Richard Scarry

1995

HARDCOVER BESTSELLERS

fiction

The Celestine Prophecy,
James Redfield

The Bridges of Madison County,
Robert James Waller

nonfiction

Men Are from Mars, Women Are from Venus, John Gray

Midnight in the Garden of Good and Evil, John Berendt

PAPERBACK BESTSELLERS

mass market

The Alienist, Caleb Carr

The Chamber, John Grisham

trade

7 Habits of Highly Effective People,
Stephen R. Covey

Chicken Soup for the Soul,
Jack Canfield and Mark Hansen, eds.

SEAMUS HEANEY (1939-) was born near Castledawson, County Derry, Ireland, and grew up on his father's farm. Educated at Queen's University, Belfast, Heaney began lecturing in English in 1966 and soon became associated with the emergence of Ulster poetry. His first collections, notably *Death of a Naturalist* (1966), were of a pastoral nature, harkening to his farming background. And it was not until his 1972 and 1975 collections, *Wintering Out* and *North,* that he began to address the Northern Irish Troubles. Heaney has been acclaimed as the finest Irish poet since W. B. Yeats, and like Yeats has found artistic enlivenment in the dilemmas and contrasts of Irish Catholic identity and an allegiance to the English literary tradition. He writes in what one critic describes as a "trustworthy, declarative voice." Since 1985, he has served as Boylston Professor of Rhetoric and Oratory at Harvard University, and between 1989 and 1994 held the coveted Professorship of Poetry at Oxford University. He was awarded the 1995 **Nobel Prize for Literature**.

THE ALFRED B. NOBEL PRIZE FOR LITERATURE

Seamus Heaney, Ireland

THE PULITZER PRIZES

fiction

The Stone Diaries, Carol Shields

nonfiction

The Beak of the Finch: A Story of Evolution in Our Time,
Jonathan Weiner

biography or autobiography

Harriet Beecher Stowe: A Life,
Joan D. Hedrick

poetry

The Simple Truth, Philip Levine

drama

The Young Man From Atlanta,
Horton Foote

DEATHS
Kingsley Amis
Robertson Davies
James Herriot
James Merrill
John Osborne
Henry Roth
May Sarton
Stephen Spender

KINGSLEY AMIS (1922–1995) was born in suburban London into a lower-middle-class family, attended City of London School and St. John's College, Oxford, on scholarships, and at an early age developed the voice of an imaginative, defiant comic. His first novel, *Lucky Jim* (1954) was a critical and popular success. In this now-famous novel, Amis depicted a new British social type, what one critic defined as "the angry young man," a lower-middle-class radical lecturer who regards the British power game as ridiculous and immoral. Amis explored similar social themes in his next three novels, and published a collection of poems, *A Look Around the Estate*, in 1967. He also wrote detective and spy novels. In 1986, he was awarded the Booker Prize for *The Old Devils*.

ROBERTSON DAVIES (1913–1995) was born in a "humble dwelling" in Thamesville, Ontario, the son of a poor but enterprising printer who became a senator and newspaper founder. He went to Queen's and Oxford universities, where he developed an interest in theater and an encyclopedic knowledge of Shakespeare, which landed him a job at London's Old Vic Theatre. In 1940, he returned to Toronto, where he worked as literary editor of *Saturday Review*, and later as editor-in-chief of his father's newspaper. *Tempest-Tost*, his first novel, was published in 1951, and became the first volume of the award-winning *The Salterton Trilogy*, which earned him a reputation as a mystical Victorian eccentric. In 1986, *The Cornish Trilogy* was shortlisted for the Booker Prize, gaining him an international readership. Davies remains one of Canada's most beloved authors, and with his Tolstoyan bearing and fondness for spiritualism lives on as a Nordic cult figure.

THE PEN/FAULKNER AWARD
Snow Falling on Cedars,
David Guterson

THE BOOKER PRIZE
The Ghost Road, Pat Barker

THE NEWBERY MEDAL
Walk Two Moons, Sharon Creech

THE CALDECOTT MEDAL
Smoky Night, Eve Bunting,
Illustrated by David Diaz

[257]

THE NATIONAL BOOK AWARDS

fiction

Philip Roth, *Sabbath's Theater*

nonfiction

Tina Rosenberg, *The Haunted Land: Facing Europe's Ghosts After Communism*

poetry

Stanley Kunitz, *Passing Through: Later Poems, New and Selected*

THE NATIONAL BOOK CRITICS CIRCLE AWARDS

fiction

Mrs. Ted Bliss, Stanley Elkin

nonfiction

A Civil Action, Jonathan Harr

biography or autobiography

Savage Art: A Biography of Jim Thompson, Robert Polito

poetry

Time & Money, William Matthews

criticism

The Forbidden Bestsellers of Pre-Revolutionary France, Robert Darnton

EDITOR'S CHOICE

the new york times best books of the year

The Haunted Land: Facing Europe's Ghosts After Communism, Tina Rosenberg

In Confidence, Anatoly Dobrynin

Independence Day, Richard Ford

The Information, Martin Amis

The Island of the Day Before, Umberto Eco, Translated by William Weaver

The Life of Graham Greene, Volume Two: 1939-95, Norman Sherry

Lincoln, David Herbert Donald

Overcoming Law, Richard A. Posner

Sabbath's Theater, Philip Roth

The Stories of Vladimir Nabokov, Dmitri Nabokov, ed.

Zola: A Life, Frederick Brown

Carol Shields, the American-born Canadian novelist and story writer, is often mentioned in the same breath with Margaret Atwood and Alice Munro . . . There is very little in the way of conventional plot here, but its absence does nothing to diminish the narrative compulsion of this novel. Carol Shields has explored the mysteries of life with abandon, taking unusual risks along the way. "The Stone Diaries" reminds us again why literature matters.

Jay Parini, review of
The Stone Diaries
by Carol Shields,
NY Times Book Review,
March 27, 1994
(1995 Pulitzer Prize winner)

1996

HARDCOVER BESTSELLERS
fiction
The Runaway Jury, John Grisham

Executive Orders, Tom Clancy

nonfiction
Making the Connection,
  Oprah Winfrey and Bob Green

*Men Are from Mars, Women Are
  from Venus*, John Gray

PAPERBACK BESTSELLERS
mass market
The Rainmaker, John Grisham

The Green Mile, Stephen King

trade
A Third Serving of Chicken Soup,
  Jack Canfield and Mark Hansen

Snow Falling on Cedars,
  David Guterson

THE ALFRED B. NOBEL PRIZE FOR LITERATURE
Wislawa Szymborska, Poland

THE PULITZER PRIZES
fiction
Independence Day, Richard Ford

nonfiction
*The Haunted Land: Facing Europe's
  Ghosts After Communism*,
  Tina Rosenberg

biography or autobiography
God: A Biography, Jack Miles

JOSEPH BRODSKY (1940-1996) was born in Leningrad to Russian-Jewish parents. The family lived in a typical subdivided communal apartment and Brodsky attended public school until quitting at fifteen. In the following decade, he worked as a machine operator at a cannon factory and at a hospital morgue where he cut and sewed up bodies. He also, like his mother, worked sporadically as a translator. In 1960, Brodsky met the poet Anna Akhmatova, who encouraged his burgeoning career as a subversive and lyrical street poet. Four years later, though, the Soviet authorities arrested and charged him with social parasitism, sentencing him to five years' forced labor in Siberia, which Akhmatova, after publicizing his case abroad, got commuted to eighteen months. Brodsky remained unrepentant, and in 1972 was expelled from the Soviet Union. He lived the rest of his life in the United States, where he led a successful career as a lecturer, essayist, and Russian poet in translation; he was awarded the 1987 Nobel Prize for literature.

[259]

DEATHS
Joseph Brodsky
José Donoso
Margaret E. Rey

THE PEN/FAULKNER AWARD

Independence Day, Richard Ford

THE BOOKER PRIZE

Last Orders, Graham Swift

THE NEWBERY MEDAL

The Midwife's Apprentice,
Karen Cushman

THE CALDECOTT MEDAL

Officer Buckle and Gloria,
Peggy Rathmann

THE NATIONAL BOOK AWARDS

fiction

Andrea Barrett,
Ship Fever and Other Stories

nonfiction

James Carroll, *An American Requiem:
God, My Father, and the War That
Came Between Us*

poetry

Hayden Carruth, *Scrambled Eggs and
Whiskey: Poems 1991-1995*

young people's literature

Victor Martinez,
Parrot in the Oven: Mi Vida

THE NATIONAL BOOK CRITICS CIRCLE AWARDS

fiction

Women in Their Beds, Gina Berriault

nonfiction

Bad Land: An American Romance,
Jonathan Raban

biography or autobiography

Angela's Ashes, Frank McCourt

poetry

Sun Underwood, Robert Hass

criticism

Finding a Form: Essays,
William Gass

GARTH WILLIAMS (1912–1996) was born in New York City, the son of English-born artists; his father drew for *Punch* as well as New York publications. At ten, he moved with his parents to London, where he developed an interest in painting and sculpture, later studying at the Royal College of Art. As a young man, he organized the Luton Art School and painted murals to earn money until 1936, when he was awarded the British Prix de Rome for sculpture. World War II disrupted Williams' blossoming art career. In 1941, after suffering a back injury during the London blitz, he returned to the United States and began working as a children's book illustrator and cartoonist for *The New Yorker*. Williams is best known for his illustrations of books by E. B. White, such as *Stuart Little* (1945) and *Charlotte's Web* (1952), but he also wrote over a dozen children's books of his own, graced by his winsome illustrations.

EDITOR'S CHOICE
the new york times best books of the year

After Rain, William Trevor

Angela's Ashes: A Memoir,
Frank McCourt

Bad Land, Jonathan Raban

*The Collected Stories of Mavis
Gallant,* Mavis Gallant

*The Life of Nelson A. Rockefeller:
Worlds to Conquer 1908–1958,*
Cary Reich

The Moor's Last Sigh,
Salman Rushdie

Selected Stories, Alice Munro

*The Song of the Dodo Island Biogeog-
raphy in an Age of Extinctions,*
David Quammen

Mavis Gallant's "Collected Stories" make abundantly clear just what an ambitous, and accomplished, anomaly she has always been . . . [Her] bold disregard of momentum and tight plot . . . is not just her method but her theme. She is a wanderingly yet acutely watchful narrator whose underlying message is that we are all destined to meander, self-destructively misinter-preting as we go . . . [She] has dared to drift in a disorienting century, always trusting her own imaginative compass

Review of
*The Collected Stories of
Mavis Gallant,*
NY Times Book Review,
December 8, 1996

This first volume of this over-size but vivid account of Nelson Rockefeller's life is the story of one long and spectaculary successful lunge for power . . . This portrait of a maddeningly elusive char-acter is probably as nuanced as any we will ever get . . . Except in style, this book might be a robust eighteenth century novel.

Review of
The Life of Nelson Rockefeller
by Cary Reich,
NY Times Book Review,
December 8, 1996

His recollections of child-hood are mournful and humorous, angry and for-giving . . . Mr. McCourt's voice is that of a fine Irish-American raconteur, aware of his charm but diffident about it, and he casts a spell with a memorable story induced by powerful circumstances.

Review of
Angela's Ashes
by Frank McCourt,
NY Times Book Review,
December 8, 1996

[*261*]

The Prizes

BESTSELLERS

The term "bestseller" was popularized in 1895 when Harry Thurston Peck, editor of the magazine *The Bookman,* began printing monthly lists of the nation's bestselling books. A book may be a bestseller in one store, one city, or for the whole country for a month, a year or, in the case of the Bible, for a century. Today, however, the publishing trade magazine *Publishers Weekly* and national newspapers, particularly *The New York Times*, set the standard for which books are regarded as bestsellers. A book is commonly considered a bestseller if its hardcover sales reach 100,000 and its paperback sales top 1,000,000.

THE NOBEL PRIZE FOR LITERATURE

Established and endowed by the will of Alfred B. Nobel, the Swedish inventor of dynamite, the Nobel Prize for Literature is the most prestigious and lucrative of all literary awards. Since 1901, it has been given annually (with the exception of 1914, 1940, 1941, and 1943) to prose and poetry writers who have achieved an outstanding body of work. Nobel laureates receive a gold medal and a monetary award worth nearly $1 million, in addition to an almost instant international readership, which is perhaps the prize's most significant outcome for its awardees. The prize is judged by members of the Swedish Academy of Literature, and award ceremonies are held in Stockholm on December 10 each year, in honor of Nobel's birthday.

THE PULITZER PRIZE

The Pulitzer Prizes were named for and endowed by Joseph Pulitzer, a Hungarian immigrant and renowned nineteenth-century newspaper publisher. Since 1917, awards have been given annually by Columbia University on the recommendation of a Pulitzer Prize board for achievement in American journalism, letters, drama, and music. The prizes in literature are for fiction, history, biography or autobiography, drama, poetry, and general nonfiction (the last two categories were not created until 1922 and 1962 respectively), and often honor books that explore American themes. Occasionally, the Pulitzer board will decide not to award a prize in a particular category. Winners receive a certificate and a five-thousand-dollar honorarium at an award ceremony held at Columbia University every spring.

THE NATIONAL BOOK AWARD

The National Book Award was initiated in 1950 by the Book Manufacturers Institute, the American Book Publishers Council, and the American Booksellers Association as a means to draw attention to exceptional works of fiction, nonfiction, and poetry by American authors. Originally run by volunteers from the publicity departments of publishing houses, the National Book Award today is administered by the National Book Foundation, which also promotes reading in the United States through author events and fundraising for literary programs. Today's prizes are given in four genres: fiction, nonfiction, poetry, and young people's literature, and every November winners receive a ten-thousand-dollar cash award at a gala benefiting the educational programs of the National Book Foundation.

THE PEN/FAULKNER AWARD

Named for William Faulkner, who used his Nobel Prize earnings to create an award for young fiction writers, and affiliated with PEN (Poets, Playwrights, Editors, Essayists and Novelists), the international writers' organization, the PEN/Faulkner Award was founded in 1980 by writers who wished to honor their peers. Every year, the award judges, who are themselves fiction writers, each read more than 250 novels and short story collections, and select five books, awarding fifteen thousand dollars to the author of the winning title and five thousand dollars to the four authors whose books are short-listed. In May, all five authors read from their works and are honored at an award ceremony held at the Folger Library.

THE BOOKER PRIZE

The UK's most prestigious literary prize, the Booker Prize is awarded annually to the best full-length novel written in English by a citizen of the U.K., the Commonwealth, the Republic of Ireland, Pakistan, or South Africa. Sponsored by the British Food Conglomerate of the same name and administered by the National Book League in England, the prize today comes with a monetary award equivalent to thirty thousand dollars. Prize-winning books have often been described as impenetrable or difficult, which likely stems from the fact that the Booker is judged by a committee of authors whose literary tastes are far-ranging. Nonetheless, the prize, which was established in 1969, has been credited with spurring on average a fivefold increase in sales.

THE NEWBERY MEDAL

Named for the eighteenth-century Englishman John Newbery, the first publisher and seller of children's books, the Newbery Medal is given annually by the

American Library Association to the most distinguished and original book written for children. Initiated in 1921 by Children's Librarians' Section of the ALA, the award today is the oldest children's book award in the world and, together with the Caldecott Medal, continues to be the best known and most influential children's book award in the country.

THE CALDECOTT MEDAL

Named for the English illustrator Randolph Caldecott, the author and illustrator of *The House That Jack Built* and *The Grand Panjandrum Himself*, this award was created in 1937 by the American Library Association to honor illustrators of children's books. It is given annually to the artist of the most outstanding American children's picture book published the previous year and, like the Newbery Medal, is considered one of the highest achievements in children's literature.

THE NATIONAL BOOK CRITICS CIRCLE AWARD

Considered the critics' pick, the National Book Critics Circle Award is the annual prize of the National Book Critics Circle, which was founded in 1974 to enable professional book critics and book review editors to collaborate and communicate with one another about common concerns. Since 1975, awards have been made in five categories—fiction, general nonfiction, autobiography/biography, poetry, and criticism—usually to established writers with a following. The NBCC is a non-cash award; winners receive a scroll and a citation as well as the honor of national critics' approbation.

The American Poet Laureate

In 1985, following in the tradition of the centuries-old British literary title, the U.S. Congress established an American poet laureateship, elevating what had previously been the position of poetry consultant of the Library of Congress. For more than a decade now, the post has been awarded yearly by the librarian of Congress to an American poet of eminent stature. The American poet laureate is not obligated to write any verse or organize any specific activities during his or her one-, occasionally two-, year term, but past poet laureates have been known to use their position to promote poetry readings, poetry publications, and literacy campaigns.

1986-1987
Robert Penn Warren

1991-1992
Joseph Brodsky

1987-1988
Richard Wilbur

1992-1993
Mona Van Duyn

1988-1990
Howard Nemerov

1993-1995
Rita Dove

1990-1991
Mark Strand

1995-1996
Robert Hass

Required Reading

From Anthony Burgess:

In 1984, the British author Anthony Burgess took it upon himself to compile a list of the best ninety-nine novels published in English since 1939. In his introduction, he wrote: "all the novelists listed . . . have added something to our knowledge of the human condition (sleeping or waking), have managed language well, have clarified the motivations of action, and have sometimes expanded the bounds of the imagination." The list is reprinted here for your perusal.

1939
Party Going, Henry Green
After Many a Summer, Aldous Huxley
Finnegans Wake, James Joyce
At Swim Two Birds, Flann O'Brien

1940
The Power and the Glory,
  Graham Greene
For Whom the Bell Tolls,
  Ernest Hemingway
Strangers and Brothers, C. P. Snow

1941
The Aerodrome, Rex Warner

1944
The Horse's Mouth, Joyce Cary
The Razor's Edge,
  W. Somerset Maugham

1945
Brideshead Revisited, Evelyn Waugh

1946
Titus Groan, Mervyn Peake

1947
The Victim, Saul Bellow
Under the Volcano, Malcolm Lowry

1948
The Heart of the Matter,
  Graham Greene
Ape and Essence, Aldous Huxley
The Naked and the Dead,
  Norman Mailer
No Highway, Nevil Shute

1949
The Heat of the Day, Elizabeth Bowen
1984, George Orwell
The Body, William Sansom

1950
Scenes from Provincial Life,
  William Cooper
The Disenchanted, Budd Schulberg

1951

A Dance to the Music of Time,
  Anthony Powell
The Catcher in the Rye, J. D. Salinger
A Chronicle of Ancient Sunlight,
  Henry Williamson
The Caine Mutiny, Herman Wouk

1952

Invisible Man, Ralph Ellison
The Old Man and the Sea,
  Ernest Hemingway
The Groves of Academe,
  Mary McCarthy
Wise Blood, Flannery O'Connor
Sword of Honour, Evelyn Waugh

1953

The Long Goodbye,
  Raymond Chandler

1954

Lucky Jim, Kingsley Amis

1957

Room at the Top, John Braine
The Alexandria Quartet, Lawrence
  Durrell
The London Novels, Colin MacInnes
The Assistant, Bernard Malamud

1958

The Bell, Iris Murdoch
Saturday Night and Sunday Morning,
  Alan Sillitoe
The Once and Future King, T. H. White

1959

The Mansion, William Faulkner
Goldfinger, Ian Fleming

1960

Facial Justice, L. P. Hartley
The Balkan Trilogy, Olivia Manning

1961

The Mighty and Their Fall,
  Ivy Compton-Burnett
Catch-22, Joseph Heller
The Fox in the Attic, Richard Hughes
The Old Men at the Zoo, Angus Wilson

1962

Another Country, James Baldwin
An Error of Judgment,
  Pamela Hansford Johnson
Island, Aldous Huxley
The Golden Notebook, Doris Lessing
Pale Fire, Vladimir Nabokov

1963

The Girls of Slender Means,
  Muriel Spark

1964

The Spire, William Golding
Heartland, Wilson Harris
A Single Man, Christopher Isherwood
The Defense, Vladimir Nabokov
Late Call, Angus Wilson

1965

The Lockwood Concern, John O'Hara
The Mandelbaum Gate, Muriel Spark

1966

A Man of the People, Chinua Achebe
The Anti-Death League, Kingsley Amis
Giles Goat-Boy, John Barth
The Late Bourgeois World,
  Nadine Gordimer
The Last Gentleman, Walker Percy

from anthony burgess

1967
The Vendor of Sweets, R. K. Narayan

1968
The Image Men, J. B. Priestley
Cocksure, Mordecai Richler
Pavane, Keith Roberts

1969
The French Lieutenant's Woman,
  John Fowles
Portnoy's Complaint, Philip Roth

1970
Bomber, Len Deighton

1973
Sweet Dreams, Michael Frayn
Gravity's Rainbow, Thomas Pynchon

1975
Humboldt's Gift, Saul Bellow
The History Man, Malcolm Bradbury

1976
The Doctor's Wife, Brian Moore
Falstaff, Robert Nye

1977
How to Save Your Own Life, Erica Jong
Farewell Companions, James Plunkett
Staying On, Paul Scott

1978
The Coup, John Updike

1979
The Unlimited Dream Company,
  J. G. Ballard
Dubin's Lives, Bernard Malamud
A Bend in the River, V. S. Naipaul
Sophie's Choice, William Styron

1980
Life in the West, Brian Aldiss
Riddley Walker, Russell Hoban
How Far Can You Go?, David Lodge
A Confederacy of Dunces,
  John Kennedy Toole

1981
Lanark, Alasdair Gray
Darconville's Cat, Alexander Theroux
The Mosquito Coast, Paul Theroux

1982
The Rebel Angels, Robertson Davies

1983
Ancient Evenings, Norman Mailer

(source: *The Book of Literary Lists*,
  Nicholas Parsons)

Controversial Books

CHALLENGED BOOKS

The following list of the most frequently challenged books in the 1995-1996 academic year was compiled by People for the American Way, a nonprofit organization that defends "pluralism, individuality, freedom of thought, expression and religion, a sense of community, and tolerance and compassion to others." Since 1983, People for the American Way has tracked censorship activities in American schools and libraries as part of its mission to promote freedom of education.

I Know Why the Caged Bird Sings, Maya Angelou
The Giver, Louis Lowry
The Adventures of Huckleberry Finn, Mark Twain
Of Mice and Men, John Steinbeck
The Color Purple, Alice Walker
The Chocolate War, Robert Cormier
Go Ask Alice, Anonymous
The Catcher in the Rye, J. D. Salinger
A Day No Pigs Would Die, Robert Newton Peck
Native Son, Richard Wright
My Brother Sam Is Dead, Christopher and James Lincoln Collier
The Bridge to Terabithia, Katherine Paterson

BANNED BOOKS

Since 250 B.C., when Confucius' work was banned by the First Ts'in Emperor for its political viewpoints, books have been censored. In A.D. 35, Homer's *The Odyssey* was banned by Caligula for inappropriately expressing Greek notions of freedom, and fourteen centuries later all of Dante's work was burned by Savonarola, the reason being: "Vanities." The following list, reprinted from *The Book of Literary Lists* by Nicholas Parsons, documents books by great authors that were banned in the first half of the twentieth century.

YEAR	WORKS BANNED	AUTHORS	REASONS	CENSORS
1911	*Love stories and plays*	Gabriele D'Annunzio	Immoral	Papal Index
1914	*Droll Stories*	Honoré de Balzac	Immoral	Canadian Customs
1914	All Works	Maurice Maeterlink	Immoral and irreligious	Papal Index
1915	*Family Limitation*	Margaret Sanger	Immoral	New York courts
1918	*Ulysses*	James Joyce	Obscene	U.S. Post Office, Irish authorities, Canadian authorities, British Customs
1922	All works	Anatole France	Immoral	British authorities
1923	*Family Limitations*	Margaret Sanger	Immoral	British authorities
1925	*On the Origin of Species*	Charles Darwin	Immoral and irreligious	State of Tennessee
1926	*On the Origin of Species*	Charles Darwin	Immoral	Soviet government
1926	All philosophical works	René Descartes	Subversive	Soviet government
1926	All works	Leo Tolstoy	Immoral and subversive	Hungarian goverment
1927	*The State and Revolution*	Lenin	Obscene and subversive	Boston authorities in U.S., Hungarian goverment
1927	*Elmer Gantry*	Sinclair Lewis	Obscene	Boston authorities
1928	All works	Immanuel Kant	Politically unsound	Russian government
1928	*Proletarian Revolution in Russia*	Lenin	Subversive	Canadian government
1928	*Well of Loneliness*	Radclyffe Hall	Obscene	British authorities
1929	*The Adventures of Sherlock Holmes*	Arthur Conan Doyle	Occultism	Soviet government
1929	*A Farewell to Arms*	Ernest Hemingway	Frank account of Caporetto	Italian government
1929	*Ulysses*	James Joyce	Obscene	British courts
1929	*The Rainbow* and *Lady Chatterly's Lover*	D. H. Lawrence	Obscene	British authorities

banned books

Year	Works Banned	Authors	Reasons	Censors
1929	*Ars Amatoria*	Ovid	Erotic	San Francisco authorities
1929	*Confessions*	Jean Jacques Rousseau	Impious and immoral	U.S. Customs
1929	All works	Emile Zola	Immoral	Yugoslav government
1930	*The Sun Also Rises*	Ernest Hemingway	Immoral	Boston authorities
1930	*Antic Hay*	Aldous Huxley	Obscene	Boston authorities
1930	*Point Counter Point*	Aldous Huxley	Immoral	Irish government
1930	All works	Emanuel Swedenborg	Politically unsound	Soviet government
1931	*The Case for India*	Will Durant	Politically subversive	British authorities
1931	*Elmer Gantry*	Sinclair Lewis	Obscene	Irish government, NY State Post Office
1931	All works	Marie Stopes	Immoral	Irish Free State
1932	*Mein Kampf*	Adolf Hitler	Politically subversive	Czech government
1932	*Brave New World*	Aldous Huxley	Immoral	Irish government
1932	*Lady Chatterly's Lover*	D.H. Lawrence	Obscene	Irish government Polish government
1933	*Memories*	Giovanni Casanova	Immoral	Irish government
1933	*The Genius* and *An American Tragedy*	Theodore Dreiser	Immoral	Nazi government
1933	All works	Lion Feuchtwanger	Subversive and Semitic	Nazi government
1933	All works	Ernest Hemingway	Immoral, etc..	Nazi government
1933	All works	Erich Maria Remarque	Subversive	Nazi government
1933	All works	Upton Sinclair	Subversive	Nazi government
1933	All works	Leo Tolstoy	Subversive	Nazi government Soviet government
1935	*Memories*	Giovanni Casanova	Immoral	Mussolini's Italian government
1935	*On the Origin of Species*	Charles Darwin	Immoral and irreligious	Yugoslav government
1937	*On the Origin of Species*	Charles Darwin	Immoral and irreligious	Greek Metaxa dictatorship
1937	*Mein Kampf*	Adolf Hitler	Politically subversive	Palestine government
1939	All works	Johann Goethe	Immoral	Franco's Spanish dictatorship
1939	*A Farewell to Arms*	Ernest Hemingway	Immoral, etc.	Irish government
1939	All works	Henrik Ibsen	Immoral and subversive	Franco's Spanish dictatorship
1939	All works	Immanuel Kant	Politically unsound	Franco's Spanish dictatorship

banned books

YEAR	WORKS BANNED	AUTHORS	REASONS	CENSORS
1939	All works	Stendhal	Immoral, etc.	Franco's Spanish dictatorship, Papel Index
1944	*Droll Stories*	Honoré de Balzac	Immoral	U.S. Post Office
1948	*Meditations* and six other works	René Descartes	Heresy	Papal Index
1948	All works	Jean Paul Sartre	Subversive	Papal Index
1949	*The Naked and the Dead*	Norman Mailer	Obscene, etc.	Canadian customs, Australian authories
1952	All works	André Gide	Immoral, etc.	Franco's Spanish dictatorship
1952	All works	Honoré de Balzac	Immoral	Franco's Spanish dictatorship
1953	*A Mummer's Tale*	Anatole France	Immoral	Irish government
1953	*The Sun Also Rises* and *Across the River and into the Trees*	Ernest Hemingway	Immoral	Irish government
1953	*Sexual Behavior in the Human Female*	Alfred Kinsey	Obscene	South African censor, Irish government
1953	*Happiness in Marriage* and *My Fight for Birth Control*	Margaret Sanger	Immoral	Irish government
1953	All works	John Steinbeck	Immoral	Irish government
1953	All works	Emile Zola	Immoral	Irish government
1953	Most works	William Faulkner	Immoral, etc.	Irish government

banned books

The Astrological Author

by Nina Straus

Hardly an exact science, the astrological categorizing of literary authors will strike the credulous and satisfy the curious in its practice of associating Zodiac signs with literary themes and story-writing with ancient mythologizing. No astrologer is surprised to find that Henry Miller's *Tropic of Capricorn* was written by an American born under the sign of the Capricorn Goat; or that the famous Scorpio Evelyn Waugh, born around Halloween in 1903, would entitle his fictions *Black Mischief*, *Vile Bodies*, and *The Sacred and Profane Memoirs of Captain Charles Ryder*.

Curiously enough, many famous authors tend to be born on or around the "cusps" of signs, straddling two tendencies as if personality conflict were a spur to writing. Take Vladimir Nabokov, born April 23, 1899, two days after the change from Aries to Taurus. As a writer both enterprisingly innovative and aesthetically possessive, Nabokov collected butterflies as well as images of women (*Lolita*, *Ada*), thus exhibiting his Taurean traits. But Nabokov also initiated literary experimentation in the bold Aries manner of a Humbert-Humbertian "I Am."

Important clues to authors and their signs are the masculine and feminine groupings. The "masculine" signs of Aries, Gemini, Leo, Libra, Sagittarius, and Aquarius are all "fire" and "air" signs, suggesting aggression and self-propulsion. The "feminine" signs of Taurus, Cancer, Virgo, Scorpio, Capricorn, and Pisces indicate interactivity and receptivity, characteristics that show up in the choice of characters or situations these "water" and "earth" authors write about.

Consider just one haunting (Taurus) image from Thomas Mann's modern classic, *The Magic Mountain*. The young Hans Castorp sits on the balcony of a tuberculosis sanitarium. He's wrapped in a blanket, enjoying a cigar, totally supine and contemplating sex, love, death, and women with a book on his lap. Consider an alternate (Sagittarius) image from Joseph Conrad's *The Secret Sharer*. A young captain steers his ship dangerously close to the shore so that another man, who's been swimming all night, can jump back in the water and save himself from court martial.

The Aries Author: March 21-April 19

As the first sign in the astrological calendar, heralding spring, Aries personifies energy, impatience, and regenerative capacities. Boldness of conception, the raw and the vital, show up in the style and choice of the Aries author's characters.

TENNESSEE WILLIAMS (b. March 26, 1911; d. 1983) is best known for his Pulitzer Prize–winning *A Streetcar Named Desire*. Focused on tensions between the powerfully sexed and violent Stanley Kowalsky and the vulnerable Blanche DuBois, the drama depicts a struggle with the primal forces of American life: sex, class, money, power, delusion, and addiction. While the "masculine" Aries quality is embodied in Kowalsky, played originally by Marlon Brando (himself a double Aries), the character of Blanche embodies the stereotypical "feminine" nebulousness of the author's near-Pisces cusp with its impressionistic nuances. See: *The Glass Menagerie*, *Cat on a Hot Tin Roof*, *Suddenly Last Summer*, *Night of the Iguana*.

FLANNERY O'CONNOR (b. March 25, 1925; d. 1964) O'Connor's brave struggle with the lupus that killed her at age forty-one informs the raw uncluttered energy of her prose. Martian metaphors associated with Aries show up in *The Violent Bear It Away* (1960), and in the primal interactions of her stories' characters. O'Connor's plots carry the reader through sin and delusion to redemption, all experienced in commonplace Southern settings and with a tragicomic sense that God's mysteries are revealed through shock, accidents, and death. See *The Collected Stories*.

The Taurus Author: April 20-May 20

Taurus authors depict their reality by working through the practical, sensual, and possessable aspects of life. The questions: what abides? what is of use—intellectually, morally, and aesthetically—engage their earthy creativity in a drive toward images of security, often lamented because lost in modernity. Obsessions with structure and form, the shapes of art imposed upon the chaos of life, are shared by Taurean authors as overtly dissimilar as Thomas Pynchon, Thomas Mann, and Vladimir Nabokov.

the astrological author

THOMAS PYNCHON (b. May 8, 1937) A recluse about whom little is known since his graduation from Cornell in 1959, Pynchon writes controversial metafictions: murky, experimental, antitechnological and hilarious. The search for the meaning of the individual self may be ludicrous and tragic, but larger forms carry Taurean significance. In his novel *V,* each character's journey forms a shape associated with that letter. In *Gravity's Rainbow*, Pynchon indicates, as does Mann and Nabokov, that artistic form is the only defense against life. With wild humor, Pynchon insists upon his grim message that atomic missiles will destroy the earth sign's beloved earth.

VLADIMIR NABOKOV (b. April 12, 1899; d. 1977) Exiled from his native Russia, the longed-for center of the world in this Taurean's imagination, Nabokov works the themes of exile and loss for all their comic and parodic worth. Humbert Humbert's love for Lolita is unapologetically sensual, but also involves a quest for the recovery of a final imaginative possession, themes mirrored again in *Pnin* and *Ada*.

The Gemini Author: May 21–June 21

Writers born in the intellectual air sign of Gemini, ruled by the volatile planet of Mercury, can be typed as "dual" in their thinking processes, as the Latin word for "twins" indicates. Mentally agile, curious, and multiform, the creations of Geminis are marked by their variety and by the tendency to polarize human characteristics for dramatic effect.

JOYCE CAROL OATES (b. June 16, 1938) Oates's work displays the variegated cleverness of Gemini, often embodied in contrasts between "deep" and superficial images of the self and the tensions between society and individual. Two book titles in particular—*Lives of the Twins* (1987) and *Do With Me What You Will* (1973)—indicate Gemini dualism.

WILLIAM STYRON (b. June 11, 1925) Styron's Pulitzer prize-winning *Lie Down in Darkness* (1968) and *Confessions of Nat Turner* (1967) explore relationships between symbolic "twins" in racial terms. Styron's black man, Turner, and Nathan (the crazed trickster Jew of *Sophie's Choice*) play opposite the white or WASP characters in these novels as Styron investigates psychological and ethnic polarities. A Gemini who "rejected" the South to live in the North, while continuing to explore the tensions between them, Styron's self-description is astrologically revealing: "I feel that the great thing about fiction as an art is that it is so mercurial, so fluid, so various."

OTHER GEMINIS: Saul Bellow, John Barth

the astrological author

The Cancer Author: June 22-July 22

Writers born under the sign of the Crab, the strongest and most feminine of the water signs, reveal an emotional sensitivity hidden under a hard shell. The tension between outer toughness and inner vulnerability in the nature makes Cancers masters of the art of passive resistance, or in literary terms, of a rhetorical persuasiveness masked either by overt simplicity of style (Hemingway) or by defensive complexity (Jean Paul Sartre).

ERNEST HEMINGWAY (b. July 21,1899; d. 1961) Born on the cusp of Cancer/Leo, the author of *The Sun Also Rises* and *The Old Man and the Sea* spent his writing career questing the "one true sentence" that would express his inner emotion without sentimentality. In Hemingway's fiction, a tough guy character is often posed against a vulnerable one. Sexual sensitivity suggesting an identity with but ambivalence about women is a major theme, dramatizing Hemingway's Cancerian instinct for protection and defense in a new style of writing that exemplifies "grace under pressure." Hemingway's crablike shell, protecting sensitive insights, was also displayed personally. Behind his roles as tough war correspondent, bullfight aficionado, marlin fisherman, and big game hunter was an Old Man of the Sea as protective of his solitude as of his reputation. Hemingway's truth mirrored the disillusioned idealism that characterized the "lost generation" between the two wars.

The Leo Author: July 23-August 22

Reclusive Leo writers may exist, but the tendency of this sign is to express authority, vitality, and willfulness in creative work. Ruled by the fiery, "masculine" power of the sun, Leo writers are obsessed by "the life force," by images of vast interconnections, and by the ideal of victory over weakness and compromise. The Leo imagination is defensively protective of its creations, the children of an imagination that also seeks, through its inspirations, to mold public opinion. Balzac's generous, all-encompassing *The Human Comedy* is a good example of Leo creativity, as is Leo Tolstoy's two-thousand-page *War and Peace*. Tolstoy's dying words offer a hyperbolic clue to Leonine ambition: "Couldn't God make just one exception in my case?"

GEORGE BERNARD SHAW (b. July 26, 1856; d. 1950) A vitalist like Tolstoy, Shaw wrote plays, literary criticism, and political and socialist tracts. An iconoclast who revitalized the English stage, a lecturer to the Fabian society about Henrick Ibsen, Shaw achieved success slowly, culminating in the Nobel Prize in 1925. With his Superman image as provocation, Shaw excoriated British conventionality in his social dramas. He propagandized for the "life force" that he embodied in his female characters, Saint Joan and Major Barbara. Controversial, oversized, and stubbornly anti-Oscar Wilde (Shaw despised "art for art's sake"), Shaw was the sun-light of his times. His titles suggest the Leonine confidence of his sign, the effort to mold matter into spirit: *The Man of Destiny* (1897), *Man and Superman* (1903), *Pygmalion* (1913).

The Virgo Author: August 23-September 22

The Virgo themes of craft, service, and healing are conveyed in sharply analyzed detail by writers obsessed with workmanship. The search for perfection, for the thing or person well-made, is manifest in prose that excels in making distinctions, in the beauty of polish, in the unraveling and analysis of complexities. Health and ways to attain it are major issues.

D. H. LAWRENCE (b. September 11, 1885; d. 1930) Famous for years as the "priest of love" and for the therapeutic sex scenes in *Lady Chatterley's Lover*, Lawrence is now being reread as a great analyst of the hetero/homo-sexual dilemmas of his characters. His greatest novel, *Sons and Lovers*, exposes his own closeness to his mother, and Lawrence's creativity stems from the (astrologically) "feminine" and "earth" qualities associated with Virgo. *Women in Love* contains the famous wrestling scene between men that aestheticizes homoeroticism while it breaks with unhealthy "bourgeois" censorship. The romantic rhythms and pastoral passions of Lawrence's prose in *The Rainbow* have intoxicated readers, but it is finally the Virgo *healing* impulses behind the rhythms and gender-torn images that guarantee Lawrence's reputation.

ROBERT PIRSIG (b. September 6, 1928). Pirsig has left us one perfect book, *Zen and the Art of Motorcycle Maintenance*. Reconciling earthly machinery with spiritual therapy (Buddhist philosophy with Kerouac's *On the Road*, the classic and the romantic), Pirsig symbolizes Virgo perfectionism in his vision of an alternative to capitalist-materialist success. What Pirsig calls his "inquiry into values" suggests the Virgo author's primary subjects: the rejection of artifice for reality, the quest for healing.

The Libra Author: September 23-October 22

The sign of Libra is associated with balancing. Libra writers are especially concerned with analyzing and resolving tensions, whether they are of a social, political, or personal nature. Like the other air signs, Gemini and Aquarius, Libras seek knowledge and new ideas with some detachment. The Libran author is less an innovator than a synthesizer, one who probes and represents what is occurring in human relationships within the present social context.

WILLIAM FAULKNER (b. Sept 25, 1897; d. 1962) Faulkner's great novels, *The Sound and the Fury*, *Light in August*, and *As I Lay Dying*, can be read as great balancing acts. Romanticism is posed against modernism, the old against the new South. The racial tensions of whites and blacks are dramatized upon a background of post-Reconstructionist transitions. Faulkner's impressionistic style, his stream-of-consciousness technique, influenced by Shakespeare and Joyce, comes into its own through the force of dramatic mediations. In Faulkner's work we recognize our peculiarly American relation to the past and our present frustrations regarding the struggle for social/racial balance and harmony.

F. SCOTT FITZGERALD (b. September 24, 1896; d. 1940) Fitzgerald's *The Great Gatsby* is a Libran novel in its negotiation of the lure of Roaring '20s wealth versus deeper values, a perspective symbolized by the East and West Egg lights of the novel's typography. Balancing reality with fantasy, romance against disillusion, Fitzgerald, like Faulkner, weighs our values upon his imaginative scales.

The Scorpio Author: October 23-November 21

Exploring fundamental transformations on all levels, Scorpion creativity is manifested in the struggle to conquer desire through willpower. Scorpion authors are interested in criminal investigation, in sacrifice, redemption, the occult, and in "Plutonian" depths (the planets Pluto and Mars rule the sign). Strong views, caustic humor or parody, as well as generosity toward victims play a big part in their literary imaginations. The titles of the works of Fyodor Dostoevsky (another Scorpio, like Evelyn Waugh, born around Halloween) suggest symptomatic obsessions: *Crime and Punishment*, *The Devils*, *Notes from the Underground*.

DORIS LESSING (b. October 22, 1919) Lessing's novels, *Briefing for a Descent into Hell*, *The Good Terrorist*, the *Children of Violence* series— as well as her classic, *The Golden Notebook*—chronicle the theme of cyclical self-rebirth that evokes Scorpio. Lessing's subjects include Communism, sexism, colonialism, and war, each explored through viscerally searing novels in which struggle is as much a central character as the fleshly characters themselves. In dramatic imaginative quests that have taken Lessing from her native Africa to distant planets (the Canopus in Argos series), she bears the spiritual scar of a writer who must self-transform: "I was defined with forceps that left a scarlet birthmark over one side of my face," she writes. "Above all I was a girl." An early feminist author, Lessing also transformed the way women imagine themselves.

OTHER SCORPIO AUTHORS: Sylvia Plath, Ursula LeGuin.

The Sagittarius Author: November 22-December 21

Symbolized by the centaur whose arrow flies directly to its mark, writers born in the fiery sign of Sagittarius are at home with abstract ideas and in love with freedom. The key phrase is "I see." The creative urge is expressed by expanding the ego toward an ideal, by exploring human motivation, and through a prophetic vision (William Blake) that is sometimes comic (Woody Allen) and sometimes dogmatic (Aleksandr Solzhenitsyn).

JOSEPH CONRAD (b. December 3, 1857; d. 1924) Known for his tales of adventure at sea (*Lord Jim, The Secret Sharer*), Conrad's fiction suggests the explorative, adventurous element of this "masculine" sign. In *Heart of Darkness,* Conrad's most famous story, the narrative "arrow" points to a modernist mystery: to a "horror" at the center of the human psyche in its pursuit of colonialist expansion. In *Nostromo,* Conrad invents a South American country, Costaguana, shaken by revolution and corruption by European investors—a tale prophetic of the racially complex, multicultural world of the late twentieth century. Distrust of political and economic solutions made Conrad one of the great literary ironists, an "impressionist" of prose who shares with another Sagittarian writer, Solzhenitsyn, an obsessive hatred of tyranny.

The Capricorn Author: December 22-January 19

Writers born in the earthy sign of Capricorn, whose key phrase is "I use," evidence a wordliness that distinguishes them from other astrological authors. Their literary works are deliberately structured, based on their use of all that they have heard, read, and seen—everything they can re-deploy from tradition. Interested in order, even in experimental narratives of a new order, Capricorns manage their own creative powers with discipline to achieve their goal of success.

E.L. DOCTOROW (b. January 6, 1931) *Ragtime,* Doctorow's philosophical meditation on history and fiction, represents a Capricornian interest in power, wealth, and fame. Doctorow confronts the era of the big industrialists, J. P. Morgan, Henry Ford, and the socialists who went up against them, like Emma Goldman. While "life at the top" is Doctorow's subject, he is also a troubleshooter and critic: a chronicler of the rise and fall of the powerful capitalists of our time.

OTHER CAPRICORNIAN AUTHORS: Henry Miller (b. December 26, 1891; d. 1980) and Susan Sontag (b. January 16, 1933) indicate two other sides of the Capricorn author. Miller may be famous for his Bohemianism, but he was the consummate litterateur, a top-of-the-line free-lover-writer, an executive of his own literary career. Sontag synthesizes Capricorn tenacity and ambition with Gemini variety, managing her talent to make it an (intellectual) "property"—the goal of Capricornian impulse.

the astrological author

The Aquarian Author: January 20-February 18

Independence, humanitarianism, and originality characterize Aquarius, and it is not surprising that many famous modern writers are born in this air sign. The key phrase for Aquarians is "I know," suggesting their interest in the intellectual life and the ideal of social fraternity. Excellent observers, often eccentric in temperament, Aquarian writers depict human communities in process. Often protean, their impulse is to transform tradition, to pioneer innovation.

NORMAN MAILER (b. January 31, 1923) The titles of Mailer's books indicate the protean and pioneering quality of his individualism: *The Naked and the Dead, Armies of the Night, An American Dream* . Compounding several genres—autobiography, fiction, film, political journalism—Mailer displays the Aquarian dimension in his compulsive self-observation matched with social commentary. His strongly provocative voice echoed as it helped to create the revolutionary voice of the 1960s. He chronicled the technical pioneering of space flight in *Of a Fire on the Moon,* exemplified the culture of narcissism (*Advertisements for Myself*), struggled with women's liberation (*The Prisoner of Sex*), and the new politics of adversity and display (*Miami and the Seige of Chicago*). Many of our popular American presidents have been Aquarians (Lincoln, FDR, Reagan), a fact that underscores Mailer's conception of himself as a writer: "I've been running for President these last ten years in the privacy of my mind."

OTHER AQUARIAN AUTHORS: James Joyce, Virginia Woolf, Bertolt Brecht, William Burroughs, James Michener, Tony Morrison.

The Pisces Author: February 19-March 20

Piscean authors are the notorious dreamers of the literary world. Interested in compassion, renunciation, the beginnings and endings of the human time cycle, they obsorb the collective unconscious and display sensitivity to suffering. "I believe" is the Piscean watchword, leading to visionary fatalism or to the transformation of the commonplace.

RALPH ELLISON (b. March 1, 1914; d. 1994) Ellison's fame rests on *Invisible Man*, the tale of a black man who retreats to a cellar in New York City, taps into the light comparny, and tells his subversive story of humiliating success, collapse, and transformation as the victim of white exploitation. A challenge to his generation, Ellison's compassionate work evokes the Piscean structure of renunciation, intuition, and redemption. *Invisible Man* dramatizes in memorable prose the underground Pisceans must negotiate before delivering themselves into the light to begin the cycle anew.

JACK KEROUAC (b. March 19, 1922; d. 1969) Author of *The Subterraneans* and *On the Road*, Kerouac typified Piscean multiformity, changeability, and the impulse toward spiritual retreat and revelation. His religious ideal, shared with Allen Ginsberg, was to merge Western media consciousness with Zen Buddhism. While the downside of his Piscean surrender to life involved drugs and alcohol, he also expressed the Beat Generation's energy and their quest for new ways of living and believing.

OTHER PISCES AUTHORS: Philip Roth, John Updike.

the astrological author

Alternate Occupations

Edward Albee	radio worker, WNYC
Sherwood Anderson	paint store manager
Maya Angelou	calypso singer
Hannah Arendt	chief editor, Schocken Books
Isaac Babel	Cossack supply officer
Louis Begley	lawyer
Paul Bowles	music composer
Joseph Brodsky	hospital morgue attendant
William S. Burroughs	marijuana farmer
Erskine Caldwell	pool hall attendant; football player; bodyguard
Rachel Carson	radio scriptwriter
Raymond Carver	janitor; sawmill worker; gas station attendant; textbook company employee; exterminator; store detective; professor
Willa Cather	high school teacher
Raymond Chandler	oil company executive; soldier; reporter
Joseph Conrad	sailor
Pat Conroy	teacher
Don DeLillo	advertising copywriter at Ogilvy & Mather
James Dickey	advertising executive; guitar player
E. L. Doctorow	editor in chief, Dial Press
W. E. B. Du Bois	economic and history teacher at Atlanta University
T. S. Eliot	bank clerk, Lloyd's of London
William Faulkner	postmaster; scoutmaster; farmer; night watchman; screenwriter
Robert Frost	bobbin-boy in Massachusetts mill; cobbler
Jean Genet	thief; prisoner
Allen Ginsberg	advertising agency marketing manager

Graham Greene	spy
Thomas Hardy	architect's apprentice
Lillian Hellman	reader for Metro Goldwyn Mayer
O. Henry	ranch hand; bank teller; bookkeeper; convicted embezzler
John Hersey	private secretary for Sinclair Lewis
Langston Hughes	cabin boy; doorman at Parisian nightclub
Henrik Ibsen	chemist's assistant
John Irving	college teacher
James Joyce	English-language teacher in Italy; bank clerk
Franz Kafka	bureaucrat for insurance agency
Milan Kundera	jazz pianist; film professor
Madeleine L'Engle	actress
John Le Carré	spy for Britain's M15
Jack London	cannery worker; gold prospector; sailor
Walter Lord	copywriter, J. W. Thompson Advertising
Archibald MacLeish	librarian of Congress
Louis MacNeice	firewatcher; BBC writer
Norman Mailer	political candidate; actor; intelligence infantryman in WWII
David Mamet	cab driver; short-order cook; window cleaner; drama teacher
Beryl Markham	horse trainer; freelance pilot
Gabriel García Márquez	foreign correspondent
Thomas Merton	Trappist monk
James Michener	high school history teacher; education professor; textbook editor
Henry Miller	manager of New York speakeasy
A. A. Milne	journalist
Yukio Mishima	civil servant
Toni Morrison	senior editor, Random House
Vladimir Nabokov	tennis and boxing coach; chess instructor; pioneering lepidopterist (moth and butterfly specialist)
V. S. Naipaul	broadcaster for BBC
Pablo Neruda	diplomat
Marsha Norman	counselor for emotionally disturbed children

Frank O'Hara	art critic; assistant curator, Museum of Modern Art
George Orwell	war correspondent
Sylvia Plath	secretary at Massachusetts psychiatric clinic
Mori Rintaro	Surgeon General of Japan
Salmon Rushdie	advertising copywriter
Antoine de Saint-Exupery	aviator
Carl Sandburg	dishwasher; itinerant guitar player; salesman; soldier; reporter; stagehand
May Sarton	director, The Apprentice Theater
Dr. Seuss	cartoonist
Anne Sexton	door-to-door makeup saleswoman
Jane Smiley	worker in toy factory
John Steinbeck	field laborer
Wallace Stevens	vice president, Hartford Accident and Indemnity Company
Donald Ogden Stewart	actor
Booth Tarkington	state senator
Dylan Thomas	radio scriptwriter
Scott Turow	Assistant District Attorney, Chicago
Mark Twain	silver prospector; journalist
Gore Vidal	television scriptwriter; political candidate
Kurt Vonnegut	teacher of emotionally disturbed children
Joseph Wambaugh	policeman
Booker T. Washington	slave; school principal
H. G. Wells	grammar school teacher
Nathanael West	hotel manager
Garth Williams	mural painter; sculptor
Tennessee Williams	show company clerk; factory worker
William Carlos Williams	medical doctor

$\mathscr{Writing}$ $\mathscr{Undercover}$

NAME	NOM DE PLUME
Kingsley Amis	*Robert Markham*
Dame Cicily Isabel Fairfield Andrews	*Rebecca West*
René Francois Armand Prudhomme	*Sully Prudhomme*
Isaac Asimov	*Paul French/Dr. A.*
Louis Auchincloss	*Andrew Lee*
L. Frank Baum	*Edith Van Dyne*
Robert Benchley	*Guy Fawkes*
Ambrose Bierce	*Dod Grile*
Eric Arthur Blair	*George Orwell*
Baroness Karen Blixen-Finecke	*Isak Dinesen*
William S. Burroughs	*William Lee*
Mary Challans	*Mary Renault*
Agatha Christie	*Mary Westmacott*
Samuel Clemens	*Mark Twain*
Sidonie Gabrielle Colette	*Colette*
Paddy Chayefsky	*Sidney Aaron*
Michael Crichton	*Jeffrey Hudson/John Lang*
Marguerite de Crayencour	*Marguerite Yourcenar*
Marie Louise de la Ramee	*Ouida*
C. L. Dodgson	*Lewis Carroll*
Frederic Dannay	*Ellery Queen*
Louis Farigoule	*Jules Romains*
Erle Stanley Gardner	*A. A. Fair*
Theodore Seuss Geisel	*Dr. Seuss*
Dashiell Hammett	*Peter Collinson*
Robert Heinlein	*Anson MacDonald*
L. Ron Hubbard	*Tom Esterbrook*
Ford Madox Hueffer	*Ford Madox Ford*
E. Howard Hunt	*John Baxter*

Evan Hunter	*Ed McBain*
Olga Katzin	*Sagittarius*
Stephen King	*Richard Bachman*
Josef Teodor Konrad Korzeniowski	*Joseph Conrad*
Jerzy Kosinski	*Joseph Novak*
Wilhelm Kostrowitzki	*Guillaume Appollainaire*
Manfred Lee	*Ellery Queen*
Doris Lessing	*Jane Somers*
Elizabeth Mackintosh	*Josephine Tey*
Kathleen Mansfield Beauchamp	*Katherine Mansfield*
Kenneth Millar	*Ross Macdonald*
Edna St. Vincent Millay	*Nancy Boyd*
David John Moore	*John le Carré*
Vladimir Nabokov	*V. Sirin*
Dorothy Parker	*Constant Reader*
Alexsei Maksimovich Peshkov	*Maxim Gorky*
Sylvia Plath	*Victoria Lucas*
William Sydney Porter	*O. Henry*
Francoise Quoirez	*Francoise Sagan*
Solomon Rabinowitz	*Sholem Aleichem*
Mori Rinataro	*Mori Ogai*
Ethel Lidesay Robertson	*Henry Handel Richardson*
William Saroyan	*Sirak Goryan*
Giorgios Seferiadis	*George Seferis*
Terry Southern	*Maxwell Kenton*
John Innes Mackintosh Steward	*Michael Innes*
Florence Rainbow Stewart	*Mary Stewart*
R. L. Stine	*Emily Cates*
Irving Stone	*Irving Tennenbaum*
Jacques Anatole Francois Thibault	*Anatole France*
Gore Vidal	*Edgar Box*
Hillary Waugh	*H. Baldwin Taylor*
Nathan Wallenstein Weinstein	*Nathanael West*
Donald E. Westlake	*Richard Stark / Tucker Coe*
J. A. Wight	*James Herriot*
Thomas Lanier Williams	*Tennessee Williams*
John Burgess Wilson	*Anthony Burgess*
Willard Huntington Wright	*S. S. Van Dine*

writing undercover

Literary Love Affairs

Russell Banks *and* Chase Twichell
Simone de Beauvoir *and*
  Jean Paul Sartre
William Rose Benet *and* Elinor Wylie
Stephen Vincent Benet *and*
  Rosemary Carr
Aline Bernstein *and* Thomas Wolfe
Jane Auer Bowles *and* Paul Bowles
Alan Campbell *and* Dorothy Parker
Raymond Carver *and* Tess Gallagher
Joan Didion *and* John Gregory Dunne
Jonathan Fast *and* Erica Jong
F. Scott Fitzgerald *and*
  Zelda Fitzgerald
Lady Antonia Fraser *and* Harold Pinter
Allen Ginsberg *and* Peter Orlovsky
Caroline Gordon *and* Allen Tate
Dashiell Hammett *and*
  Lillian Hellman
Gilbert Highet *and* Helen MacInnes
Ted Hughes *and* Sylvia Plath
Georgiana Hyde-Lees *and* W. B. Yeats
Pamela Hansford Johnson *and*
  C. P. Snow
Faye Kellerman *and*
  Jonathan Kellerman

Walter Kerr *and* Phyllis McGinley
Stephen King *and* Tabitha King
Sinclair Lewis *and*
  Dorothy Thompson
A. J. Liebling *and* Jean Stafford
Robert Lowell *and*
  Elizabeth Hardwick
Robert Lowell *and* Jean Stafford
Katherine Mansfield *and*
  John Middleton Murry
Joyce Maynard *and* J. D. Salinger
Mary McCarthy *and*
  Edmund Wilson
Henry Miller *and* Anaïs Nin
Harold Nicolson *and*
  Vita Sackville-West
Anne Rice *and* Stan Rice
Salman Rushdie *and*
  Marianne Wiggins
Vita Sackville-West *and*
  Virginia Woolf
Gertrude Stein *and* Alice B. Toklas
Diana Trilling *and* Lionel Trilling
Anne Waldman *and* Lewis Warsh
H. G. Wells *and* Rebecca West
Leonard Woolf *and* Virginia Woolf

Acknowledgments

High Tide Press wishes to express its gratitude to Tamara Straus for writing the author biographies; Adele Q. Brown for making facts come alive; Lisa Hartjens and Katharine Marx for locating many of the photographs in this book; Jennifer Bomze for her diligent research; Nina Straus for making astrology a literary discipline; Glenn Horowitz and Laura Barnes, Glenn Horowitz Booksellers, for providing their collection of first edition book jackets; Farrar, Straus, Giroux, Inc., Little, Brown and Company, and Wendell Minor for providing their book jackets; Frederick G. Ruffner, Omni Graphics, for his sound counsel; Clark Evans, The Library of Congress; Deborah Goodsite and Jocelyn Clapp, Corbis Bettmann; Larry Schwartz, Archive Photos; Christine Schillig for acquiring this project; and Jake Morrissey for his patience and unswerving support.